Huguenot Heritage

The Author

Educated at Pembroke College, Cambridge, and at University College London, Robin Gwynn is Reader in History at Massey University, New Zealand. He was Director of the 1985 national commemoration of the Huguenots' contribution to British life, also called HUGUENOT HERITAGE.

24-5

I still flung to Eng(& ic
~ A.S's Lifetime

Huguenot Heritage

*The history and contribution of
the
Huguenots in Britain*

Robin D. Gwynn

SENIOR LECTURUER IN HISTORY,
MASSEY UNIVERSITY, NEW ZEALAND

ROUTLEDGE
London and New York

For
John David Gwynn

First published in 1985
Reprinted in 1988 by
Routledge
11 New Fetter Lane
London EC4P 4EE

Published in the USA by
Routledge, Chapman & Hall, Inc.
29 West 35th Street
New York NY 10001

Set in Linotron 202 Bembo, 10 on 12 pt
by Hope Services, Abingdon, Oxon
and printed in Great Britain
by Hartnoll Print
Bodmin, Cornwall

Library of Congress Cataloging in Publication Data
Gwynn, Robin D.
Huguenot heritage.
Bibliography: p.
Includes index.
1. Huguenots – England – History – 17th century.
2. Minorities – England – History – 17th century.
3. England – Church history – 17th century. I. Title.
BX9458.G7G99   1985   942'.0088245   84–16005

British Library CIP Data also available

ISBN 0-415-00277-X

Contents

Illustrations

Illustrations

Maps

Tables

Preface

The inspiration for this book derives from the Huguenot Society of London, which has long been aware of the need for a modern work to replace the outdated classics by J. S. Burn and Samuel Smiles. It is appropriate that it should appear on the eve of 'Huguenot Heritage', the commemoration in 1985 of the contribution made to Great Britain and Ireland by the French-speaking Protestant refugees who crossed the Channel between the sixteenth and eighteenth centuries. The year 1985 was chosen both as the tercentenary of the Revocation of the Edict of Nantes – an event which inspired many Calvinists to leave France and seek sanctuary elsewhere – and as the centenary of the foundation of the Huguenot Society itself. The stream of publications emanating from the Society over the last century has made it possible to reconsider the impact of the refugees and the subsequent history of their descendants in their new homeland. It is high time, for the Huguenots have been shamefully neglected by English historians.

My thanks are due to members and officers of the Society for their encouragement and assistance, freely given to an author not himself of Huguenot descent. Especially I would thank Miss Irene Scouloudi and Mr Charles Marmoy, respectively its Hon. Secretary and Hon. Librarian, whose labours have helped open new windows on the refugee community. Few learned societies can have enjoyed such continuous and devoted service over the last quarter of a century. Without their support, it is unlikely that this book, the fruits of twenty years of research, would ever have appeared; they have helped create a lifetime interest. It is impossible to recall, let alone adequately acknowledge, all the kindnesses I have received over so long a period in archives and libraries in England, France and New Zealand, but I am particularly indebted to successive ministers (especially M. Dubois) and the Consistory of the French Church of London for allowing me free access to their library, and to the staff of the Rare Books room at University College, London, who put themselves out to accommodate me when I was on sabbatical leave in 1976.

While a doctoral student at London University in the 1960s, my initial steps were guided by the late Professors Joel Hurstfield and T. F. Reddaway. Later, I benefited from the advice of Dr H. G. Roseveare, Dr I. Roy, Professor Valerie Pearl, and especially Mr R. C. Latham. In revising drafts of this book, I have been assisted by comments from Peter Lineham, the Lady Monson, John Muirhead, Tessa Murdoch, Neil Rennie, Morton Rodger, John Ross, Andy Trlin, Jean Tsushima and Randolph Vigne. Natalie Rothstein, Hugh Tait and Peter Thornton helped with the selection of plates 13, 8 and 6(b) respectively.

I am further indebted to the illustration studio of Massey University, New Zealand, which prepared the maps of London; to the Massey University Council, for financial assistance towards my research; and to the Geography and History departments of University College, London, for facilitating my work in recent months. Also to the editors of the *Proceedings of the Huguenot Society of London*, the *English Historical Review*, and the *Journal of Historical Geography* for permission to incorporate material from my articles published in those journals; and to Dr D. W. Jones for table 4.

My heartfelt thanks go too to my family. To my parents and my wife I owe a very special debt of gratitude. Without encouragement and financial assistance from my parents, I would never have started this work. Without my wife's tolerance, good humour, moral support and practical help, it would never have been finished.

Robin Gwynn

Note on Quotations

Abbreviations and contractions in quotations have been extended, and capitalization and spelling have in many cases been modernized. Most French passages have been translated.

Date Chart

1517   Luther publishes his Ninety-Five Theses
1523   First French Protestant martyrdom
1536   Calvin settles in Geneva (–1564, except 1538–41)
1545   First Calvinist community founded in France, at Meaux
1548   Earliest mention of an organized French Protestant congregation in England
1550   Foundation of French and Dutch Churches of London
1551   Edict of Châteaubriant: persecution of Protestants intensifies in France
1555   Missionaries leave Geneva for France
1559   First French Calvinist National Synod, held in Paris
1559   Peace of Cateau-Cambrésis
1560   Conspiracy of Amboise: word 'Huguenot' first used around this time
1561   Colloquy of Poissy: failure of attempt at reconciliation
1562   Outbreak of first war of religion in France
1562–3   Influx of refugees to England
1566   First revolt of Netherlands against Philip II of Spain
1567   Alva arrives in Netherlands: reign of terror there
1567–8   Influx of refugees to England
1570   Peace of St Germain ends third French war of religion
1572   Second revolt of Netherlands
1572   Massacre of St Bartholomew
1572–3   Further marked influx of refugees to England
1581   First Colloquy of French churches in England
1589   Assassination of Henry III of France
1593   Henry of Navarre (Henry IV) abjures Protestantism
1598   Edict of Nantes
1604   First Synod of Dutch and French churches in England
1610   Henry IV assassinated
1628   Fall of La Rochelle
1629   Peace of Alès: end of French wars of religion
1634   Archbishop Laud attacks foreign churches in England

Date Chart

1642	Outbreak of English Civil War (–1646)
1660	Restoration of monarchy in England
From 1660s	Increased legal pressures against Huguenots in France
1679	Attack on Huguenots in France intensifies
1679–81	Exclusion crisis in England
1681	*Dragonnades* begin in France
1681	Large influx of refugees to England: first brief for financial collection on their behalf
1685	Revocation of the Edict of Nantes
1686	New brief for collection for Huguenot refugees in England
1687	James II publishes Declaration of Indulgence: maximum period of Huguenot immigration to England
1688	William III invades England
1689–97	England at war with France
1690	Battle of the Boyne
1694	Foundation of the Bank of England
1697	Peace of Ryswick
1702–13	England at war with France (War of Spanish Succession)
1702	Camisard Protestant peasants rebel in the Cévennes
1709	Protestant refugees from Palatinate reach England
1713	Peace of Utrecht
1718	Foundation of French Protestant Hospital
1762	Last execution in France of a Huguenot minister
1762	Execution in France of Jean Calas, whose case is taken up by Voltaire
1787	Huguenots tolerated in France
1852	Foundation of French Protestant Historical Society, Paris
1885	Foundation of Huguenot Society of London
1985	Commemoration of 'Huguenot Heritage'

Introduction

To a world that has witnessed the atrocities committed by Hitler's Germany on the Jews or the plight of the boat people from Vietnam, the word 'refugee' is charged with emotion. Yet the fears, pains, emotional as well as physical upheaval, destitution and sometimes sheer panic experienced by those seeking refuge are not easily conceived or shared by others fortunate enough to lead a comparatively secure and sheltered existence. This book is about the fugitives who first gave the word 'refugee' to the English language, the Huguenots. They were French-speaking Protestants, or more precisely Calvinists. Large numbers of them fled to neighbouring Protestant states, especially the Netherlands and England, to escape religious persecution in France between the sixteenth and eighteenth centuries. So many, indeed, crossed the Channel that it is statistically probable that over three-quarters of all Englishmen alive today have some Huguenot blood in their veins. People in the British Isles did not start talking about 'réfugiés' or refugees until the 1680s, but this book encompasses also an earlier wave of French-speaking Protestants who came from the Continent during the reigns of Edward VI and Queen Elizabeth in the sixteenth century.

Over the years, many immigrant groups have contributed to English society: amongst others, Flemish, Huguenot, Jewish, Welsh and Irish. Of these peoples, only the Jews have been adequately studied. The Huguenot refugees of the later Stuart period have been accorded more attention than Irish or Welsh migrants, but in general such groups are ignored, or summarily dismissed, or confined to the pages of specialist journals. Consider the content of advanced school and university courses. A sixth-former who had studied the Stuarts would not be surprised to be faced by an examination question on English Catholics, and an undergraduate might be confronted by one on, say, the Quakers. Both would probably be appalled to find before them a question about the refugees from Louis XIV's France. Yet the English Catholics were only slightly more numerous than the Huguenots in England, and there were fewer Quakers. Moreover the

I

French refugees were far more important for England's survival in a threatening world, and for her future, than either the Catholics or the Quakers of the period. So this is a study of a seriously neglected minority.

The origins and earliest applications of the term 'Huguenot' have always been, and still remain, obscure.[1] Some explanations belong to the world of myth: a sixteenth-century Catholic apologist, for example, suggested that John Calvin nightly summoned a devil named Nox to his side, using the words 'Huc Nox', and that their son 'Hucnox' was the sire of the Huguenots. Others are more plausible, but still cannot be accepted. Into this category fall the sixteenth-century French attempts to make political capital out of the name; the Catholic faction under the Duke of Guise sought to derive 'Huguenot' from the German 'Eidgenossen' (Leaguers, confederates bound by oath), while the Protestants loyal to the Duke of Condé claimed that the Huguenots were faithful royalists, devoted adherents of the line of the medieval French king Hugues Capet who had died nearly six centuries before. While 'Huguenot' is known to have existed as a French surname in the fourteenth and fifteenth centuries, the nickname does not lead back to any one individual. Another explanation connects the term with King Huguet's gate at Tours, a supposed meeting-place of local Protestants. Yet another derives it from 'Hausgenossen', meaning brethren and fellow-sufferers in the faith. Whatever the true explanation, the name was in common use to describe French Protestants by the 1560s. From the point of view of ordinary Englishmen it was difficult to distinguish between French Protestants and Walloons from the southern Low Countries (now Belgium and northern France), who spoke a related dialect. This book therefore uses 'Huguenots' in the widest possible sense to cover all French-speaking Protestants, including Walloons who arrived on English shores in Tudor times and refugees from the Principality of Orange who crossed the Channel a century later.

Cut off from their home backgrounds, refugees in all ages have shared similar characteristics. Confronted by new surroundings, they are forced to make exceptional efforts, as well as sacrifices, in order to carve out a niche for themselves. Unused to the political and social customs as well as the language of the host society they tend to cluster together, forming a distinct minority element, perhaps for several generations, before slowly being assimilated. The Huguenots conformed to this pattern. In London, Canterbury and other centres in the south-east and south-west of England they formed communities of their own which lasted far longer than it took the refugees to acquire a reasonable knowledge of spoken and written English, communities within which they frequently intermarried and – as far as they were allowed – created their own church and work environment. Their psychological need for such support was the greater because of the blinkered horizons of Tudor and Stuart Englishmen. Although the word 'foreigner' has been used in this book with its modern meaning, the way it was used in early modern Europe reveals a very provincial outlook. To a seventeenth-century Kentishman, for instance, the term meant someone not from beyond England's borders but from outside Kent, while a man described as from 'the western parts' would have come not from Devon or Cornwall but from west Kent.

The picture conjured up in our minds by refugees is one of destitute hordes. It is valid enough; but, except in the case of sudden calamity, there are always likely to be a few farsighted men and women who anticipate disaster and strive to keep themselves one jump ahead of it. Thus a minority of Jews escaped from Nazi Germany early enough to take with them a substantial part of their wealth, and a minority of Huguenots acted with similar foresight in early modern Europe. It was as well for their less fortunate brethren that they did, for there were no refugee camps or international aid agencies in the sixteenth and seventeenth centuries, and those who left early – often men of substance as well as vision – attracted later migrants to settle round them. One of the characteristics of Huguenot settlement, in England as in Holland or New York[2] or elsewhere, was the marked disparity of wealth within the refugee group.

The host society stood to gain much, both from the minority of Huguenots who came with substantial resources and from the large majority who brought little other than their hands and acquired skills. The assets of the wealthy were far more significant than their mere value might suggest because the capital in question was liquid, not tied to land or property like that of their hosts but available for industrial and commercial investment and banking. The artisans who formed the bulk of the refugee population provided cheap skilled labour and came with valuable new techniques. They facilitated the production of such manufactures as glassware and the 'new draperies' of the late Tudor-early Stuart period, and silks and white paper in the 1690s. Whether blessed by economic good fortune or not, the refugees were likely to share an exceptional degree of determination and to have particular reason to work long and hard to create for themselves a new life in a strange land. Consequently they proved to be a productive people, highly motivated, who provided a major economic impetus to Britain, as to other countries wise enough to adopt them.

The value of the Huguenot refugees to their host nations is now widely accepted, but not all their contemporaries viewed them favourably. To a king like the Roman Catholic James II they were anti-monarchical. In the eyes of high church Anglican authorities they gave undesirable encouragement to English Presbyterians and Non-conformists. Poor native workers, especially in the weaving trade in the overcrowded eastern suburbs of later Stuart London, were likely to find them a source of competition for scarce employment opportunities. Xenophobia was often present, occasionally breaking out in acts of open hostility and violence against the refugees. Conflict was also likely to develop as second- and third-generation refugees became assimilated and took a more active part in the affairs of the host nation. Consequently it should not be thought that the troubles of the Huguenots ended when they crossed the Channel, although their lot improved.

What prepared English public opinion to receive them with considerable humanity and sympathy (and saved them from further and more prolonged attack) was their religion. In an age when religion and politics were well-nigh inseparable, here were fellow Protestants whose sufferings for their faith lent them an aura of martyrdom. Well-publicised atrocities such as the Massacre of St Bartholomew (1572), the attacks on the Protestant Vaudois in Cromwell's day, and the *dragonnades* of the 1680s invited the generous response to the needs of the refugees that was, on the whole, forthcoming. Even the urban clothworkers, whose personal interests were most adversely affected by the arrival of the Huguenots in England, were far from singleminded in expressing opposition to their employment, since they tended to be strongly Protestant in sympathy. The general feeling of the nation was revealed by the favourable popular response to public collections on behalf of the refugees in the 1680s.

Yet the strong religious beliefs of the Huguenots were also bound to strain their relations with the Anglican Church. When the first Protestant refugee congregations were established in England during the reign of Edward VI, it was uncertain what form the English Church would eventually take; indeed the Dutch and French Churches of London may have been – as their founder thought – intended as a model for future English national developments. But Queen Elizabeth insisted that the old ecclesiastical hierarchy (apart from the pope) and much former ritual be retained, and thereby created a permanent barrier between the structure of the Anglican Church and the more democratically organized refugee congregations. By the 1630s Archbishop Laud was seeking to prevent the perpetuation of the foreign churches, but he was foiled by their stubborn resistance and the outbreak of the Civil War. They never again faced so resolute a challenge. However, after the Restoration, the churches

4

adhering to the forms and services of the French Reformed Church were joined by others conforming to the Anglican liturgy translated into French. The unwillingness of Charles II and James II to license new nonconformist congregations must have discouraged many refugees from coming to England. Both types of French church persisted into the twentieth century, with the nonconformist congregations proving the more resistant to the process of assimilation.

Between the late 1670s and the first decade of the eighteenth century, some forty or fifty thousand Huguenots settled in England. Their contribution was very substantial, and embraced many spheres – political, military, diplomatic, economic, commercial, artistic, intellectual and fashionable. Historians have begun to examine their role in the economic transformation of England that took place in the years around 1700. Two vital aspects of their immediate impact on their new homeland, however, have generally been neglected. Their plight, their stories of persecution, above all their very presence as witnesses to what might happen to Protestants in a country ruled by a Catholic monarch, helped form the climate of opinion in which it was possible to dispossess James II without bloodshed during the Glorious Revolution. And subsequently, England might well have proved unable to defeat Louis XIV without the Huguenot influx.

'The history of the Huguenots in exile is a history of high interest, but it lacks unity.' Reginald Lane Poole's words,[3] penned more than a century ago, highlight the problems confronting the author of a book such as this. The Huguenots came at different times and in different ways. Should we study their forms of worship, so important in their own eyes, or should the emphasis be on their adjustment to English society? What about the economic or the military contribution of the refugees, their relationship with the government, their impact on intellectual life and the professions? No single work can hope to treat all these themes exhaustively, but to a greater or lesser extent all have been considered here in the hope that this book will open doorways to further reading. Unfortunately it is often difficult to find reliable information about the refugees. No book on the history of the Huguenots in England has appeared this century. The nineteenth-century works by Burn, Smiles, Agnew and others, too often still cited as authoritative, are uncritical and have been superseded by more recent research, while valuable theses and articles often pass unnoticed except by specialists. A bibliographical note has therefore been provided as a guide to the available literature. Readers wishing to follow up any argument should refer to this in preference to the occasional footnotes to more obscure references. An appendix examines some of the problems involved in tracing Huguenot ancestors.

1

An Exposed Minority

Jean Migault, a successful and law-abiding schoolmaster of Mougon in Poitou, was leaving the Protestant church of which he was reader and secretary on 22 August 1681 when he and his wife Elizabeth witnessed the arrival of an intimidating troop of mounted dragoons. 'Would they change their religion and adopt Catholicism?' the quartermaster demanded of them abruptly on their return home. When they refused, they were visited by the commander of the troop, who asked what they would pay him to limit the number of troops billeted on them. When they explained they had little cash, he inspected their house from end to end, and departed.

Within minutes, two soldiers arrived with billeting orders, made themselves at home and demanded an enormous dinner. Meanwhile two more soldiers turned up, then another, then four more, then another six: all insolent, menacing in their demeanour and insatiable in their demands. As it became obvious that nothing short of their total ruin was intended, the Migaults abandoned their home and fled, though not before Elizabeth had been forced into a corner of the fireplace while the soldiers made the fire burn more and more fiercely, blaspheming and threatening to burn her if she did not abjure her faith, until she lost consciousness. Fortunately a Catholic vicar and neighbours who had no liking for such behaviour connived at her escape, so that she and her husband were able to join some twenty other Protestant families from the neighbourhood who had taken to the woods when the dragoons arrived.

They were free, and had maintained the purity of their faith at the cost of most of their possessions, which were sold off for next to nothing by the soldiers. But what were they to do next? They were burdened with twelve children, with ages ranging from 17 to only a few days, and could hardly hope to leave the country undetected. They tried returning to Mougon after the troops withdrew, but the folly of such a design soon became apparent. The sudden reappearance of the dragoons nearly trapped the Migaults, but again they escaped.

Once more their goods were seized, and this time their house was left a ruin, its partitions demolished and all its thirty-six windows broken. Accepting the inevitable, they left in search of Protestant gentlefolk sufficiently influential to be able to protect them. For a time there were some to be found, but in the end rank ceased to matter and, as Jean recorded in the *Journal* he wrote for his children, 'there was no one left who did not feel the iron hand of despotism'. Meanwhile his wife died, shortly after giving birth to their fourteenth (and twelfth surviving) child in 1683. He finally decided to make his escape from the country, but how was he to do it? The laws against emigration were severe, and every effort was made to enforce them; the Migaults were in the same position as Jews in Hitler's Germany, persecuted at home yet refused permission to leave.

Still, news leaked back that three of Jean's four eldest sons had crossed the frontier, two by land to Germany and the Netherlands, the third by sea to Holland. The fourth abandoned his apprenticeship, quarrelled with his father, would not settle to anything, and in 1687 left for the New World. A daughter had died, but Jean still had most of his family with him when he tried to escape on a cold, black night in January 1688. He had arranged to go by ship, but to get to the beach where his family was to be picked up was no easy matter. He left La Rochelle with one horse, with the two youngest children riding in panniers, a third seated, the others walking. One of the elder daughters was left behind to arrange their affairs and then make her own escape. Heavy rain had made the paths almost impassable, and in any case the open road had to be avoided. The family crossed meadows that had become quagmires, clambering over vines, sinking deep in mud at every step and narrowly avoiding unseen precipices as they struggled to their embarkation point, where seventy-five fugitives waited to board the vessel they hoped would carry them to freedom. 'Soldiers on the beach!' someone cried. 'Save yourselves!' There was little that Jean Migault could have done, but fortunately it proved to be a false alarm, and panic abated. Thirty-six refugees were taken off on a longboat, but the family was too large a unit to get on board. Twenty-five more were rowed out to sea, but again the Migaults were unsuccessful. Tension grew. Dawn broke to reveal two patrolling guard boats, cutting off the English rescue ship and forcing those left on the beach to return to La Rochelle as fast as their weariness and terror, and the conditions underfoot, would allow. The Migaults were lucky and had not been missed or reported by their neighbours, but it says much for their resolution that they were prepared to try again three months later. This time the roads were dry, and crowds arriving for Easter celebrations masked their movements. On Tuesday 19 April they successfully embarked, and nineteen days later they reached Brill in Holland.

The story of Jean Migault and his family underlines the importance that French Calvinists placed on the ability to worship as they chose, the suffering that was often their lot in their home country, and the determination that was a notable characteristic of the Huguenot refugees. But to understand how such useful citizens came to be hounded from their home, we need to go back to the early years of the Reformation and consider the development of Protestantism in France. In August 1523 an Augustinian hermit, Jean Vallière, met his death on a stake at Paris, burnt alive for heresy, for 'blasphemy' against the Virgin Mary. From the time Martin Luther nailed his Ninety-Five Theses to the door of the castle church at Wittenberg, it had taken less than six years for France to produce her first Protestant martyr. Her earliest known Protestant refugee, Lambert of Avignon, had already fled, crossing the Swiss border the previous year. In French-speaking areas, as elsewhere in Europe, individuals were deeply concerned for the safety of their souls; finding traditional ways of salvation vain, Luther had asked 'How can I be saved?' and his question reverberated around the Continent. Vallière was the first of many French Protestants to die, Lambert the first of many to choose exile, for the sake of their faith. In the end their fellow countrymen were to refuse to accept their beliefs, and French Protestantism as a national movement was to be rejected, consigned to the scrapheap of historical lost causes. But this happened only after a long and bitter struggle, and after French Protestantism itself had undergone marked change and development.

The nature of French Protestantism was unformed during the early decades after the Sorbonne in 1521 declared Luther to be a pernicious enemy of the church of Christ, who had 'thrown up a pestilential doctrine full of execrable errors'. Some adherents of the new ideas were Lutheran. More, however, were followers of Zwingli or of Farel: reformers closer to hand in Switzerland than was Luther in Wittenberg, less tied to German speech and culture, and inclined to admit only what the Scriptures included rather than (as Luther) accepting anything they did not prohibit. Early French Protestantism lacked any national structure or organization. Opposed by the Church, the Sorbonne and the Parlement of Paris, it badly needed royal support, but no such encouragement from the Crown was likely; the strong degree of royal control over the Gallican Church had been reaffirmed and acknowledged by the Papacy as recently as 1516. Nevertheless Zwingli dedicated his *On True and False Religion* and

John Calvin his *Institutes of the Christian Religion* to Francis I, and Protestant hopes doubtless grew as it became evident that the German Lutherans were the king's natural allies in his long struggle with the Emperor Charles V. In practice Francis was determined to allow no concessions on fundamental issues like the sacrament of the Eucharist. He showed himself more moderate in his dealings with the Protestants than his Parlements would have liked, but during the 1530s the royal judiciary and administration began to assert themselves, and it gradually became clear that official policy would not accept Protestantism. In consequence an increasing number of the adherents of the new faith chose to leave France, among them Calvin himself and those for whom he founded his first French refugee congregation at Strasbourg in 1538.

By the 1560s, the children of the founding fathers of French Protestantism were living in a different environment, more regulated, more full of hope and yet more fearful. Where their parents had been Protestants they were, specifically, Calvinists, sometimes referred to as 'Huguenots', a word first used around 1560. The first Calvinist community in France had been founded at Meaux in 1545. From 1555 on, a formal Calvinist missionary effort was conducted from Geneva, from whence came trained ministers, advice and assistance, diplomatic support and printed Bibles. The church at Paris also provided inspiration and leadership. Gradually, spontaneous Protestant congregations became what Calvin called *églises dressées*, fully constituted churches led by pastors. Local, provincial and national synods linked individual congregations with other Calvinist churches in a national network. The first national Synod was held in 1559 in Paris, and agreed on a Confession of Faith and an Ecclesiastical Discipline.

As French Protestantism became more closely organized, it became ever more deeply enmeshed in politics. Given sixteenth-century conditions, any movement that undermined the legally sanctioned Church was bound to cause political waves. The Church was vitally important to the State in many ways, so that no attack on its structure or status could be welcome. It was enormously wealthy, and from its wealth the Crown derived not only taxation revenues but a major source of patronage through which its servants might be rewarded. Moreover, by preaching obedience and emphasizing that the established authority was ordained by God, the Church provided the regime with an essential ideological foundation. Support for government action from the pulpit could go a long way towards defusing potentially dangerous situations; absence of such support could be disastrous. The Church also dominated the fields of education, poor relief and social welfare. At a local level, it provided much that helped society cohere. It was the centre of life, a place where God was worshipped, but also where news might be exchanged and the will of the authorities made known. Normally the church building was the largest in the village, while the great cathedrals dominated the cities. Sixteenth-century men might occasionally find themselves in court-rooms or at military gatherings, but for most people, and especially for women and children, church services were usually the only occasions when they joined a group of people larger than might gather together in an ordinary house.

For all these reasons, the stability of the Church was invariably of grave concern to the State everywhere in early modern Europe; the political orthodoxy of the sixteenth century was summed up in Lord Burghley's remark that 'state could never be in safety where there was toleration of two religions'. But there were special reasons why Calvinism posed a more substantial threat than other brands of Protestantism to authorities sympathetic to Catholicism. It was a second-generation reform movement, clear-cut in its beliefs and certain of its role; not for Calvin the feverish insecurity that underlay Luther's search for truth in the Scriptures, not for his followers the excited meanderings that had accompanied early attempts to define exactly what the new protest involved. Hand in hand with its precision of belief went organization and missionary impact. Two features made Calvinist missionary activity especially dangerous: its external planning, and its successful tactic of aiming at the top.

Between 1555 and 1563 some 88 missionaries were trained in Geneva and sent into France. Of 42 whose status is known, 10 came from an aristocratic background, only 4 were artisans; 62 of the 88 came from France and so had personal experience of conditions there. Before being sent out, they underwent strenuous training at Geneva, where the Academy was presumably founded with the foreign situation in mind. After examination, they left with accrediting letters – implying a continuing Genevan influence on French Protestantism – for the areas where they would do most good. When they went to France, they did so secretively, under assumed names. This was not because Calvin wanted to establish a network of *agents provocateurs* to stir up rebellion. Far from it; he desired that peace be maintained, spoke and wrote strongly against those of his followers in France who became involved in 1560 in the *coup d'état* known as the Conspiracy of Amboise, and consistently set his face against armed resistance. As he wrote to the Church of Aix in 1561, the 'whole duty' of Christians under persecution was 'to possess our souls in patience'. The reason for the secrecy was simply that if the missionaries had entered France openly, they would promptly have been arrested. Yet from the authorities' point of view, they could only be considered subversive. They were also alarmingly successful. Often they were sent to work in areas where sympathetic local lords could provide protection. Calvin himself was in touch with many important aristocrats. Some of these, frightened by the ambitions of the powerful Catholic Guise faction at Court, stood to gain materially from an alliance with Protestant elements. Others were motivated by genuine religious conviction, like the Seigneur of la Ferté-Fresnel who in 1561 believed that 'God has placed me in authority over many men and by this means one of the most superstitious parts of the realm can be won for Christ'. Whatever their motivation, more and more nobles turned towards Calvinism, and by the beginning of the civil wars which racked France from the 1560s to the 1590s, about half the French nobility had already declared their allegiance to the Reformed Church.[1]

Yet the Huguenots remained only a small minority of the total population of France, never more than an eighth, and aristocratic leadership alone would not have sufficed to ensure their survival. Even more important was Calvinist ecclesiastical organization. Calvin believed that, 'as doctrine is the soul of the Church for quickening, so discipline and the correction of vices are like the nerves to sustain the body in a state of health and vigour'.[2] Consequently he provided the means of reaching out to govern the lives of every individual Christian. At parochial level stood the Consistory, composed of ministers to preach God's Word and elders to oversee the maintenance of the church and discipline its members. The Consistory sent ministerial and lay representatives to the Classis or Colloquy, a gathering representing a number of churches in one area. To ensure that uniformity of belief and action was maintained in a country as large as France, Colloquies in turn sent representatives to a Provincial Synod, and Provincial Synods to a National Synod.

Calvin had devised his system so that God should be more faithfully worshipped, but it became used for a very different purpose in the tense situation in France. In 1560 the Provincial Synod of Clairac, foreseeing a military threat, determined that each of its seven Colloquies should raise troops. The following year another Provincial Synod, at Sainte-Foy in Agenais, elected 'protectors' for the Bordeaux and Toulouse areas and ordained that their Colloquies should be led by 'colonels' who had charge over the 'captains' of the individual churches. Thereafter it became apparent that Calvin's church structure was remarkably well equipped to serve secular purposes. Because the elders were initially elected, there was some degree of 'democratic' participation at the local level. Because of the hierarchical system

Consistory – Colloquy – Provincial Synod – National Synod, it was possible for information and requests to move from the locality to the apex or vice versa, and for troops to be raised and co-ordinated. Because the members of the National Synod had connections at Court and were in touch with Geneva, the whole body was well informed about potential threats and current national and international developments. The value of the structure was shown very clearly in 1562, when the Guises attempted to suppress Protestantism by force. They found that there was already a Huguenot army in the field before them, led by the Prince de Condé, who assumed the title of 'Protector General of the Churches of France'.[3]

Calvinist organization thus provided a cement to link province with province in a national movement, while Calvinist belief offered a means of binding together the interests of artisans and nobles. As a result, in the Netherlands and elsewhere as well as in France, rulers found themselves confronted by a new and frightening phenomenon. In earlier times, groups in revolt had tended to be composed of people of the same status; rebellion in the Middle Ages is associated with peasants' revolts, baronial revolts and the like. Now monarchs encountered whole *regions* in rebellion, linked by ideology and a firm organizational structure, and led by the ruling class. It is this development that explains how a minority like the Huguenots in France could continue to resist for so long.

It also helps explain why such bitterness existed in France on the eve of the civil wars, but other considerations are relevant here. Rome had not been idle in the face of the Protestant threat, and in the 1540s and 1550s the first two sessions of the Council of Trent had clarified and codified Catholic belief. The situation was becoming more polarized, a trend that would continue towards the end of the century. In France, persecution of Protestantism had been intensified after the Edict of Châteaubriant of 1551. By that time French Protestant influence was already infiltrating some neighbouring areas where French or the related Walloon was spoken: the Channel Islands and, more significantly, the southern Netherlands. Such ties confirmed the international nature of the problem confronting the authorities, but they could not devote their full attention to its solution because the country was at war. It was not until the end of the decade that the Peace of Cateau-Cambrésis (1559) brought some lasting peace between the French Valois rulers and their rivals for European power, the Habsburgs. The Peace was ominous for French Protestants, for shortly before it was signed King Henry II swore that if only he could order foreign affairs satisfactorily, he would make the streets run with the blood of what he called 'this infamous Lutheran rabble'.[4] If he meant his words seriously, however, he never had the chance to put them into practice. During a tournament held to celebrate the Peace and two ensuing royal marriages, a lance penetrated the slit in his visor, and France had a new ruler.

Henry II had not been a great king, but he possessed certain undeniable, if basic, advantages. He was adult; he was a man, in a male-dominated world receptive to John Knox's *First Blast of the Trumpet against the Monstrous Regiment of Women* (1558); he was a competent military leader; and he possessed sufficient personality to hold in check the factions at his Court. Those who followed him lacked these fundamentals, with disastrous results. Henry left behind him four boys, the eldest of whom – his successor Francis II – was only 15. When he died at the end of 1560, he was replaced by the 9-year-old Charles IX, who was dominated by his mother, not only, as a woman, untrained in the arts of war, but a foreigner, the regent Catherine de Medici. Charles in turn died young, at the age of 24. Historians disagree about the personality and abilities of the last of Catherine's sons to rule, Henry III (1574–89), but on any assessment he proved unable to win the trust of his subjects, and his reign is ·notable for intrigue, assassination and bloodshed.

There was, then, a serious and enduring failure in the quality of royal leadership, and it came at a most unfortunate time. The Peace of Cateau-Cambrésis had largely been occasioned by the economic exhaustion of all the European powers which had been engaged in war. The French monarchy had for many years been tightening the financial screws on its subjects. Yet the Peace offered no compensation for past sacrifices. Rising prices, a European phenomenon of the century, placed additional burdens on most members of the population, including many of the nobility who had spent years fighting for the Crown and now looked to it for some reward, which it was in no position to provide. Weak central leadership provided the opportunity for ambitious aristocrats like the Catholic Guises and Protestant Condés to vie with one another to control Crown patronage; and religious divisions ensured that their conflict would be accompanied by an unprecedented degree of bitterness and violence.

Catherine de Medici attempted to find religious agreement by summoning Catholic and Calvinist leaders to the Colloquy of Poissy (1561). When the Colloquy failed, Catherine and her royal offspring found themselves squeezed in a vice. On the one hand was the 'Triumvirate', a militantly Catholic political association led by the Duke of Guise, the Marshal de Saint-André and the Constable Montmorency. This possessed sufficient power and influence to control most of the army, and it was prepared to look to Philip II of

Spain for external support. On the other hand stood the Huguenots with their Genevan ties and organization, led by the Prince of Condé and Gaspard de Coligny, Admiral of France. Such nobles had great regional strength. Especially influential were the houses of Guise, in Lorraine and the east and also in Brittany; Bourbon, in the south-west and in Normandy; and Montmorency, in central France and Languedoc. True, even in the heartlands of their strength these houses were confronted by opponents and noble families outside their clientage system, but that merely intensified their desire to see that crown patronage did not fall into the hands of their rivals. Faced by such power and determination, there was little that Catherine could do but try to maintain the independence of the crown and hope for military stalemate; as her chancellor Michel de l'Hôpital observed, the Crown might in theory hold absolute authority, but it lacked hands and feet.

In the end the Regent's aims were achieved, but the road to their fulfilment proved to be drenched in blood. Again and again during the rest of the century France suffered the agonies of civil war, with sporadic outbursts of open hostilities, in which the two sides demonstrated that neither was strong enough to destroy the other, interspersed with precarious periods of peace. From time to time hopes of some more lasting settlement arose, only to be dashed by renewed and escalating violence. The Peace of St Germain (1570) at the end of the third war offered the most acceptable solution from the Huguenot viewpoint; military guarantees were introduced to protect the Protestant minority, which was allowed a measure of toleration and reintegration into French society. This peace, however, was no consensus decision but rather the outcome of a great cavalry sweep by Coligny that had snatched victory from the jaws of looming defeat. Consequently it endured only a few short months. Any hopes of a more lasting peaceful future were soon destroyed by the Massacre of St Bartholomew in 1572.

This massacre was neither the first nor the only atrocity of the wars, in which both sides were guilty of brutal acts against the other. Treacherous attacks on individuals had begun before open warfare even started; the Guises would have succeeded in masterminding Condé's execution but for the early death of Francis II in 1560. The first war of 1562–3 ended in Protestant retaliation with the assassination of François, Duke of Guise. Such personal attacks gathered momentum as positions polarized, and all the Henries who gave their name to the 'war of the three Henries' in the 1580s were to die by the hands of assassins – Henry of Guise in 1588, Henry III the following year, and Henry of Navarre (after surviving over twenty previous attempts on his life) in 1610. The nature of warfare in general also became more horrific. When a Catholic military leader, Blaise de Monluc, captured Rabastens in 1570, for instance, he put the place to the sword to such effect that

> there were two only saved who were hid and such there were who offered four thousand crowns to save their lives, but not a man of ours would hearken to any ransom; and most of the women were killed who also did us a great deal of mischief with throwing stones.

This slaughter, Monluc explained in his memoirs, was ordered not so much in revenge for an arquebus wound he had received in the face while leading an assault 'as to strike terror into the country, that they might not dare to make head against our army'.

Yet amidst all the dreadful violence of the late sixteenth-century wars, the Massacre of St Bartholomew stands out: partly for its extent, partly for its duration – begun in Paris on the eve of St Bartholomew's Day in 1572, it spread from the capital to the provinces and, as Michelet remarked, was 'not a day but a season' – and partly for its enduring effects. It can no longer be maintained that the Massacre was the outcome of Catholic premeditation and the Machiavellian cunning of Catherine de Medici. To understand why it took place, one has to appreciate that on France's northern border another Catholic power was confronted by a Protestant problem. The Netherlands were part of the dominions of Philip II of Spain, a king who had no desire to rule over heretics. Although both Lutheranism and Anabaptism had long existed in the Netherlands, Calvinism arrived there late, initially in the large cities of what is now Belgium. Its links with the Huguenots in France were close, and indeed the problems facing the governments of the two areas were very similar. The Netherlands too had a discontented nobility, a crown short of money, neighbours prepared to fish in troubled waters, and a population split by religious differences and afflicted by rising prices; and the Netherlands also had a regent, for though Philip was no minor he preferred to remain in the Iberian peninsula. In 1572 his regent was the Duke of Alva, a military man renowned for putting his faith in force of arms.

As far as Philip and Alva were concerned, it was imperative to secure their southern borders, to isolate their rebellious Calvinist subjects from Protestants in France who had been lending them assistance. To achieve this end they were prepared to wage war if they must. In Paris, King Charles IX – who had been toying with designs for the invasion of the Netherlands – was faced by an awkward situation and conflicting advice. The Huguenot leader Coligny urged war with Spain in the Netherlands, war against Philip, the ally of the militant French Catholics, and in support of his own co-religionists. He was isolated in his advocacy. Catherine de Medici would contemplate hostilities only if English backing was assured, and it was not. In the end, having wavered this way and that, Charles found himself cornered, finally seeing the war as undesirable, but unable to frustrate Coligny's intention of leaving for the Netherlands. The decision was therefore taken – by whom is still uncertain – to eliminate first Coligny and then, to prevent them turning against the government for its failure to protect their leader, other prominent Huguenots. What actually happened was far more frightening: the Parisian militia and mob got out of hand. Made discontented by their ideological fervour and by current high grain prices, they vented their passions in a bloodbath that continued for nearly a week (plate 1a). By the end of that time some 3,000 people had been butchered in the capital, and the scenes in its streets were re-enacted in various provincial centres like Bordeaux and Lyons so that an estimated further 10,000 lost their lives.

Because of its scale and extent, because of its unexpectedness, above all because of royal involvement, the Massacre of St Bartholomew transformed Huguenot attitudes and prospects. It had hit the Protestant nobility particularly hard, since they had been concentrated at Paris for the imminent marriage of the Protestant Bourbon Henry of Navarre with Catherine de Medici's youngest daughter, Marguerite de Valois. After the Massacre many of the survivors emigrated or withdrew from the front line, and the leadership of the Huguenot cause fell increasingly into the hands of the great towns of the Protestant south and west: La Rochelle, Nîmes and Montauban. The resistance that they led was bitter, and given theoretical justification far beyond anything that Calvin had ever approved.

It was widely believed that the Crown was responsible for what had occurred in 1572. This is how the Roman publicist Camillo Capilupi presented the Massacre in a work entitled *The Stratagem of Charles IX*:

> One should not pass over this splendid deed without examining it closely, without carefully considering the excellence of the king, the queen–mother and their counsellors in having made so noble and generous a decision, as well as having had the skill to manage it, the tact and the intelligence to disguise it, the wisdom and the discretion to keep it silent and unknown, and lastly, the boldness and the courage to carry it out and the great happiness to bring it to a successful conclusion. . . . This wonderful act was premeditated,

planned and considered many months before and not merely
pitched upon by chance or hazard.[5]

Not only were Catholic authors prepared to write in such a vein,
but medals were struck applauding what had happened (plate 2, top).
Moreover the Crown issued confusing and contradictory statements
and finally acknowledged responsibility. Given the belief that their
king desired their extermination, the Huguenots could hardly
continue to espouse doctrines of non-resistance. The 1570s saw the
production of a series of Calvinist writings arguing that the king had
responsibilities to his subjects and could and should be opposed if he
forsook them; amongst these were François Hotman's *Franco-Gallia*,
Théodore de Bèze's *The Right of Magistrates over their Subjects* and the
influential *Vindiciae contra Tyrannos* ('A Defence against Tyrants'),
probably written by Philippe Duplessis-Mornay and Hubert Languet.

Despite such publications, it was in the interest of the Huguenots to
stay loyal. They were, and were likely to remain, a minority; and how
else, in the long run, could a minority hope to survive but through the
protection of the ruling house? The closing decades of the century
were marked by dogged perseverance, for Protestant hopes of
national success were evaporating and Calvinism had been thrown on
the defensive. As the cities took control, it became clearer that French
Protestantism was a regional movement, strong in the crescent which
had La Rochelle and Lyons at its tips and Guyenne, Gascony and
Languedoc at its heart, but elsewhere confined to Normandy and a
scattering of small pockets. It was not accidental that Protestantism
was strongest in the extremities of the realm and in areas with a
marked desire to maintain a large degree of provincial autonomy.
From the mid-fifteenth to the mid-sixteenth century, French political
development had been marked by an increasing centralization of
power. Huguenots became more and more closely associated with the
inevitable regional reaction. So strong indeed was the regional
foundation of Calvinism that the distinguished French historian Jean
Delumeau has been moved to speak of the 'United Provinces of the
Midi'.

Not that all was in harmony within those 'United Provinces'. Two
of the great southern cities, Bordeaux and Toulouse, remained
predominantly Catholic. So, too, did the rural peasantry. Even in the
Protestant south, the Huguenots were not a microcosm of French
society. In their ranks were many artisans, especially cloth workers,
and members of the *petit bourgeoisie* – teachers, notaries, lawyers: but
they included few peasant farmers. They were, therefore, unusually
literate, but (except in the Cévennes and one or two other confined

areas) they lacked any popular base. Modern French historians like Emmanuel Le Roy Ladurie and Janine Garrisson-Estèbe find in the wars of the late sixteenth century a clash of cultures, with Calvinism disliked by the peasantry not so much for its doctrine as for its work ethic and its new forms of behaviour. Its strict moral discipline attacked the dancing and taverns and games and carnivals, the pleasures that injected an element of joy into hard, bleak rural lives.

In so far as the Huguenots were able to raise their sights beyond regionalism and self-preservation in the generation after the Massacre of St Bartholomew, their hopes rested heavily on Henry of Navarre. A Protestant leader from his youth, Henry was of high birth but possessed an unfailing common touch. He was a competent and brave soldier, capable of inspiring trust and loyalty. Time was to show that he was also politically astute. As long as Henry commanded the Huguenot armies there remained prospects, however distant, of a Calvinist France. The death of the Duke of Alençon in 1584 – a cynical historian once remarked of him that his death was of greater importance than his life had ever been – caused a realignment of political thinking, for it made Henry heir to the throne. The Huguenots promptly abandoned those theories of resistance they had developed during the 1570s, and the supporters of the militant Catholic cause now adopted them. Nevertheless the Gallican Church and Catholic League were too strong, the Catholicism of Paris and of its Parlement too pronounced, and the Huguenots too small a minority for Henry to ascend the throne as a Protestant. On 23 July 1593 he received 'instruction' from a select body of Catholic bishops, and two days later he renounced Calvinism (plate 1b). Early the following year he was crowned king. With the aid of moderates both Catholic and Protestant, *politiques* who put a negotiated political settlement involving some measure of religious toleration before absolute religious claims, he was able eventually to meet the need of his country for peace and internal order.

As was to be expected, his conversion alarmed and embittered the Calvinists who had fought for him. All the same, Henry was the most favourably disposed king the Huguenots could hope for. As long as they could be guaranteed security, most were anxious to demonstrate their loyalty; and security came in 1598 with the Edict of Nantes. In many ways an updated version of the Treaty of St Germain of 1570, this famous 'perpetual and irrevocable' edict offered them toleration, limited freedom of worship, physical protection and guarantees of a normal social life. It consisted of no fewer than 92 general and 56 'secret' articles (in practice the latter were not secret at all) and two royal *brevets*. The Huguenots were allowed freedom of conscience, and the exercise of public Calvinist worship and organization wherever it had been established in 1577 or in 1586 and 1597, and in the houses of the great nobles as long as the latter were personally present. They were given civil equality, and were not to be excluded from educational or employment opportunities or from any professions. Colloquies and Provincial and National Synods were permitted if authorized by the king. Arrangements were made for the fair administration of justice, with special chambers established in most Parlements. The two royal *brevets* set aside money for the payment of Calvinist pastors and allowed the Huguenots to maintain as *places de sûreté* 'all the fortified places, towns and châteaux which they held up to the end of last August'.[6] Moreover the king undertook to pay a substantial sum towards the upkeep of the garrisons in these places.

The Edict of Nantes is normally, and perhaps rightly, regarded as favourable to the Huguenots. That was certainly the feeling of the French Catholics of the time, who took particular exception to the clause (specifically confirmed by one of the secret articles) that made Protestants eligible for all public offices and councils. But it must also be recognized that the edict demanded a high price in return for the security it gave: abandonment of all hopes of missionary expansion. Protestant churches and schools were allowed only in certain locations, and Protestant books might only be printed and publicly sold in Calvinist towns. The edict thus imprisoned the Huguenots in a straitjacket and made their protection dependent (since the guarantee clauses were temporary) on the continuance of royal favour.

It was never likely that monarchs lacking Henry IV's Calvinist background would accept the 'state within a state' concept, which the edict in theory sought to abolish but in practice embodied. If his successor Louis XIII needed any reminder of its unacceptability, it was constantly provided by Catholic churchmen embued with a new spirit of reform and vigour. The Counter-Reformation was slow in having its full effect on France, but in the early seventeenth century it took firm hold. An Oratory for the improvement of the clergy was founded by Bérulle in 1611; new orders spread, old ones were improved and reinvigorated; the Jesuits were allowed back into France in 1603 after a brief period during which they had been banned; the influence of François de Sales and later Vincent de Paul penetrated deeply. Mounting Catholic pressure against the provisions of the edict was harnessed by royal servants like the Cardinal de Richelieu who would brook no provincial or aristocratic resistance to the claims of central government.

Once effective Crown control had been re-established, the aristocratic adherents of Calvinism were bought off with surprising speed, systematically enticed into state positions or military service, or at least discouraged from lending active political and military support to the Protestant cause. By the early 1620s only the Duke of Rohan, the official Protector of the Huguenots, and his brother Soubise stood firm: and they were acutely aware of their isolation. When Louis XIII attacked the Huguenot 'state', it was not the nobility but the cities that stood in his way. First Montauban, then Montpellier, finally La Rochelle with its formidable fortifications, showed remarkable capacity for resistance, but the fall of La Rochelle in 1628 spelt the end of Huguenot military and political power. It had not been conceded lightly. Of a population of some 25,000 when the blockade of La Rochelle began, a fifth had fled and three-fifths had died before the 5,000 survivors ('ghosts, not people') finally surrendered. The figures are all the more startling since there were potent antagonisms within the city between its old ruling oligarchy, the more militant bourgeisie and the artisans. By the end of the siege there was no food, and the dead lay in the streets with the living physically incapable of burying them. Richelieu had besieged La Rochelle with an army of 25,000; when he ordered the armed men of the city to leave, there marched out only 64 Frenchmen and 90 recently arrived English reinforcements.[7]

The Duke of Rohan continued to resist in the south-east for a few months after the fall of La Rochelle, but the Peace of Alès (1629) brought to an end the French wars of religion. All Huguenot fortifications were razed, all *places de sûreté* surrendered. The defeated Calvinist party could no longer be of any political advantage to the aristocracy, and its political involvement ceased abruptly. Thereafter the Protestants were model subjects; even in the 1620s there had been no resumption of the contractual ideas of the *Vindiciae contra Tyrannos*, and in the mid-century disturbances known as the *Fronde* the Huguenots were notably loyal. Now more than ever confined to the bourgeoisie and artisan classes (although there were still a few faithful nobles like Ruvigny, Schomberg and, until 1668, Turenne), they wanted only to live in peace. It seemed, at first, that they could. Louis XIII and Richelieu, anxious to break the encirclement of France by Habsburg power, reaffirmed the freedom of conscience, exercise of public worship and civil equality granted by the Edict of Nantes, and turned their attention abroad. After their deaths Richelieu's successor Mazarin was grateful for Huguenot assistance to the royal cause during the *Fronde*, and the young Louis XIV promised the Calvinists that 'they will be maintained and kept, as in fact we maintain and keep them, in the full enjoyment of the Edict of Nantes'.

During the youth of Jean Migault, then, the Huguenots were

enjoying an unusually tranquil period. As late as 1666, Louis XIV was assuring the Elector of Brandenburg of the falsehood of any rumours that acts and edicts in favour of the Protestants were not being observed. 'I take care', he wrote, 'that they be maintained in all . . . privileges . . . to this I am engaged . . . by my royal word.'[8] Yet the mere fact that the king felt obliged to give such an assurance was ominous, and the attitudes that would bring about the *dragonnades* of the 1680s were already apparent. The Catholic revival, begun early in the century, continued unabated, and was symbolized by the canonization of François de Sales – an effective agent in the conversion of French Protestants – in 1665. The dislike of Calvinist doctrine and worship by the Catholic clergy was matched by the hatred of the Huguenots' civil equality by the Catholic laity. The Court was no longer distracted by such acute foreign pressures; and, in keeping with the political orthodoxy that had been hammered out in Europe since the Reformation, it believed that the State would be more secure if all the king's subjects shared the same religion. Louis himself may have become a more devout Catholic under the influence of Bossuet and Madame de Maintenon, and – since he often found himself at loggerheads with the pope – there was political advantage in showing by his actions that he was indeed a staunch Catholic defender, truly the 'Most Christian King' of France. Possibly, too, he was deluded by his officials so that he failed to realize the continuing strength of Calvinism in his realm. Whatever the reasons, it is certain that from the 1660s onwards the Huguenots came under increasing pressure to abjure their faith and return to the Catholic fold.

Between 1661 and 1679 there was a steady erosion of the privileges granted by the Edict of Nantes. Synods ceased. By the time the Edict was finally revoked in 1685, the number of Calvinist *temples* had been reduced from 813 to 243, 570 having been destroyed. The Huguenots were subjected to petty annoyances: their ministers were not allowed to wear clerical garb outside their churches; psalms could be sung only during worship, and then only softly and not if a Roman Catholic procession including the sacrament was passing by outside; their dead were to be buried, in special cemeteries, only at 6 a.m. or 6 p.m. in summer and at 8 a.m. or 4 p.m. in winter. More serious were regulations such as those prohibiting Protestant ministers from marrying a Catholic to a Protestant if anyone objected, and forbidding Huguenots to persuade servants or employees to turn Protestant. In several cities it was ordained that aldermen must be Catholic; Protestants could occupy only such positions as clock-keeper or porter. Huguenots found it harder to enter crafts, whether as apprentices or masters. A fund was founded to buy conversions.

From 1679 onwards, oppressive interpretation of the Edict of Nantes was superseded by more direct action. The rate of destruction of Protestant *temples* increased, while the pretexts for their demolition grew weaker. The legal guarantees in the Edict of Nantes were withdrawn. Huguenots were ejected from various towns like Châlons-sur-Marne and Dijon because they had never been explicitly allowed to reside in them. Greater control was exercised over the movement of Protestant pastors, who were also subjected to increased taxation and severe legal penalties for minor offences. Marriages between Catholics and Protestants were prohibited. Two moves by Louis in 1681 aroused particular indignation: his order (soon repealed) that Protestant ministers were not to visit dying members of their flocks, and his decree that children aged 7 or over in Protestant families could be converted without their parents being able to interfere. In economic as well as religious matters, the Huguenots were harassed by an ever-increasing stream of edicts preventing their entry into various guilds and restricting them in the exercise of their professions. They were excluded from all public office, from posts in the royal household or on aristocratic estates. They were not to be admitted into the legal profession, not to practise medicine, not to act as midwives, not to print or sell books. If on the other hand they accepted conversion, they were offered substantial tax relief and did not need to pay their debts for three years.

While intelligent Protestant leaders could read the writing on the wall by 1679, it was the events of 1681 which opened the eyes of most to what was likely to happen. When the royal *intendant* of Poitou, Marillac, quartered dragoons on Protestant households he was doing nothing new in principle, but the licence given them to indulge themselves and their systematic employment as agents of conversion were novel, horrifying, and – as we have seen in the case of Jean Migault's community – effective. What persuasion, bribery and intimidation had failed to do was achieved, at least superficially, by the combination of force, brutality and a crushing financial burden. The resultant flood of abjurations was so great that the *intendant* at Montauban complained in 1685 that when troops approached towns in his district, the Protestants converted so rapidly that it was difficult to find enough homes to lodge all the soldiers for the night.

On 22 October 1685, the 'perpetual and irrevocable' edict that had given shelter to the Huguenots for nearly a century was revoked. Before then, even in decrees licensing its subversion, Louis XIV had always repeated that he intended the Edict of Nantes to be observed. Now, perhaps so that Huguenot ministers could be banished, perhaps to relieve the treasury of the financial burdens imposed by bought 'conversions', it was annulled. All Protestant services were forbidden, all *temples* ordered to be destroyed. Ministers were exiled unless they accepted conversion; Huguenot laymen, however, were forbidden to leave the country, and their children were to be baptized and brought up as Catholics. The Gallican Church trumpeted its delight (plates 2, 3). Its champion Bossuet wrote:

> Let us not fail to proclaim this miracle of our age and to perpetuate its record. . . let us pour out our hearts in praising the piety of Louis. Let us raise our acclamations even to the skies, attributing to this new Theodosius, this new Marcion, this new Charlemagne the words of the six hundred and thirty Fathers of the Council of Chalcedon: 'You have confirmed the Faith; you have exterminated the heretics. This is the crowning achievement of your reign which hereby gains a character all of its own. Because of you heresy is no more: God alone could have achieved this marvel. King of Heaven, preserve the King on earth. This is the prayer of the Church; this is the prayer of the bishops.'[9]

But Bossuet's claim that heresy had been 'exterminated' was ill-founded. A final general clause in the Revocation assured surviving Huguenots that they could live freely in the kingdom as long as they held no religious gatherings. Some 'new converts' thereupon with-drew their enforced abjurations and tried to resume Protestantism, in the belief that persecution was at an end. They were soon undeceived, as the *dragonnades* were renewed and intensified; but Louis was left with hundreds of thousands of subjects who remained Protestant at heart and deeply resented what had been done to them. About 200,000 – many of them younger people – left France as refugees against the will and despite the deterrent measures of its government, and went to live in the lands of Louis' enemies.

The conservative figures shown on map 1 are based on the suggestions of Samuel Mours.[10] The estimates for Germany, the Netherlands and America are likely to be low, and none of the figures take account of fugitives intercepted while trying to leave France. They add up to less than 200,000, but other historians consider that a total between 200,000 and a quarter of a million would be reasonable. In any case, the Huguenots who stayed behind in France were far more numerous. Some 700,000 remained, only nominally (if at all) Catholic, abstaining from church attendance and ceremonies when-ever they could, an alien and hostile element in the Gallican Church. By the 1690s a handful of ministers had returned, risking the fate of the best-known of their number, Claude Brousson, who was broken on the wheel at Montpellier in 1698. In the early years of the

23

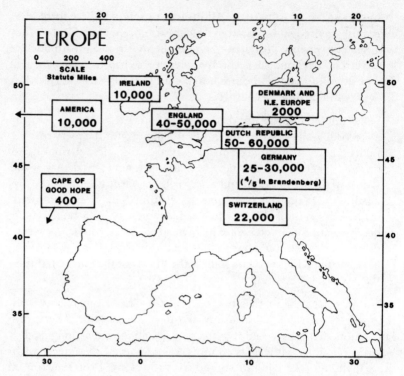

Map 1   Destinations of refugees from Louis XIV's France

eighteenth century Huguenot resentment in the Cévennes broke out into the Camisard rebellion, which for years tied up royal armies under the Marshals Montrevel and Villars, and in 1715 Antoine Court organized a Protestant Synod in the area. Though men found themselves condemned to live as galley slaves and women were confined in prisons as terrifying as the Tour de Constance at Aigues-Mortes for taking part in Huguenot worship, services continued to be held *au Désert*, that is, in secluded secret locations. Catholic missionary endeavour had considerable success, but Calvinism survived. Indeed it was given a new structure, and in 1744 a National Synod in Languedoc drew ministers from all parts of France.

News that this Synod had been held sparked off renewed persecution, and even in the 1760s Protestants could suffer the ultimate penalty. François Rochette was the last minister to be hanged in France for his faith, in 1762; deeply imbued with the psalms in the best Calvinist tradition, at the scaffold he sang the verse, 'This is the day that the Lord has made; let us rejoice and be glad in it.' But times were changing, and in the same decade Voltaire mounted his famous and successful campaign in support of the innocence of Jean Calas, tortured and put to death on account of his Protestantism by the Parlement of Toulouse. There was growing revulsion against cruelties practised in the name of religion, and Huguenot liberty increased in the generation before the French Revolution. In 1787 an Edict of Toleration permitted Huguenots to live freely and practise the trades and professions from which they had been excluded, although only Catholic public worship was permitted. Finally the French Revolution enshrined the equality of all citizens before the law, and insisted that no one should be troubled for their religious opinions unless public order was infringed. Special rights were given to descendants of Huguenot refugees wishing to return to France, rights which were to persist until the 1939–45 World War.[11] French Protestants could once more live in their homeland with hope and dignity. But for almost all the descendants of those who had fled during the previous two centuries and more, it was too late; their change of national loyalty was irreversible.

2

The Huguenot Settlements in England

Given the chronology of persecution in France, it is not surprising that French Protestants were to be found seeking refuge abroad from the 1520s onwards, especially in the 1560s and 1570s. Emigration diminished in the early seventeenth century, briefly reviving in the 1620s, but it intensified sharply from the late 1670s and peaked in the 1680s. Thereafter it was more sporadic, intensifying anew in the late 1740s and early 1750s, then dying away altogether during the second half of the eighteenth century. Jean Migault was typical of the Huguenots in fleeing his country only when faced by an emergency. Although men sometimes left ahead of, or separately from, their families, there was no conscious process of chain migration whereby refugees, as they settled in a new land, sponsored the migration of kinsfolk or fellow villagers from their homelands until a section of the original community had been transplanted. Nor did the countries to which the refugees fled appoint state officials to assist their passage, in contrast to the case of Salzburg in 1731 when all Protestants over the age of 12 were expelled and Prussia promptly appointed special commissaries to organize their relief and transport. In the sixteenth and early seventeenth centuries Huguenot refugees often hoped to return home when conditions improved, but after the *dragonnades* and the Revocation the decision to emigrate was likely to be permanent.

Their French background could hardly have been more effective in preparing the Huguenots for a refugee environment. They had never been anything other than an exposed minority. Every official document reminded them of their isolation, since they were always referred to as belonging to the 'so-called reformed religion' or RPR (*Religion Prétendue Réformée*). They were used to living in fear, and their survival depended on the development of inner certainty and fortitude. We have seen that they were not a microcosm of French society as a whole, but were mostly artisans or bourgeois. They possessed, therefore, commercial and craft skills and an unusually high degree of literacy. Such assets were portable; they could readily be taken from country to country and from town to town as opportunities beckoned. Had the Huguenots been predominantly a rural, landed or peasant group, their history in exile would have been very different. As it was, they were welcomed in many parts of Europe and the wider world, and for good reason: they blessed the lands that adopted them with commercial advantages as well as with a rare combination of integrity and determination.

One outcome of their education, their beliefs, their commercial interests and Calvinist international co-ordination, was that even while in France the Huguenots developed contacts elsewhere. Calvinism in Geneva, in La Rochelle, in London, in Amsterdam was interlinked. This made the decision to emigrate more acceptable, the process of taking refuge that much easier, the choice of destination greater. Before the world of international Calvinism had developed, the earliest refugees slipped across the border to other French-speaking areas, notably the southern Low Countries and parts of Switzerland. Their impact on the places to which they went was considerable, indeed was partly responsible for the development of Calvinist internationalism. It can be encapsulated by a brief look at the fascinating history of the Reformation in another area they evangelized, the islands of Jersey and Guernsey.

The Channel Islands were in a very curious political and religious position in the first half of the sixteenth century. They were small, rather isolated, and much closer to France than England, yet still in the hands of the Tudors after almost all the continental mainland possessions once ruled by their predecessors had fallen to the French king. The islands were fortified frontier posts in sight of enemy country. Their inhabitants spoke French, used *livres tournois* and not pounds sterling, and were subject to Norman law; but they were as anti-French as they were un-English. As part of their Norman heritage, their ecclesiastical links were with Normandy rather than England. Their bishop was the Bishop of Coutances, and continued to be so throughout the Henrician and Edwardian Reformations, the Catholic reaction under Mary, and part of the reign of Queen Elizabeth.

Protestant ideas, and hostile counter-measures, developed more swiftly in France than in England, and Normandy was affected at an early stage. In 1528 laymen were burnt for heresy at Rouen and Coutances, and three women at Avranches. Both because of their closeness and because they spoke French and therefore had no educational opportunities in England, Channel Islanders were inevitably influenced by events in Normandy. Although we cannot name French Protestant teachers active in Jersey and Guernsey before Edward VI's reign, there is good reason to believe they had been at work for years. The Channel Islanders had a long tradition of vocal and pertinacious defence of their rights, and were well aware that in the last resort it was both difficult and impolitic for the English Privy Council to insist on its own way in such a remote, foreign and beleaguered part of the realm. At the time of the Reformation they were protesting loudly about various political matters. Yet only one or two lone voices were raised against the Westminster acts introducing Protestantism. Parish fraternities, obits (endowments left for masses to be said on the anniversary of a person's death) and chantry chapels abounded in the islands, but their suppression gave rise to no apparent protest. Wayside crosses were destroyed with a will. And when in 1549 the Act of Uniformity did away with Latin services, these were at once abandoned; indeed the Privy Council wrote to thank the islanders for their speedy action. They can hardly have adopted Cranmer's English prayer book, which they would have found even less intelligible than Latin. The historian of Jersey, G. R. Balleine, suggests that Calvin's *Prières Ecclésiastiques* were used instead. During Mary's reign, when an attempt was made to resume the Maundy procession at St Helier, two youths marched in front carrying a dead toad on a gibbet. Such an offence would surely have merited the death sentence in France, probably too in Marian England. In Jersey all that was required of the offenders was that they find security for good behaviour. Clearly Protestantism was too strongly entrenched for more forceful action to be acceptable. The Huguenot bridgehead that had been established in the Channel Islands was of enduring value to refugees escaping France, and we will see later that the forms of worship developed there over the next century exercised an important influence on the nature of later Huguenot churches in England.

While the earliest French Protestants to reach England included those leaving Normandy for Jersey and Guernsey, the first major influx of refugees came not from France at all, but from the southern Low Countries. These were, therefore, Walloon-speaking rather than French-speaking Huguenots, but they were rapidly joined by Frenchmen alongside whom they worshipped and with whom they shared, in English eyes, a common identity. From the time Lutheranism first spread until just before the end of the century, the conglomerate of provinces that made up the Low Countries was ruled by only two monarchs, Charles V (until his abdication in 1555) and Philip II. Both were staunch defenders of Catholicism. Their willingness to use the Inquisition to enforce their desires ran counter to the wishes of their subjects, who held an unusually tolerant point of view. Lutheranism and Anabaptism reached the area early. When Calvinism arrived, it first took root in the great old towns of the south, and, as we have seen, its development in France and the Low Countries remained closely intertwined.

After the English Reformation the long-standing close trading links between England and the Low Countries, as well as the proximity of the Channel, made it inevitable that those fleeing persecution would head for London. A few Protestants from the area arrived even before the Henrician Reformation, following closely on the heels of the earliest Lutheran books, which are known to have reached England by 1519. It was to be another decade before the French king was calling on Henry to repatriate French heretics who had sought refuge in his realm.[1] Persecution in the Low Countries became acute only after the accession of Philip II. Calvinism grew rapidly in the Netherlands in the 1560s, and large numbers of Calvinist refugees reached England in 1562–3, after the outbreak of religious wars in France. Many more followed in 1567–8, after the first revolt in the Netherlands failed and the Duke of Alva arrived there with Spanish and Italian troops and implemented policies based on fear and bloodshed. Another large influx occurred at the time of the second revolt in 1572–3. The provinces of the Low Countries under Spanish control remained unsafe for convinced Protestants, and many left during the remainder of the century, seeking sanctuary either to the north, where the Union of Utrecht eventually joined a group of provinces in a fighting alliance against Spain, or across the Channel.

Since Henry VIII was as happy to burn Protestant heretics as he was to hang Catholics who denied royal supremacy over the church, England was not a safe refuge for continental Protestants while he lived. With his death, however, the situation changed dramatically. The religious immigrants who crossed the Channel during Edward's brief reign founded England's earliest foreign Protestant churches, even though most were obliged to move on again when Mary came to the throne. When Elizabeth succeeded her sister in 1558 the country once more became a haven, just at the right time to offer hope to many caught up in the continental turmoils of the 1560s and the 1570s. It remained a sure refuge thereafter.

It is impossible to state precisely how many religious refugees were in England at any one time. Numerous returns of aliens in the London area were compiled under Elizabeth and the early Stuarts, inspired either by government fears about possible riots in the capital and plots against the royal person, or (since aliens were heavily taxed) by economic motives. The evidence seems ample, but it is difficult to interpret. Contemporaries had problems defining the word 'alien'. Extant returns are not always concerned with the same region. It is not always clear whether the returns relate only to men, or to women and children as well. Above all, it is hard to know how many of the aliens were inspired to come primarily by religious motives. For the purposes of this book, the most relevant of the early returns is that for 1573, the year after the Massacre of St Bartholomew in France and the outbreak of the second revolt in the Netherlands. It suggests that there were then 5,315 members of the various foreign churches in and about London, of whom just under a half had come for reasons of employment rather than religion.

As a result of the troubles on the Continent, substantial numbers of refugees came to England in 1572 and 1573. At Southampton, where a foreign church with 116 communicant members had been formed in the winter of 1567–8, the civic authorities now ordered references of newcomers to be listed in case spies tried to take the opportunity to enter the country; while from Rye the Mayor reported to Lord Burghley that 641 refugees arrived between 27 August (just after the Massacre) and 4 November 1572. There is no evidence that any newcomers swelled the large stranger community at Norwich, which in 1571 already numbered nearly 4,000, or getting on for a third of the city's population. (Almost a half of the 4,000 were children; and about a sixth had been born in England.) Nor does the much smaller Dutch settlement at Maidstone seem to have been affected. On the other hand the community of 406 foreign Protestants originally settled in Sandwich in 1561 grew greatly, and was about to spawn the Canterbury settlement; it had previously been responsible for that at Colchester where, according to a return of 1573, there were 534 foreigners.[2]

These figures show that the foreign Protestant churches in England had well over 10,000 members as early as 1573, and the majority of them were religious refugees. Over the next generation the number of aliens in the country grew substantially, peaking in the 1590s both in the capital and the provinces. The Norwich community grew despite the loss of 2,482 members to plague in 1578–9, and was numbered at 4,679 in 1582. Plague likewise hit Southampton with great severity in 1583–4, but although over 70 members of the foreign church died – there had been only 25 deaths in the previous five years – it still had 186 communicants in August 1584. The other congregations increased too. It was certified from Colchester in 1586 that there were 1,293 Dutch settlers, of whom 504 were children born in England. Although the community at Rye had returned to France by the 1590s, the Canterbury settlement was flourishing, and when the Consistory there investigated the situation in 1597 it found the church had more than 2,000 members; there may have been as many as 3,000 a few years earlier. The total figure for all the foreign churches in the realm at the time must have exceeded 15,000.[3]

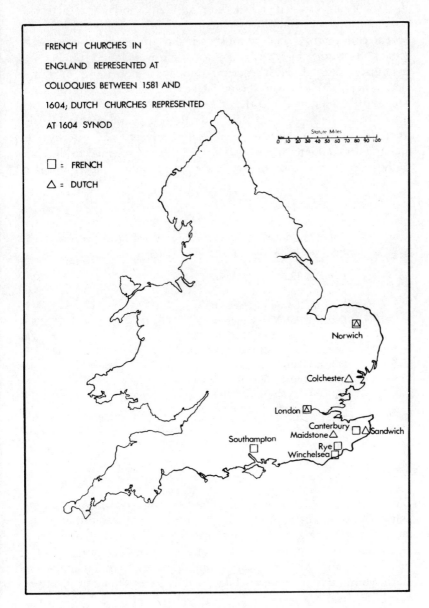

FRENCH CHURCHES IN
ENGLAND REPRESENTED AT
COLLOQUIES BETWEEN 1581 AND
1604; DUTCH CHURCHES REPRESENTED
AT 1604 SYNOD

☐ = FRENCH
△ = DUTCH

Statute Miles
0 10 20 30 40 50 60 70 80 90 100

Norwich

Colchester△

London ☐△

Canterbury
Maidstone△   ☐△Sandwich

Southampton
☐

Rye☐
Winchelsea☐

Map 2 French and Dutch churches in England at the close of the sixteenth century

The creation of the independent United Provinces, formed from the seven northernmost provinces of the Low Countries, was in practice recognized by the Spanish king when he agreed to a twelve-year truce in 1609. Thanks to that and the Edict of Nantes in France, there was less need for continental Protestants to cross the Channel in the early seventeenth century. The size of the foreign communities accordingly shrank as some of their members returned home or became assimilated into English society, and were not replaced. Some newcomers arrived from France when Louis XIII and Richelieu attacked the Huguenots in the 1620s – the Southampton Consistory admitted 42 refugees from the Ile de Ré to communion in January 1628, for instance – but they were comparatively few in number. In the mid-1630s the foreign churches in England presented to the state authorities the breakdown of communicant numbers shown in Table 1.

Table 1   *Statement of sizes of French and Dutch congregations in England, 1630s*[4]

French Church of London	1,400
Dutch Church of London	840
French Church of Canterbury	900
Dutch Church of Colchester	700
French Church of Norwich	396
Dutch Church of Norwich	363
Dutch Church of Maidstone	50
Dutch Church of Sandwich	500
Dutch Church of Yarmouth	28
French Church of Southampton	36
Total	5,213

Two things should be noted about this list. It was composed at a time when the congregations were under attack, and was produced by them – not by state or civic authorities – specifically to show that Englishmen thought they were far more numerous than was really the case. And it purported to list only communicants; to find the total size of the community, including children, the figures should probably be nearly doubled.

We can conclude, then, that a generation before and again a generation after 1600, there were in all some 10,000 members of the foreign Protestant communities in England; but that at their peak in the 1590s, there were over 15,000. These figures include all worshipping foreign Protestants, Dutch (and, in London, a few Italians and Spanish) as well as Walloon and French. Before the 1620s the Dutch were always more numerous, at times much more numerous, than the French and Walloons; table 1 provides the first indication of the reversal that was to take place over the rest of the seventeenth century. What the terms 'Dutch', 'Walloon', 'French' represented is not always clear but, although nationalities were vague, the refugees (with far greater certainty than their English hosts) did sometimes differentiate between themselves. Thus the minister of the Walloon/French Church of London, Jean Castel, described his congregation to the Archbishop of Canterbury in 1591:

> One part, and that the least, were Frenchmen . . . but such as were of better condition long since returned, to defend their own seats . . . the other part, and that the greatest, were Hannonii, Artesii, Flandri, Gallicani, that is, sprung out of the countries which obey the Spaniard; and in less need and want (some few excepted) than the rest.

Castel's assertion that the Walloons were in the majority probably holds good for the French-speaking congregations founded under the Tudors and enduring long thereafter – those of London, Norwich, Southampton and Canterbury. It is hard to be sure. When Francis Cross analysed a thousand individuals married at Canterbury between 1590 and 1627, he found that most came from within a few miles of the Franco-Belgian border, especially from the region between Armentières and Valenciennes.[5] The short-lived French-speaking church that existed alongside the Dutch or Flemish one at Sandwich in the late 1560s and early 1570s was predominantly Walloon. Other small groups of Walloons, too small to found their own congregations, joined the Flemings at such places as Maidstone and Colchester, just as some Dutch joined the French-speaking Canterbury community. The church at Rye (and its offshoot at nearby Winchelsea) was purely French, but its sporadic history supports Castel's observation that the French were more likely to return home than the Walloons; intimately connected with Dieppe, its fortunes fluctuated according to the situation there, as its members sailed back and forth between France and England.

During the early seventeenth century, two changes took place in the composition of the Huguenot communities. The percentage of their members who had been born in England increased; and they became ever more French and less Walloon, as emigration from the southern

Low Countries dried up but that from France continued. Of the 111 men known to have served the French Church of London as elders or deacons or both during the 1640s and 1650s, the place of birth of 104 has been established. Of these, 41 were born in England, 30 in France,

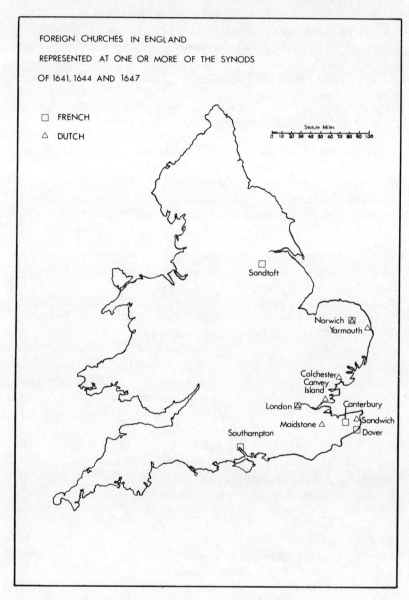

Map 3 Foreign churches in England in the 1640s

23 in the Spanish Low Countries and 10 elsewhere. Closer examination shows that the number of English-born officers peaked in the 1640s and declined slightly in the 1650s, while the number of those who had been born in France was rising sharply.[6] The move to French predominance was completed during the later Stuart period, as refugees flooded in from Louis XIV's dominions. The same stages of development can be discerned in the churches of Canterbury and Southampton, but perhaps not at Norwich, which attracted comparatively few newcomers in the late seventeenth century.

By the time of the Civil War and Interregnum, other French Protestant communities had been established. Dutch, French and Walloons were all involved in projects, conceived by Cornelius Vermuyden, to drain fenland. These produced settlements first in the Level of Hatfield Chase in the Isle of Axholme, later in the Great Bedford Level in the Isle of Ely. From the Hatfield Chase area was drawn the congregation of Sandtoft (Lincolnshire), from the Great Bedford Level the Cambridgeshire congregations of Whittlesey and Thorney. All three viewed themselves as primarily French rather than Dutch. There was also a French church at Dover from the time of the Civil War to the Restoration, following in the footsteps of a Flemish congregation that had existed in the town in the later sixteenth century and a French one which had met there briefly at the close of James I's reign.

So French Protestantism and French-speaking communities had existed in England for over a hundred years before they were so strongly reinforced by the new refugees of the later seventeenth century. Of the Huguenots who left France during Louis's reign, some 40,000 to 50,000 settled in Britain.[7] The timing of their emigration reflects conditions in their homeland. During the 1660s and 1670s there was a growing trickle of refugees; from 1679, as oppressive edicts increased sharply in number, a stream; in 1681, with the onset of the *dragonnades*, the stream became a river. After the Revocation of the Edict of Nantes, though with a slight timelag, the river turned into a torrent. Thereafter the volume of immigration diminished, increasing anew from time to time during the eighteenth century whenever fears of persecution intensified.

On arrival, the newcomers naturally tended to gravitate towards the two large existing centres of London and Canterbury. London – using the term to embrace the cities of London and Westminster and the built-up area around them – was the heart of Huguenot settlement in England. There they congregated in the outskirts, where food and housing were cheaper and guild control less effective, although many came into the City proper to worship at the French Church of London

Table 2   *New Members of the French Church of London, 1680–1705*[8]

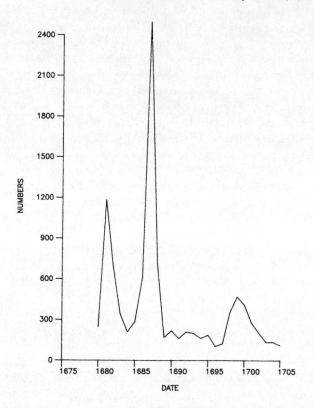

in Threadneedle Street. In the 1680s a fair number may have been living to the north of the City, but by 1700 refugee settlements formed a pattern along an east-west axis with two distinct communities based on Spitalfields in the eastern suburbs and the Leicester Fields/Soho area in the west. In 1685 there were only two French congregations in the western environs, the Savoy church (officially sanctioned in 1661) and its annexe 'des Grecs', and none at all in the eastern suburbs; by 1700 there were fourteen in the western area, nine in the eastern (see maps 6 and 7). At this time, it has been conservatively estimated, there were some 15,000 refugees living in the City and eastern environs and 8,000 in Westminster and the western suburbs, as well as more distant settlements at Chelsea, Greenwich, Wandsworth and Wapping. The French exiles thus comprised about 5 per cent of London's population, at a time when one in every ten inhabitants of England lived in and around the capital. It is interesting to compare these figures with those

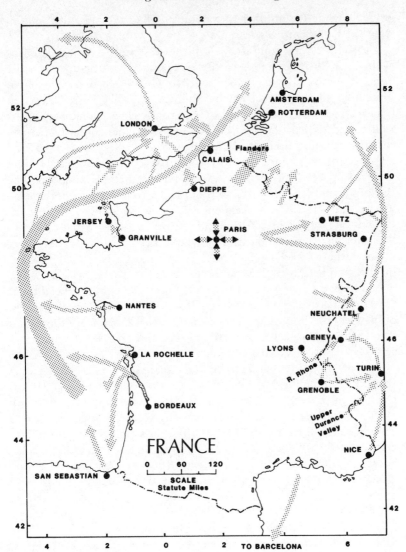

Map 4 Some popular Huguenot escape routes from France

for Elizabeth's reign. Then, too, in the early 1570s, aliens had comprised 5 per cent of the London population – but at that stage London had only about 100,000 inhabitants, while by the end of the seventeenth century it had over half a million. In between the two periods the percentage declined, with London's overall population growing while the number of foreigners fell as the rate of migration from the Continent lessened.[9]

Clearly, the very rapid growth of the western and eastern suburbs in the later Stuart period – hardly to have been anticipated after the devastations of plague in 1665 and the Great Fire in 1666 – owes something to the arrival of the Huguenots. They were drawn to London for a variety of reasons. Through merchants, members of the Court, and its existing foreign communities, the capital had many continental connections. It was a centre of relief assistance, and offered prospects of employment. Once some had come, newcomers were attracted in search of friends, news, advice and companionship. The Bishop of London, Henry Compton, had a well-deserved reputation for his support for the Huguenot refugees. And both the French Church of London in Threadneedle Street and that of the Savoy in Westminster were willing to help where they could.

The earliest of the new Huguenot settlements were established at Ipswich and Rye in 1681, within months of the first *dragonnades*. They were organized from the capital, the fruit of the combined efforts of the Threadneedle Street church, the Bishop of London and (in the case of Ipswich) the English philanthropist Thomas Firmin. By the end of the century many other French communities existed: at Colchester and Thorpe-le-Soken in Essex; at Faversham and Dover (the fourth foreign group to exist in the town in the space of a century) in Kent; at Bristol; at Edinburgh in Scotland; and at Barnstaple, Bideford, Dartmouth, Exeter, Plymouth and nearby Stonehouse in Devon. All of these had their own ministers and congregations, there being two churches at both Exeter and Plymouth. Ephemeral congregations also existed briefly at Soham (Cambridgeshire), Maldon (Essex), Hollingbourne and Boughton Malherbe (Kent), Salisbury (Wiltshire), Taunton (Somerset) and Falmouth (Cornwall), but disappeared before the end of the century. At the same time the old settlements of Canterbury and Southampton derived new strength from the refugees, as to a lesser extent did the one at Norwich. The groups created by the efforts to drain the Fens were not affected by the influx; the Sandtoft church actually ceased to exist a matter of months before the Revocation, although that of Thorney (which had absorbed the Whittlesey congregation in the 1650s) continued to flourish into the eighteenth century. Some refugees may have stayed in the south coast ports where they landed. Others went to the Channel Islands, where they had no need of a separate identity and merged quickly into the French-speaking environment.

Some significant conclusions can be drawn from this distribution. The refugees were in the south-east and, to a much lesser extent,

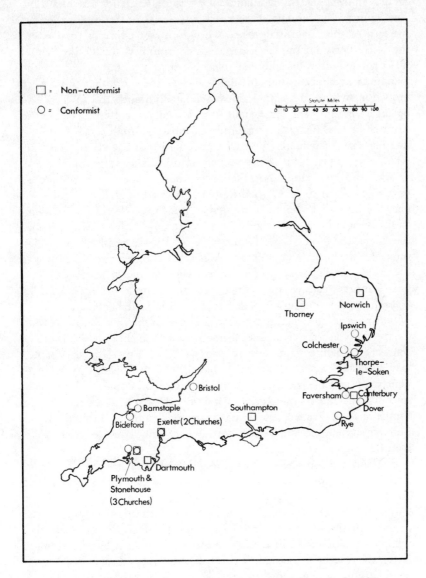

Map 5 French churches in England (excluding London), 1700

south-west of England; all their communities lay south of a line drawn
from the Severn to the Wash except for the one in Edinburgh and a
small later one at Chester, which seems to have become a transit point
for Huguenots travelling to and from Ireland. There were no other

French churches in the Midlands or north of England, nor in Wales. The country settlements were much smaller than those of either the western or the eastern suburbs of London, and many of them were short-lived. By far the largest foreign community outside the capital was that at Canterbury, housing nearly a third of all the refugees in the provinces (excluding the Channel Islands). About another third were in Devon, where the main groups were at Plymouth and Exeter. The balance were in Kent, Essex and East Anglia, or scattered around the country in ones and twos or family groups too small to be visible to the historian. Normally the refugees settled near the coast, and thus retained the options of cheap transport and further migration.

Why did the Huguenots settle in these places? What, indeed, motivated them to come to Britain at all? For England was only one place of refuge – if the most popular – after the Netherlands. Switzerland, Brandenburg and other parts of Germany, Ireland, Scandinavia, the Cape of Good Hope, America, even Russia became homes for those fleeing Louis XIV's France. Whatever choice of destination was eventually made, some preconditions were obviously necessary. The host country had to be sympathetic to them as refugees and as Calvinists. It seems certain that Britain would have become the home of far more refugees had the ruler at the time of the Revocation in 1685 not been a Catholic, James II. It is most striking that the main influx across the Channel came not in 1685 or 1686 but in 1687, after James had published his Declaration of Indulgence promising his subjects liberty of conscience and the free exercise of religion. Economic support, the means of making a livelihood, was also a necessity; in England as in France, the Huguenots tended to be located not in isolated rural regions but in towns, where they could exercise their commercial and craft skills.

England had long been a home for Flemish weavers, and had from time to time since Edward III's day deliberately invited them, but historical considerations on their own mattered little. Far fewer Huguenots went to Scotland, for instance, than might be anticipated in view of the strong traditional medieval Franco-Scottish alliance, whereas many settled in Ireland, which had no such historical links. Geography, when coupled with economic opportunity, was much more important. For those escaping by sea from south-western France or Normandy or the southern Low Countries, England was an obvious destination. Once uprooted, many refugees were prepared to migrate more than once, but the western settlements in England were a more likely initial home for those coming from the south-west of France than those escaping from the north-east. At Bristol, four out of every five whose place of origin is known came from Aunis,

Saintonge and Poitou.[10] By contrast Huguenots from Normandy were more likely to head for London or Canterbury.

It is noteworthy that the first communities to be formed in the English provinces after the *dragonnades* were to the east of London, not in the west country. Does this mean that the earliest group of new refugees came from the north rather than the west of France? So little is known of the history and composition of the Devonshire settlements that we cannot tell. Or was it, rather, that the capital was immediately perceived as the obvious hope for work opportunities or charitable relief? One factor of unquestionable importance was the pre-existence of a French/Walloon community and church organization. Not only did this offer reassurance of freedom of worship in the immediate future, but work might be found through the goodwill and connections of the descendants of earlier refugees. Families such as Delmé, Desbouveries, Houblon, Lefroy, Le Keux, Lethieullier or Papillon were indeed well-placed to give help, being by now well-established in English society and of formidable means. Pierre Delmé, for example, was a Common Councilman of London; his eldest son became Lord Mayor and Governor of the Bank of England, and was worth over £250,000 on his death in 1728. In later chapters we will see that the forces of earlier Walloon/French and later Huguenot combined to develop enterprises in linen, silk and paper-making, and to help in the establishment of the Bank of England. But first we should acquire a new perspective by examining how the refugees were viewed through English eyes.

3

The Refugees and the English Government

In 1551, five commissioners appointed by the Privy Council inspected a Flemish and Walloon refugee settlement at Glastonbury in Somerset. There they found 44 families and 6 widows, rather over 200 foreigners in all, who struck them as godly, honest, poor folk of quiet and sober conversation, willing to teach their craft of weaving to others. The refugees were Protestant, their minister and chief organizer being Valérand Poullain, previously pastor of the French-speaking church at Strasbourg. They had been settled in the grounds of the recently dissolved abbey by the Duke of Somerset, but his present fall from political favour had left them exposed to exploitation by the Englishmen among whom they lived. They were ill-housed, having only six habitable dwellings, although twenty-two others lacking roofs, doors and windows could in time be improved.

This cameo suggests that certain conditions were necessary for the refugee settlements of the later sixteenth century to thrive. They had to be composed of Protestants; they must promote trades which the authorities felt would benefit the English economy, and be prepared to teach their skills to Englishmen; and they needed both initial encouragement and support, and continuing protection from the Privy Council. The last condition might seem least likely of fulfilment, for the later Tudor Privy Council was gravely overworked. During the reign of Queen Elizabeth its effectiveness increased as its membership was pruned and it came to meet daily rather than three times a week, but the range of business it transacted was so great that it was always overburdened. Major matters of policy mingled with the arbitration of petty disputes, foreign policy with the enforcement of law and order at home, judicial concerns with the defence of the realm. Given such pressures, it might be anticipated that the Council would have had little time to spare to consider aliens. But in fact it found them relevant to a number of issues central to its deliberations: religion, commerce, and the maintenance of external peace and internal concord and good order.

Tudor councillors would not have defined their interests as

precisely as modern historians, who tend to be experts in ecclesiastical or commercial or foreign affairs, but rarely in all three. In 1564, for instance, the English ambassador in France, Sir Thomas Smith, thought it worthwhile to send a copy of the proceedings of the French Reformed Synod recently held at La Ferté-sous-Jouarre to the Secretary of State William Cecil, with the suggestion that the Archbishop of Canterbury and the Bishop of London might like to know 'the fashion of their synods'.[1] Cecil himself was thoroughly sympathetic to the cause of foreign Protestant refugees in England, and proved a most constant and valuable patron. He saw as inseparable the economic benefits they offered the country and God's blessings that would accompany them. In reflection of that attitude, the Council developed a policy which, broadly, welcomed a substantial but controlled number of Protestant strangers to England; protected them after their arrival; encouraged settlements of skilled artisans where they could best inject new life and expertise into English manufactures; governed them as far as possible through their fellow-countrymen and their own church organization; and sought to reduce local English hostility by distributing them around the country in groups of limited size.

In 1570, when thirty Flemish aliens asked whether they might settle at Rye, the Council directed that should the local authorities find after enquiry

> that they be come out of their country for religion and for
> safeguard of their conscience, and that they be such as may be
> beneficial to that town, and be also comprised within the number
> of strangers limited by the Queen's Majesty to inhabit there, that
> then they do receive and suffer them to remain with them.

It will be noted that the first requirement was the religious one. Some 1,500 strangers in London who could not show appropriate Protestant credentials were ordered out of the realm in 1574. The same year, it was discovered that there were far more foreigners in Sandwich than had been authorized. Unlike those in the capital these were Protestant, and therefore acceptable; they were merely to be 'removed into other places more remote from the sea side' so that national security was not endangered. Canterbury was chosen as their new residence, and the Privy Council directed that those who went there were not to be 'of the meanest sort, but choice to be made of such as be makers of bays, grograines etc'; provided they behaved in orderly fashion, they were to be used 'charitably and favourably'. The Council continued to protect foreign Protestants when the need arose. As it wrote to the Judge of the Admiralty in 1581, it was anxious that 'a special regard should be had' for 'such as shall be repaired hither for the cause of religion'. It continued to frown on aliens who lacked the qualification of Protestantism, and in 1586 ordered the banishment of strangers 'not being of any church or congregation' in London, Maidstone, Sandwich and Dover.[2]

If the Edwardian and Elizabethan governments practised positive discrimination in favour of Protestant aliens, the Stuarts did not. Faced by complaints from Norwich in 1613, the Privy Council explained that it desired a balance between the rights of citizens and of strangers. Under Charles I, particularly in the time of Archbishop Laud's ascendancy, the foreign communities came under hostile scrutiny and feared for their survival. With the Interregnum that pressure was removed, but the established foreign congregations in England with their Calvinist discipline found less support than they hoped from the new Puritan regime. The accession of Charles II did not bring any return to Laudian harassment, but the government decided to license new congregations only if they adopted the Anglican liturgy translated into French, while James II's attitude to the Huguenots was fundamentally unwelcoming. Only with the accession of William and Mary, and later of Anne – strongly Protestant monarchs engaged in a long struggle with Louis XIV – could foreign Protestants in England once again look forward with optimism to the favourable treatment they had enjoyed in the later sixteenth century.

What were the advantages discerned at different times in welcoming aliens to England? Traditionally, it was for economic reasons that various groups of aliens had been suffered to cross the Channel. Some medieval immigrants, notably the Jews before their expulsion by Edward I, were money-lenders. Others were skilled foreign craftsmen like weavers or shipbuilders, miners or armourers – masters of techniques which monarchs were anxious to see introduced in England. From Ireland and Scotland came herders of sheep and cattle. Fewer in number, but striking in their wealth and their importance to medieval English trade, were merchants, Flemings, Lombards, and members of the German Hanse who had their own guildhall and warehouses and churches in the 'Steelyard' in London. None of these groups met an enthusiastic response from ordinary Englishmen. The Jews were particularly badly maltreated, and the savagery they encountered might even, as at York and London and Bury St Edmunds in the winter of 1189–90, involve large-scale massacre. Christian alien merchants and artisans were rather better respected and protected, but could still fall victim to mob fury. Flemings and Lombards were both targets of Wat Tyler's men in the Peasants' Revolt of 1381: having executed Archbishop Sudbury, the rebels went on to the banks of the river Thames where the majority of the Flemings lived; and they beheaded all the Flemings they found without judgment and without cause. For you could see heaps of dead bodies and corpses lying in the squares and other places. And so they spent the day, thinking only of the massacre of Flemings.[3]

Untypical indeed, but such treatment reveals the suspicion of Englishmen that these foreigners were growing rich at their expense. The Huguenots were never assaulted in so violent and unrestrained a manner. Perhaps this was partly because late Tudor, Stuart and Hanoverian governments wielded more authority than their four-teenth-century predecessors. The ferocious punishments meted out after the 'evil May Day' tumult of 1517, when fifteen Londoners were hung, drawn and quartered for their part in an anti-alien riot, may also have had a deterrent effect. All the same, there were far more immigrants in the sixteenth and seventeenth centuries than ever before, so a corresponding increase in hostility might have been expected. But there was a new element in the situation, religion.

As long as Henry VIII lived, the conservative inclinations of that frightening monarch hindered the expansion of European Protestant ways within the English Church. His death in 1547 changed the situation, for he left behind him a young son who was in the care of Protestant tutors, a Council in which control was rapidly seized by the Protestant Duke of Somerset, and an Archbishop of Canterbury, Thomas Cranmer, whose thoughts were moving in an increasingly Protestant direction. In the six years before Edward VI died a significant continental contribution was made to the development of the English Church. Martin Bucer, an often under-rated reformer, had exercised an important influence on Calvin's thinking about church organization in the later 1530s. Now he was brought over from Strasbourg on Cranmer's invitation and established as Regius Professor of Divinity at Cambridge, where he made a lasting impression on the future Archbishop Grindal and other English Protestants. The Italian Peter Martyr filled the equivalent chair at Oxford. Other notable visitors of lesser influence included Bernardino Ochino, the Hebrew scholar Paul Fagius, and Valérand Poullain. It is in a letter to Fagius in November 1548 that an organized congregation of foreign Protestants in England, at Canterbury, is first mentioned. The early Canterbury congregation was short-lived, as was Poullain's at Glastonbury, but within two years a far more important develop-ment had occurred in London. This was the work of another invited guest: John à Lasco or Laski.

Laski was one of that group of reformers of the second rank, so vital to the spread of Protestantism, who were highly regarded in their own day but whose originality, impact and merits have been buried beneath the mountain of scholarly writings on Luther, Melanchthon, Calvin and Zwingli. Since he left a lasting mark only in Emden and London, the neglect is more understandable in Laski's case than Bucer's. His early potential had seemed great; as nephew of a namesake who had been Archbishop of Gniezno and Primate of Poland, and later as friend of Erasmus and a promising humanist scholar, doors opened for Laski more readily than for many others. By 1543, when he became based at Emden in Frisia as Superintendent of all churches in the territories of the Countess of Oldenburg, he had been converted to Protestantism and stood in the Zwinglian tradition. In 1548 he visited England at Cranmer's invitation; it is an interesting comment on the regard in which he was held that the Archbishop's letter spoke of Laski and Melanchthon in the same breath. Two years later, finding his position at Emden undermined by political developments, he returned to London with his family. On 24 July 1550, largely as a result of his efforts, letters patent established what were to become the French and Dutch churches of London.

The nature of the letters patent was most unusual. In an age which set immense store on stringent religious conformity, they authorized foreigners in London to worship – in a church restored at royal expense – according to their own ecclesiastical discipline, freed even from the jurisdiction of the Bishop of London. No wonder that Jan Utenhove, a leading member of the Flemish ('German') congregation, wrote to Calvin that the concessions obtained by Laski exceeded all expectations. What or who lay behind such an extraordinary grant? Certainly not the bishops, for Ridley of London, convinced leader of Protestant reform though he was, vehemently objected to the separate existence of congregations whose different form of worship and church discipline might entice native Protestants and thus destroy uniformity within the English Church. His stance was supported by other bishops, but Cranmer and the extreme Zwinglian John Hooper of Gloucester were friendly with Laski and Utenhove and encouraged the project. Moreover Hooper and Laski both had connections at Court. Hooper was chaplain to the Duke of Somerset, deposed as Protector but by mid-1550 again a member of the Council and a gentleman of the king's chamber. Laski, during his earlier visit, had become friendly with well-placed men including William Cecil, who had acted as secretary to Somerset, and Cecil's relation by marriage Sir John Cheke, one of the king's principal tutors. However, connections with the entourage of the deposed Duke of Somerset would not on their own have been sufficient to protect Laski against episcopal attack.

The king, for all his tender years, may well have been the decisive influence. Although not quite thirteen, he was precocious, versed in continental Protestant thinking, and acutely aware that he was the first English king to have been crowned as Supreme Head of the Church. Hooper saw a good deal of him, and in the autumn of 1550 reported to the Zurich reformer Bullinger that should Edward live he would be 'the wonder and terror of the world'. Writing five years later, Laski was certain both of Edward's influence and his intentions: the foreign congregations were only founded in the form they took because of the desire of the king and his ministers to establish an official English church, step by step, on the basis of primitive evangelical purity. As for Edward, he was the keenest champion of this design. Historians will probably never get much closer to the truth behind the formation of the 'stranger churches'. If Laski was right, as seems likely, then their structure and government are of the greatest interest; they were to be the model, the blueprint, for a pure, reformed Church of England. The twin refugee churches of London offer us a window into the future envisaged by Edward, a future in which there might be superintendents but not bishops.

'Superintendent' was the office Laski had held in Emden, where he had exercised a kind of reformed episcopacy. It was a rather curious position for an ardent reformer, yet it suited Laski's background and may have suggested a convenient way for incorporating the episcopate into an English church reformed along continental lines. As superintendent, Laski instituted the first example in England of fully-fledged reformed Protestant discipline, based on elected, ordained 'elders'. Some of these, paid for their services, preached and taught. Others, unpaid, supervised their congregation, while deacons were appointed to look after poor relief. Laski's discipline was unusually democratic in its operation, stressed preaching, and featured weekly 'prophesyings' or Bible study groups considering questions arising from sermons.[4]

Whatever plans were hatching in the mind of the young Edward, his death meant that they were doomed. His successor on the throne was Queen Mary, whose depth of commitment to the Catholic cause matched that of her half-brother to Protestantism. Laski and a large section of his congregation retired to the Continent, as did several hundred prominent English Protestants, and not until Mary in her turn had died and been replaced by Elizabeth could England again be viewed as a place of sanctuary. In terms of doctrine and prayer book and personnel, the Elizabethan religious settlement involved a return to Edwardian days, so it is not surprising that London's foreign congregations were also restored. But just as the 1559 prayer book was modified in a conservative direction by comparison with its 1552

47

predecessor, so one important change took place affecting the refugee congregations: they were subjected to the authority of the Bishop of London. Gone was any thought that they might act as a blueprint for the future English church; from the Queen's point of view their degree of democratic participation would have been reprehensible, while some of the English Protestants returning from exile had more advanced continental models in their minds.

It was fortunate for the foreign congregations that the new appointment to London was Edmund Grindal. He had spent Mary's reign at Strasbourg, and was deeply sympathetic to their cause both theologically and because their members were exiles for the sake of their faith. London was a notoriously difficult diocese to govern, constantly under the eye of the Court and with strong-minded clergy and a large and volatile population. 'The Bisop of London is always to be pitied', remarked Grindal himself, while his successor observed that the holder of the office needed to be 'furnished as Samuel, or rather as Solomon, with all graces and gifts of learning, policy, wisdom and knowledge of things belonging to both God and man'.[5] Coping with the foreign churches in the capital certainly demanded such gifts. The very determination that had driven English Protestants abroad in Mary's reign had meant that, under the hothouse conditions of exile, comparatively minor disagreements between them had frequently flared into bitter and painful arguments, and continental authorities had found them hard to handle. Similarly, successive Bishops of London were to find the foreign congregations in their care challenging and troublesome. Dealing with them required tact and circumspection, since they often had powerful patrons at Court and always had strong connections abroad, and any attack on their privileges could be represented in a much wider frame as a reflection on relations between the Church of England and the Reformed communities overseas. As foreign churches were established in other English dioceses, their bishops turned for advice to the capital, and the Bishop of London found himself determining national policy.

Grindal's episcopate was, therefore, of special importance because it set the pattern for his successors to follow. When Queen Elizabeth made the Bishop of London superintendent of the foreign congregations in his diocese, she expected him to work towards the uniformity of religious observance in her realm that was so dear to her heart; the church of Austin Friars was now made available to the refugees specifically 'so as no rite nor use be therein observed contrary to our law'.[6] But Grindal had been heavily influenced by Bucer, and was a confidant of Calvin and his successor Theodore Beza. He had no quarrel with the types of organization of reformed churches overseas, and was content to allow the congregations in his charge to follow the form of government they wished. His successor Edwin Sandys – who had also spent Mary's reign in exile, at Strasbourg – followed Grindal's example, and the precedent they set was never reversed. As a result the foreign churches developed an increasingly Calvinist organization during Elizabeth's reign, even while the Queen was steering the English Church along a conservative path and insisting on the retention of old ways of church government.

At the combined request of the French Church of London and Bishop Grindal, Calvin agreed to release one of his most trusted lieutenants, Nicolas des Gallars, for service in the English capital. The ecclesiastical *Discipline* that des Gallars drew up was based on the Genevan model, adapted to fit circumstances in England. Modified by Robert le Maçon de la Fontaine in 1578 and later revised anew in 1641, it came to be used in all the French churches of the realm. Before a uniform type of church government could be agreed, however, there were two essential preconditions. First, the foreign churches in England had to believe themselves permanently separated from continental Protestantism; this was decided when an informal assembly of representatives of the French-speaking congregations met in London in 1572 and agreed they should not take part in the continental general Synod of Emden. And second, they had to develop their own organization. The first Colloquy, or gathering of formally appointed delegates of the French churches in England, was held in 1581; it considered disciplinary matters, and decided that further meetings should be held. The following year it agreed that 'it would be expedient for the churches to be united as far as possible in one single form of government', and in 1588 the seventh Colloquy formally accepted des Gallars's *Discipline*, as revised by Fontaine. Fourteen Colloquies assembled between 1581 and 1598, establishing in England by the end of Elizabeth's reign a good part of the hierarchical system of church government so characteristic of continental Calvinism. In London, where the existence of several foreign churches made possible more frequent local gatherings, representatives of the Dutch, French, Italian and Spanish Consistories met regularly in a body known as Coetus. Finally, the pyramid of Consistory-(Coetus)-Colloquy was crowned in 1604 by a meeting of the first Synod, a gathering of deputies of the Flemish as well as the French-speaking congregations.[7]

Whether the Privy Council knew about all these developments may be doubted. The Colloquy itself was well aware that it was unwise to flaunt its existence before a Queen who had little love for the forms of continental Protestantism, and decided in 1598 not to advertise the convocation of meetings but simply to alert the parties directly involved. Nor did Colloquy wish to antagonize the authorities who sheltered its members from the storms of continental persecution. Yet the Privy Council too had no desire for a public clash with the foreign churches in the country, fearing that it might encourage local disorders in places where there were settlements of aliens. Besides, European esteem and prestige was at stake. Elizabeth was known as the protector of continental Protestants; this was one of the grounds for the papal bull excommunicating her in 1570. Public rebuke of the form of government of the foreign churches in England could have had diplomatic repercussions overseas.

In 1604, by meeting openly and jointly as a Synod, the French and Dutch Colloquies took a calculated risk. The ostensible reason for the Synod was the preparation of a joint petition from all the foreign churches to the new king, James I, for the preservation of their liberty and privileges. Surely there was a deeper motive. James came from Scotland, a Presbyterian country closely linked with continental Protestantism; might he not wish to see a national church in England with a more distinctly Reformed flavour than that which he had inherited from Elizabeth? If the leaders of the refugee churches were thinking along such lines, they were doomed to disappointment: despite welcoming words from James, the new royal dynasty was to prove a source of anxiety, not support, to their congregations. But for the moment, the calling of the Synod had been an astute move. Once assembled, it could not be unmade; the precedent had been set and the organization of the foreign churches in England completed.

The cost of these moves towards worship on the best Reformed models was increasing tension between the foreign churches in England and the Anglican episcopate. This worsened as the descendants of refugees became more involved in English society and local parish churches, forcing the two different church systems to take more notice of one another. Protestant foreigners were not needed now that Protestantism had been firmly established in England. The Catholic threat seemed less pressing once peace had been made with Spain and the Gunpowder Plot exposed. Furthermore, positive support for the Anglican *via media* existed by the early seventeenth century in a way it had not in the 1560s. John Whitgift, Archbishop of Canterbury from 1583 to 1604, defended episcopacy far more forcefully than Grindal or Sandys would have done when he expressed the wish that France and Scotland 'as far as religion goes were in the same state and condition as England'. Supporters of Anglicanism viewed the foreign churches with increasing suspicion. Their misgivings could only be increased when fringe groups like Brownists and

Barrowists, who rejected the notion of a national church, pleaded for 'the same liberty granted us in the worship of God' as the foreign congregations in the country enjoyed.[8]

At the same time, the Privy Council became less willing to support the presence of the aliens for economic motives. Their sheer numbers had never been welcome, since Elizabethan Englishmen considered their country overpopulated. Tudor government *was* troubled by a rising population, caused by a high birth-rate, with its associated problems of unemployment, poverty, and disruption of good order. But William Cecil and other intelligent and influential men of his time greatly valued the skills foreigners brought with them, and their trading contacts on the Continent. Through these skills, they hoped, English manufacturing and industrial projects would be encouraged and the English poor gainfully employed, while fewer English resources would be drained abroad to pay for imports. Towards the end of Henry VIII's reign, Frenchmen had assisted in the rapid development of ironworks, originally for military purposes, later used for the production of more homely wares as well. After Henry's death, the way was open for projects which would kill two birds with one stone, fostering Protestantism while providing an economic boost. The Duke of Somerset's settlement at Glastonbury was composed of weavers and dyers. That project did not last, but the thinking behind it was resumed under Elizabeth. The making of worsteds was revived at Norwich; copperas was exploited in dyeing at Colchester; linen thread was developed as a Maidstone speciality. In each case the role of foreign Protestants was critical. Joan Thirsk's recent researches, published in 1978 under the title *Economic Policy and Projects*, suggest that this was true in a number of other significant areas such as the promotion of woad growing or the development of the stocking knitting industry, the latter eventually employing more handicraft labour than any other manufacture except the New Draperies. From 1560 on patents were repeatedly granted to foreigners introducing new manufactures or methods of manufacture to England. These covered a wide range of products from hard white ('Castile') soap to saltpetre, and from ovens and furnaces to white salt.

The influence of aliens on English economic development is an important subject, to which we will return in the next chapter. William Cecil also made use of their help and overseas connections in steering the ship of state through the troubled waters of European trading politics. An overwhelming proportion of English foreign trade in the mid-sixteenth century was dependent on one commodity – unfinished woollen cloth, exported from one city (London) to another (Antwerp). Consequently Tudor England was vulnerable to external manipulation, or so Philip II's minister in the Netherlands, Cardinal Granvelle, calculated when in 1563 he prohibited the English cloth trade with Antwerp. Granvelle's action doubtless encouraged Cecil to redouble his attempts to encourage native manufactures. It certainly spurred English merchants and politicians to seek ways of abandoning the semi-colonial relationship that had previously tied London to Antwerp's apron strings. Their earliest effort was to start an alternative mart at Emden. It was not a success; while it was the German port nearest to London, Emden lacked the size, glamour and international connections of Antwerp, and did not have the same facilities for dyeing and finishing the cloth. But that Emden should have been chosen at all is an interesting commentary on the inter-relationship of religion and commerce, and provides insight into Cecil's outlook and network of contacts.

From a secular twentieth-century perspective, it seems surprising that religion should play any part in the choice of a cloth market. Nevertheless, the selection of Emden was due to the fact that it was Laski's home before he came to London in Edward VI's reign. When Mary came to the throne Laski retired there once more, taking with him part of his congregation; by 1554, Emden had become a major centre of anti-Marian propaganda. Amongst those who were with Laski was Jan Utenhove, who returned to London after Elizabeth's accession, bearing Edward's precious charter establishing the strangers' churches. He came from Ghent, where he had been born into a learned family of the minor nobility. His deep concern for religion – he was, for instance, a translator of the Psalms – combined with his birth to make him the natural lay leader of the London foreign Protestant community, but his rank and connections gave him wider importance. He was a close friend of the ruler of Emden, Countess Anna, and her sons; and, in England, of Bishop Grindal. He must also have known William Cecil, if only through his nephew Charles who was well acquainted with the Cecils. When in 1563 closer political and commercial ties between England and Emden were sought, it was through Utenhove, with Grindal as his intermediary, that Cecil made his overtures. Religious considerations thus made possible the Emden experiment, although commercial realities undid it.[9]

Granvelle's threat to the English economy was one piece of the political jigsaw that preoccupied Elizabeth and her advisers in the early 1560s. Because the peace treaty of Cateau-Cambrésis (1559) brought to an end a long period of rivalry between France and the Habsburgs, it seemed to Protestant Europe that the path was now clear for a Catholic onslaught on heresy. In the ensuing cold war atmosphere of fear and suspicion even the queen's reluctance to commit herself was

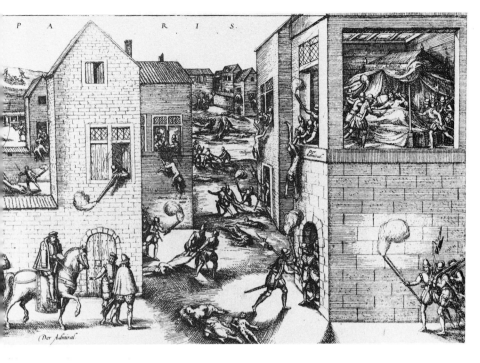

1 (a)   Scenes from the Massacre of St Bartholomew, including the murder of
from a later engraving

1 (b)   Abjuration of Henry IV

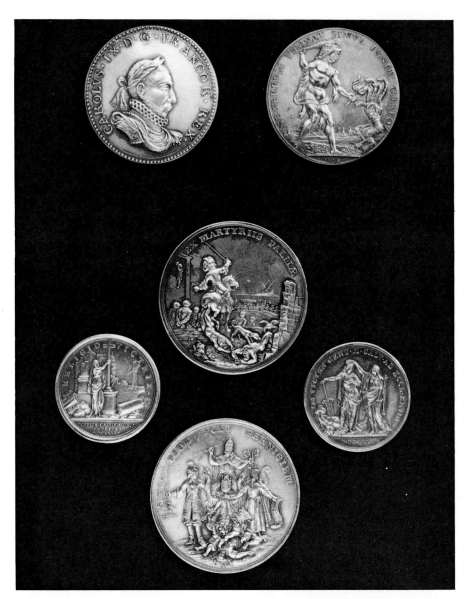

2 (*top*) Medal commemorating the Massacre of St Bartholomew, struck in Paris, 1572:
obverse, Charles IX; reverse, Hercules [Charles] struggling with the hydra [heresy]

2 (*bottom*) The Revocation of the Edict of Nantes: the smaller medals show (a) a Cross
erected before demolished Huguenot temples, and (b) Religion crowning Louis, who sets
his foot on Heresy; the larger medal is a contemporary satire struck in Holland, showing
(obverse) a scene of execution, torture and deportation of Huguenots and (reverse) the
pope, supported by a Jesuit and a dragoon, riding upon a many-headed monster which
devours Huguenots

3 'Heresy Unmasked by Truth', from a French calendar of 1686. At the top, Louis acts against Calvinism; below, bottom left, Calvinists abjure, while bottom right, their temples are destroyed

4 (a) *Mereau* or communion token; on one side a shepherd calls his sheep, while the reverse bears the text 'Do not fear, little flock'

4 (b) Artist's impression of Huguenots landing at Dover, 1685

5 (a)   French Church of London, Threadneedle Street

5 (b)   French Church of Canterbury, crypt, Canterbury Cathedral

6 (a)   Royal coat of arms, affixed to the wall of the French Church of London after the Restoration

6 (b)   Detail of the headboard of the State Bed at Melville House, Fife. Made c. 1697–1700, probably by Francis La Pierre, to a design by Daniel Marot. Pine frame with hangings of crimson Italian silk velvet lined with Chinese silk damask

GOOD BROTHER,

IN purfuance of His Majefties Commands, this comes to recommend to your care, the Brief for the FRENCH PROTESTANTS. You have fuch an Object of Charity before you, as it may be, no cafe could more deferve your Pity. It is not a Flight to fave their Lives, but what is ten thoufand times more dear, their Confciences. They are not fled by Permiffion, (except the Minifters, who are banifhed,) but with the greateft Difficulty and Hardfhip imaginable. And therefore it will be an act of the higheft compaffion to comfort and relieve them, as being perform'd to Perfons whofe afflictions it is hard to fay, whether of Mind or Body are the greater. When we reflect upon that Defolation that has been made before their eyes, of all their Goods and Stores, the Barbarity of Ufage, both to their Bodies and Eftates, and their quiting their whole Subfiftence with their Native Soil, through all forts of Peril, one would imagin it the greateft Hardfhip. But when we come to examin that Anguifh which is brought upon their Minds, it is incomparably greater ; their Wives, Children, and Relations imprifoned, clapt into Monafteries, put down into Dungeons, inhumanly tormented and afflicted, till they renounce their Faith, or perifh in the Trial. All men are not required to be wife enough to judg of the fecular Confequences of this accident in the peopling our Country, increafing Manufactures, Induftry, Trading, and the like: But God excufes no man from being good and charitable. They who have no Mite to give, have hearts to pray ; and this occafion requires, with an equal neceffity, our Prayers for thofe who ftill lie in Mifery and Irons, as it does our Benevolence for fuch as are efcaped. Exhort then your People whilft they have time, to do good ; and to blefs God for the opportunity, and to honour the King for his gracious encouragement, who is not content himfelf to give fuch as fly to him for fuccour, Safety and Protection, but calls upon all his loving Subjects, to partake in the accomplifhing fo good a Work. Remember how it is written, He that has pity upon the poor, lendeth unto the Lord. And I pray God in this and all things elfe, to direct you and your Flock, and

Your affured Friend

FULHAM,
Apr. 2. 1686.

and Brother,

HENRY London.

7 Circular from Bishop Compton to the clergy of his diocese, commending the 1686 Brief

8 (a) Silver cup and cover by Louis Cuny, 1703

8 (b) Ewer

8 (c) Silver wine-cooler by Philip Rollos, 1712

finally overcome, and by the treaty of Hampton Court she gave military support to the Huguenots in France in 1562. Refugees in England played little part in such high politics, only occasionally becoming involved, as when Nicolas des Gallars reported from the Colloquy of Poissy (at which his participation had been invited by Admiral Coligny) to the English ambassador and Bishop Grindal.[10] Nevertheless, their presence had diplomatic value in promoting England as a champion of Protestantism. After the Massacre of St Bartholomew, in a dignified and perfectly stage-managed protest, Elizabeth kept the French ambassador waiting for three days and then, surrounded by courtiers, received him in total and devastating silence. But in the longer term her favourable reception of Huguenot refugees was a more effective statement, falling short of direct intervention in France on behalf of the Protestant cause (though in the early 1590s she again had recourse to that) but making her position plain.

The combined force of religious, economic, commercial and diplomatic considerations encouraged the Elizabethan Privy Council to lend its support to the foreign churches in England, even when those churches hindered attempts to integrate their members into English society. A burgess in the 1593 Parliament was guilty of exaggeration when he complained that the strangers to whom the country played host 'will not converse with us, they will not marry with us, they will not buy any thing [from us]'; but his remarks had some foundation. Consistories discouraged intermarriage and strenuously opposed any attempts by members of their congregations to withdraw and join the English Church. Both Privy Council and the episcopal authorities were well aware of this stand, and under Elizabeth supported it, for the churches were useful units of administration through which refugees could be controlled and their good faith ensured. When Jean Cousin, minister of the Threadneedle Street church, asked Grindal what to do about foreigners seeking to join their local English churches, the bishop immediately instructed all parishes in his diocese not to receive foreigners withdrawing from the discipline of their own congregations, even promising to excommunicate offenders to enforce his decision if necessary.[11]

Time wore down such early goodwill. The Church of England developed its own identity; other considerations that had motivated the Privy Council lost their importance. The wars with Spain and involvement in the Netherlands ceased. The Edict of Nantes gave protection to Huguenots in France. In 1625, when Charles I married the French princess Henrietta Maria, he even agreed to an expedition to help suppress the Protestants of La Rochelle. English merchants extended their overseas contacts and corridors of trade, and grew in confidence; there was no longer any need for intermediaries like Utenhove. Englishmen mastered the aliens' crafts and skills. Gradually, therefore, the priorities of the Privy Council changed. It became more inclined to listen favourably to complaints against aliens, and less willing to accept the permanent existence of churches and communities distinct from the Church of England and English society.

After William Laud became Archbishop of Canterbury in 1633, the foreign churches came under direct attack. Laud believed that bishops were divinely instituted, and necessary for good order in any church. He also thought that Presbyterianism must of necessity be opposed to monarchy. The sermon he preached at the opening of Parliament in February 1626 illustrates his views:

> I know there are some that think the Church is not yet far enough beside the cushion, that their seats are too easy yet, and too high too. A parity they would have, no bishop, no governor, but a parochial consistory and that should be lay enough too. Well, first, this parity was never left to the Church by Christ; he left Apostles, and Disciples under them. It was never in use with the Church since Christ; no church ever, anywhere (till this last age) without a bishop. If it were in use it might perhaps govern some petty city, but make it common once, and it can never keep unity in the Church of Christ. . . . And there is not a man that is for parity, all fellows in the Church, but he is not for monarchy in the State.

The foreign congregations practised the 'parity' Laud disdained, and by their very existence disturbed the 'unity in the Church of Christ' he prized so highly. He found that their discipline was 'the occasion of many factious persons in his diocese'. Everything about them was anathema to him, not least their presence in substantial numbers at his successive headquarters of London and Canterbury.

In 1632 Laud submitted his first report to the Privy Council on the dangers resulting from the foreign churches in the realm. At that time he was Bishop of London. After being promoted to archbishop, he moved fast. In 1634 the churches of Canterbury, Sandwich and Maidstone were ordered to answer questions about their liturgy and the number of their members who had been born in England. The reply from Canterbury claimed exemption on the grounds that the foreign congregations were 'in the diocese but not of the diocese'. It was ignored, and in December the three churches were ordered to adopt the Anglican liturgy translated into their native tongue and to instruct their members born in the realm to retire to their local Anglican churches. The second synod, hastily convened, decided that these were matters on which it simply could not compromise, whatever the cost. The situation of the foreign congregations was desperate. The bishops of their dioceses (Laud himself, Juxon of London, Wren of Norwich, Curll of Winchester) were all hostile, and they could raise little support at Court although they tried to obtain Charles's aid through the influence of the Duke of Soubise whom he had invited to England. After receiving unsatisfactory answers from the king, and after awkward interviews with Laud and his vicar-general Sir Nathaniel Brent, the deputies advised the Kent churches to continue their normal activities and simply ignore the archbishop's injunction.

During the course of the synod Laud had withdrawn his demand for the Anglican liturgy to be used in the foreign churches, and by September 1635 he was prepared to make further concessions: aliens and their first generation descendants could keep their privileges, and all other members – although having to attend their parish churches – were to remain liable for the support of the ministry and poor of their old congregations. This was as far as the archbishop was prepared to compromise, and his position was still quite unacceptable to the foreign congregations. They probably doubted both Laud's intentions and his ability to enforce the clause preserving their financial stability. In any case, they were not prepared to advance any plan aiming at their eventual destruction. They fought a delaying action, retreating nominally when forced to do so while preserving their worship and ties with second generation supporters as best they could. When publication of the injunction became unavoidable, the ministers showed what they thought by refusing to read it; it was read instead by the clerk of the weavers' hall in Canterbury and by the 'chanter' at Sandwich. Their congregations were well adapted to such delaying tactics; they had not taken refuge from the fire and sword of continental persecution to be frightened into the Anglican Church by mere words from the archbishop. And the ministers themselves gave a strong lead, fiercely declining Brent's invitation to them to receive communion in the Church of England. Only the weaker churches, like the Dutch Church of Colchester and the French Church of Southampton, submitted immediately. The others were determined to struggle on as long as they could, and in the event it was Laud who ran out of time: he was impeached on a charge of high treason by the Long Parliament in 1640, and committed to the Tower the following year. One of the charges brought against him was that he had tried to cause division between the English Church and other Reformed churches, and to that end had suppressed the privileges enjoyed by the foreign congregations in the realm.[12]

'It is merry with lambs when the wolf is shut up', wrote one of the Canterbury ministers, Jean Bulteel. The foreign churches had good reason to be pleased at surviving a dangerous attack without a single casualty; to the synods of 1641 and 1644 came representatives of the French churches of London, Canterbury, Norwich and Southampton, and the Dutch of London, Norwich, Sandwich, Colchester, Yarmouth and Canvey Island. It seemed that they could look forward to a period of peace and quiet, and they celebrated by revising their discipline so as to exclude any suggestion of episcopal domination.

Alas, appearances proved deceptive. While the congregations had united in opposing Laud, their apparent unity concealed internal tensions. Many of their members were well on the way to being assimilated, and thought in an English rather than continental way. Unable to stay aloof from the Civil War and English debates about Presbyterianism and Independency, the churches of London, Canterbury and Norwich each split into rival factions. In London in 1643 the pulpit at Threadneedle Street must have provided an amazing spectacle, for it was shared by the ultra-royalist Louis Hérault from Alençon and the equally strong parliamentarian Jean de la Marche from the Channel Islands, who only two years later was to be calling for the king's execution. Hérault called for obedience, loyalty, peace; de la Marche thundered that Parliament was pregnant with the child of reformation of the state, which would deliver the country from the burdens under which it groaned. It soon became apparent that both the congregation and political circumstances favoured de la Marche, and Hérault was forced to withdraw to France. The congregations at Canterbury and Norwich were also mostly parliamentarian, but political differences only partly explain the splits that developed in these places. There was also a wish to replace ageing and unpopular ministers by more exciting preachers. Only the small French congregation at Southampton was not sharply divided, and its poverty and insignificance drove its minister to drink.

In 1644 Parliament convoked the Westminster Assembly to construct a new scheme of church government for England on the model of the 'best Reformed churches'. It seemed that the parliamentarian victory had produced an ecclesiastical climate favourable to the foreign congregations. Not so. The Westminster Assembly, dominated by Scottish rather than continental influence, took little interest in the foreign churches closest to hand. Worse, by the time the Assembly's recommendation of a form of presbyterianism was turned into law, the Scottish army was no longer essential to the parliamentarian cause. English army interests took over, backing not presbyterianism with its ordered church hierarchy, but the independence of each individual congregation. Without a state authority to reinforce its decisions, Colloquy could not operate effectively. Yet this was a time when its member churches were deeply divided about the interpretation of their discipline as revised in 1641. So the Interregnum proved to be a time not of peace but of bitter division both within and among the foreign churches.

The mid-century decades were in many ways a time of transition for the French communities in England. Before the Civil War, their background had been Walloon as much as French, and they had been growing smaller as assimilation occurred. After the Restoration in 1660, especially from the late 1670s, the influx of new refugees meant that they expanded once more, becoming almost wholly French in the process. The restored monarchy developed a new policy; while it never resumed Laud's outright attack on the old-established churches, it decided to license new congregations only if they accepted the Anglican liturgy translated into French. This meant that the Huguenots were to face a choice of environment in England which their Walloon predecessors had never been offered. Colloquy fell into disuse, partly because it could not incorporate the new congregations, partly in reaction to the divisions that had beset it in the 1650s, partly because it was no longer possible even to hope that the state authorities would enforce its decisions. The churches felt obliged to stress their loyalty to the Crown in an attempt to wipe out the past; the Threadneedle Street Consistory, for instance, recalled Hérault and erected the royal arms on the wall of the church above the Ten Commandments (plate 6a).

Something that did not change was the vital necessity of government support for the refugees. Without it, had they been able to enter the realm at all, they would have been exposed to the full force of insular hostility. As it was, the positive steps by which the government assisted them were of great value. Two of these steps (in addition to physical protection) were especially significant. Government had the right to grant patents of denization, just as Parliament had the right to pass acts of naturalization. Whether through executive or legislative action, the intent of these processes was the same, to make their recipients Englishmen. In practice, naturalization provided superior status, conveying rights of inheritance and trade advantages denied to a mere denizen. Nevertheless a foreigner was far more secure as a denizen than as an alien. He was also better off; if, for example, he was a master weaver in London, he could employ an extra loom and take an extra apprentice.[13] Since no general naturalization act was passed until 1709, it was most important that the government proved willing to make mass grants of free denization when the *dragonnades* began in 1681.

Second, a series of briefs ordering parish collections for Protestant refugees was issued between 1681 and 1703, providing much-needed emergency relief. They were especially valuable during the late 1680s. But even the substantial sums collected as a result of these briefs – those between 1681 and 1694 produced over £90,000 – could not sustain the mass of poor refugees for long after the Revocation, and eventually further efforts had to be made. The great good will of William and Mary towards the Huguenots could not have been more clearly shown than in the £39,000 they allocated them from the Civil List between 1689 and 1693. Parliamentary acts later in the decade embodied their generosity, providing a precedent for further grants to be made throughout the eighteenth century. The 'Royal Bounty' was not removed from the Civil List until 1804, and the last pensioner, Sara Pignon, died only a little over a century ago, in 1876. By then more than one and a quarter million pounds had been handed over to destitute refugees and their descendants, in a charitable action of quite unprecedented generosity and longevity. Moreover, for the first time in English history a body had been set up to distribute relief on a national scale to people from all social classes. Funds found their way to Barnstaple, Bideford, Bristol, Canterbury, Colchester, Dartmouth, Dover, Exeter, Jersey, Norwich, Plymouth, Rye, Southampton, Stonehouse and Thorpe-le-Soken, as well as being distributed in London and its environs. The origins of the body responsible for their administration go back to 1681, and in its mature form it comprised three tiers: the Lords Commissioners, who supervised the whole process, an 'English Committee' which scrutinized the accounts, and a 'French Committee' which actually administered relief.[14] The need for such administrative arrangements reflects the sheer numbers of Huguenot refugees and the new problems confronting the government. Old ways simply would not do. Censuses of aliens, common under Elizabeth and the early Stuarts, were not resumed in the later seventeenth century. And the foreign churches, while still used as a channel of communication and deeply involved in refugee relief, no longer sufficed on their own.

An early Elizabethan councillor recalled from the grave to participate in Council debates under Charles II and James II would have been struck by a change of emphasis. The reason why the refugees poured across the Channel remained religious, and diplomats continued to be horrified by the treatment meted out to the Huguenots in France. But the authorities were more obviously primarily concerned with their possible economic contribution to the country. The Huguenots were welcomed for their economic and manufacturing skills in the same way that their sixteenth-century predecessors had been, but also for two important additional reasons. Whereas informed Elizabethans had believed their country overpopulated, during the later Stuart period Sir William Petty and others were arguing that England was, on the contrary, short of manpower. The refugees could therefore be seen as contributing a desirable national resource. 'There is nothing so much wanting in England as people', especially 'the industrious and laborious sort, and handicraftmen,' Carew Reynell suggested in *The True English Interest* (1674). 'No country is rich but in proportion to its number,' the author of the preface to *An Apology for the Protestants of France* reminded his readers in 1683.

Even more important, the Huguenots benefited from widespread acknowledgment that their French and Walloon predecessors had increased England's prosperity. This feeling was summed up by a 1681 newsletter which argued

> If it be considered how populacy and riches once made several
> towns happy, which now are poor and depopulated, witness
> Dover, Sandwich, Winchelsea, Southampton and others, it will
> appear their best condition took its rise from such a sort of
> industrious strangers, who had their churches there, and their
> decay from discouragements put on them and their then departing
> those places.[15]

As a matter of fact Southampton had been declining before any foreign Protestant settlers reached the town, and those at Winchelsea had not been there long enough to work the effect attributed to them. Nevertheless, long before the *dragonnades* began in France, there was a well-established tradition that playing host to aliens rendered homeless for the sake of their religion brought practical blessings in return. And the tradition was justified – so well justified, indeed, that it is remarkable that the Huguenots from Louis XIV's dominions should have been able to equal and surpass the formidable contribution made by the earlier wave of Protestant refugees to England.

4

Crafts and Trades

The historian has to sail troubled waters in assessing the significance of the aliens' economic contribution. Dangerous reefs of error and miscalculation have to be avoided: these are partisan contemporary argument, and historical judgment subsequently based upon it without due allowance for bias. A surprising number of groups had reason to emphasize or to belittle the Huguenots' contribution. Within France, Louis XIV's *intendants* were likely to minimize the part played by Protestants in their reports on local conditions, since it was part of the rationale behind the Revocation that there were supposed to be only a handful of Huguenots in the country in 1685. Bonrepaus, the French agent sent to the Netherlands and England to seek the repatriation of skilled refugees, was equally bound to report negatively on their impact abroad; by doing so he could disguise the failure of his mission. In England, the refugees themselves would naturally stress the value of their presence to obtain the governmental and local support they needed, but native craftsmen who found their employment threatened belittled any achievement. English historians have tended to accept the reality of a major economic contribution from the Huguenots; but the detailed work of W. C. Scoville has shown that the emigration of the 1680s did not on its own destroy the economy of Louis XIV's France.

Clothing and Textiles

Sixteenth-century Frenchmen and Walloons and seventeenth-century Huguenots did not necessarily share the same skills, but both groups were urban artisans rather than workers of the land. The closest approximation to an industrial proletariat at the time was the labour employed in cloth production; so it is not surprising that both groups of refugees should be best known for their contribution to the textile and clothing trades. The earlier French and Walloons, together with the more numerous Flemings, provided the skills needed to establish the 'New Draperies', made from mixed fabrics which were lighter and softer than traditional English woollens and therefore better suited for export to southern Europe and warmer climes. With varying degrees of success, these New Draperies were established at many places in south-eastern England where there were alien communities, such as Canterbury, Colchester, Halstead, Maidstone, Norwich, Sandwich and Southampton. In European terms, the draperies were not in reality so very 'new'. Rather they were mutations of Italian models and established peasant techniques. But they certainly transformed the English clothing industry, and contemporaries accepted that the refugees were responsible. As Leake commented in 1577,

> by reason of the troubles grown in other countries, the making of 'baies, friesadowes, tuftmoccadowe', and many other things made of wool, is mightily increased in England. . . . For this cause we ought to favour the strangers from whom we learned so great benefits . . . because we are not so good devisers as followers of others.[1]

Concern to establish the New Draperies caused the Privy Council to encourage specific skills in specific places, free the new products from taxation burdens, and protect foreign settlers from local attack. For instance, when informers molested refugees at Canterbury trading in 'the making of bays and other stuffs, whereby the realm doth reap great benefit and commodity', the Privy Council repeatedly intervened to suspend proceedings. Industrial regulation was a tricky matter. On the one hand, refugees complained of their poverty and of the need to employ their own people so that standards were maintained. On the other, English craftsmen objected that their employment and livelihood were threatened. The differing perspectives of aliens and local authorities are shown in documents of 1567 drawn up when a body of Walloons offered to settle at Southampton. They asked leave to carry out their trades of whatever kind; the local Corporation wanted only trades hitherto unknown, remarking that there were too many English tailors and shoemakers already. The refugees wanted to employ their own people; the Corporation insisted that English servants be employed.

At the heart of such exchanges lay the question of apprenticeships. This had two aspects. New arrivals who already possessed a desirable craft skill could not reasonably be asked to serve an English apprenticeship, and from time to time the Privy Council stepped in to defend foreign communities from prosecutions based on infringements of English apprenticeship statutes. Second, if the English were to acquire new skills for themselves, they had to have access to the 'mysteries' practised by the strangers. It had long been official policy that immigrants must teach Englishmen, and should neither employ more than two alien journeymen nor take alien apprentices other than their own children. So it was a considerable concession when each refugee family bound for Southampton, allowed ten servants per household, was ordered to keep and instruct only two English apprentices and, after seven years, one Englishman for every two strangers. The Privy Council also granted tax concessions, and its generosity was rewarded by enduring benefits for the English economy.

The textile industry in the south-east of England benefited greatly from the arrival of aliens in the late sixteenth century. That in the West Country did not; repeated claims that Flemish refugees established lacemaking at Honiton have recently been shown to be false. Dutch and French settlers produced woollen and silk cloths for a generation from the 1560s at Maidstone in Kent; by 1605 English inhabitants had taken over, and by 1620 the small surviving Dutch community was concentrating on the manufacture of linen thread. (Maidstone retained a monopoly of this for most of the Stuart period.) Colchester (and, briefly, Halstead) concentrated on bays and says, and the craft was still known there as the 'Dutch work' in the mid-seventeenth century. The effect of the introduction of the New Draperies was particularly striking in this area of northern Essex, transforming an economy previously dependent on traditional broadcloth manufacture. Fifty weavers were brought over from Holland under royal patronage in 1619 to establish a tapestry factory at Mortlake, where they used Raphael cartoons as the basis for their work. This venture, which lasted for the rest of the century, was inspired purely by economic motives and did not employ existing refugees. At Canterbury the strangers were entitled to make 'bays stammells and cloth after the Flanders fashion' but not 'cloth or kersies such as the English do make at this present'. Woolcombing rapidly became important here, as also at Dover and Sandwich. In Canterbury, as in London, silkweaving increased steadily in importance from the end of the sixteenth century onwards, at the expense of the older materials wool and linen. At Southampton, too, the foreign community came to concentrate its endeavours, and in 1590 the French church claimed its congregation 'consisteth altogether of sergeweavers'. The widest range of New Draperies was produced at Norwich, where the refugees were settled to exercise their 'faculties of making bays, arras sayes, tapesterie, mockades, stamins, kersye, and such other outlandish commodities as hath not been used to be made within . . . England'.[2]

It is not surprising that Norfolk became such a significant centre of the New Draperies, for here worsteds were already established – indeed 'worsted' drew its name from a village north of Norwich. But there can be no doubt that the impetus provided by alien settlers was necessary, for under the early Tudors worsted exports had steadily declined. The different groups of foreigners concentrated on different fabrics, the Dutch on 'wet greasy goods' and Walloons on 'dry woven goods'. Within a comparatively short time the Norfolk economy was reviving, spearheaded by the New Draperies and associated industries like lacemaking, ribbonmaking and stocking-knitting. Because the New Draperies were hybrids, marrying the qualities of worsted and woollen cloth, it was easy to produce a 'new' product by varying the mixture or length or breadth. A galaxy of names for these manufactures evolved, confusing to contemporaries and impossible for scholars to define with precision. Three 'proper' kinds of bays alone were described at Colchester in 1579, and bays existed in five degrees of fineness in James I's reign. In 1611 the manufactures of the foreigners at Norwich covered

> bays, fustians, parchmentiers, camientries, tufted mockadoes, currelles, tooys, bussins, mockadoes, valures all of linnen cruell, carletts, damaske, says of dry cruel (after the fashion of Lille, of Amiens, and of Muy), dry grograynes, double mockadoes, ollyet bumbasines of taffety, *all silk*, striped says, broad lyles, Spanish sattins, cross billets of silk, serge de boyce, silk saye, striped tobines figuratoes, bratos, purled and other outlandish inventions.

Weird names indeed, designed specifically to imply exotic foreign origins. No wonder English craftsmen at Norwich complained that the strangers there invented new names just to make their products 'more vendible':

> In demonstration thereof, a buffyn, a catalowne, and the pearl of beauty are all one cloth; a peropus and paragon all one; a say and pyramides all one; the same cloths bearing other names in times past. The paragon, peropus and philiselles may be affirmed to be double chambletts; the difference being only the one was doubled in the warp, the other in the weft. Buffyn, catalowne and pearl of beauty, etc., may be affirmed single chambletts, differing only in their breadth. The say and pyramides may be affirmed to be that ancient cloth . . . called a bed; the difference only consisting in the breadth and fineness.

Undoubtedly the argument had substance. Between 1608 and 1618, for instance, the Walloons at Norwich applied for rules to be drawn up governing the manufacture of no fewer than five 'new' sorts of cloth: satin cotton or 'bumbazie', made of a mixture of silk and cotton wool; the 'figurato', part silk and part white spun yarn; the 'cheveron', derived from a cloth formerly made called the 'Bird's Eye'; the 'Pearle and Bewty', wrought on linen derived from another earlier cloth, the 'trisses'; and the 'quadramidis'.[3]

Such sensitivity to shifts in the wind of fashion was one reason why the New Draperies were so successful both in England and abroad. There were others. The New Draperies met the needs of the day. They may have been less durable than the heavier cloths they displaced, but they were cheaper. This brought them into the range of a larger market at home as well as overseas, while their lighter nature made them more suitable for export to Mediterranean areas. Another important aspect of their appeal was their colour. Dyeing was therefore a critical craft, and again the necessary expertise was injected by foreigners. At Southampton those wishing to settle in 1567 requested that, should they be too few to support a dyer and his family, they be allowed to export their fabrics undyed; clearly they did not believe that native skills would suffice. At about the same time it was agreed in Norwich that while English dyers should have a monopoly of dyeing in blue, dyeing in other colours as practised in Flanders was to be in the hands of Anthonye de Pottier, and was to be certified by a seal. Half a century later it was still necessary for the new Merchant Adventurers' Company to keep foreign dyers on contract, though that was to dye wool cloth. Meanwhile the dyeing of worsteds had greatly improved, so that an observer in 1593 suggested it was approaching perfection. And as the craft spread, so too did the growing of woad and madder (developed respectively with French and Dutch help), the digging of alum and the gathering of copperas.

These activities provided employment opportunities at a time when the population increase of the sixteenth century made them desperately needed. So of course did the New Draperies themselves. Initially at least, they seem to have been more labour-intensive than the old. As early as 1576, Customer Thomas Smith argued that 'it cannot be that such number [of New Draperies] can be wrought in this realm by strangers only, but that they must set many of the poor people of this realm on work.' In 1616 the Privy Council commended the industry because indeed it did 'set many poor on work'. The Canterbury authorities concurred, certifying in 1622 that the Walloons there were 'a poor and painful people' who had given employment to the English as well as maintaining their own poor. The stocking-knitting industry, which developed in the train of the New Draperies as an allied fashionable product, also came to employ an astonishing number of people. By the 1690s, it has been estimated, 100,000 part-time knitters would have been needed to make two pairs a week for fifty weeks a year to satisfy the demand of the home market for ten million pairs; and another one and three-quarter million pairs a year were being exported. Once established, the New Draperies themselves continued to provide employment long after the time was past when they could even remotely be called 'new'. Defoe testified in the early eighteenth century to the enduring effect they had had on the prosperity of Norwich and Colchester and their surrounding countryside. Between 1660 and 1749 almost exactly half the freemen of Norwich were employed in the textile industry; and of these, 86 per cent were worsted weavers.[4] Firms like Gurteen and Sons of Haverhill, Suffolk, and Courtaulds, founded in Essex by the great-great-grandson of the Huguenot refugee Augustine Courtauld, owed their lasting success to expertise brought into being by the establishment and spread of the New Draperies.

In addition to offering employment opportunities, the textile manufactures implanted in Elizabeth's reign greatly assisted English exports during the early Stuart period. In 1640, a year for which we happen to have figures for exports by English merchants from London (by far the most important port), textiles accounted for some 87 per cent of the total; and by this date the value of New Draperies was approaching that of the old.[5] About 17,000 bays and 3,000 says were shipped from London in 1612; nearly 40,000 bays and over 20,000 says in 1640. The rise was not continuous, being interspersed with years of disruption and uncertainty, but the general trend is not in doubt. Its significance is accentuated by the heavy predominance of textiles in national exports.

When the Huguenots from Lous XIV's France arrived, they were helped by the enviable reputation earned by their predecessors. Moreover the earlier French/Walloon concentration on textiles provided an environment in which Huguenot skills could flourish. Over the thirty years before the tidal wave of refugees was washed on to British shores in the 1680s, there are many signs that influential sectors of English society were willing to encourage skilled weavers to cross the Channel. Protestations about their value were frequently accompanied by comments on the contribution to the national economy that had been made by earlier immigrants.

If the requirements of fashion had assisted the expansion of the New Draperies in Elizabethan England, a century later they helped the Huguenots sell their wares. By then new fashions were expected every year, and it was France that set them for others to emulate. This was a stock subject for satirical comment, and George Etheredge's *The Man of Mode, or, Sir Fopling Flutter* (1676) can be taken as representative:

EMILIA	He wears nothing but what are originals of the most famous hands in Paris.
SIR FOPLING FLUTTER	You are in the right, madam.
LADY TOWNLEY	The suit?
SIR FOPLING	Barroy.
EMILIA	The garniture?
SIR FOPLING	Le Gras.
MR. MEDLEY	The shoes?
SIR FOPLING	Piccat.
DORIMANT	The periwig?
SIR FOPLING	Chedreux.
LADY TOWNLEY AND EMILIA	The gloves?
SIR FOPLING	Orangerie: you know the smell, ladies. . . .

The government, English merchants and others from time to time objected to such aping of French fashions, and sometimes satire was tinged with envy and hostility:

> The richest silks we with regret put on,
> If made by skilful artists of our own:. . .
> But to a tawdry stuff in Paris made,
> Such store of praise, and moneys often paid.

But it is next to impossible to legislate on matters of taste. French fashions continued to hold sway, and the Huguenots were well placed to profit by them.[6]

During the later 1670s and 1680s, and again after 1714, calicos from the East Indies posed a severe challenge to the English textile industry. In the intervening period, however, wartime conditions encouraged its resurgence; and this was precisely the time when the Huguenots were settling into their new home. Demand for cloth was high both in England and abroad, with declining exports to the Levant in the 1690s more than offset by sharply rising exports to the Spanish peninsula and areas of Europe close to the Channel. Consequently textile manufacturing provided good employment opportunities for large numbers of new refugees, and, like their sixteenth-century predecessors, they established and refined branches of the clothing industry almost everywhere they settled, with the striking exception of the western suburbs of London. Even Bristol, often viewed as housing Huguenot seafarers, received amongst the French Protestants settling there more weavers than any other single trade category. Although the relevant French church registers contain no information about trades, new refugee weavers surely also went to the West Country, to the flourishing serge industry at Exeter and perhaps to Bideford and elsewhere. They certainly settled at Southampton, where they established a silk manufacture. At Norwich they were responsible for the one new fabric developed in this period, Norwich crape. Linen and silk were intended to be the main trades of the Huguenot colony planted at Ipswich, but this was in trouble by 1685 and never developed as its organizers hoped. In the end it was Ireland rather than England that became the home of linen and sailcloth production at Lisburn, Waterford, Cork and elsewhere, thanks particularly to Louis Crommelin after the earlier efforts of Nicholas Dupin had failed to achieve their objective. Crommelin came from St Quentin. So too did Nicolas D'Assaville, who attempted with much less success to found a linen manufacture in Scotland, at Broughton near Edinburgh, in the years after 1727.[7]

The principal centres for the clothing industry involving new refugees in England were at Canterbury and in the East End of London, where the most exciting new developments were associated with high quality dress materials, costly and distinctive silks. French refugees first established a viable industry at Canterbury and then migrated to the Spitalfields area, where they helped create a thriving manufacture that reached its peak in the mid–eighteenth century (plate 13). The boom period enjoyed by the Canterbury community in the 1680s and early 1690s was followed by a fairly sharp and enduring decline, so that although some silkweavers in reduced circumstances still remained in 1765, 'the history of the Canterbury industries throughout the eighteenth century is a melancholy record of almost continuous decay'. By contrast the fortunes of the industry in Spitalfields prospered over the first two generations of the century, assisted by a growing export trade to America and the proximity of the main domestic market in the capital. Important to the success of flowered silks were the silk designers, who devised the complex patterns for the rich material; for it was not the cut of costumes but their patterns that determined fashion by changing every year. Of seven identified designers working at the time, five, including Christopher Baudouin and James Leman, were Huguenots.

If the patterned silks were the chief glory of the silk industry, most of its output was plainer and aimed at a cheaper market; and the refugees contributed quantity as well as quality. Alamodes and lustrings were pioneered in England by Huguenot immigrants. The Royal Lustring Company, a joint-stock company incorporated in 1692, was masterminded by a group of prominent new refugees including Louis Gervaise and Hilaire Reneu; a few years after its foundation it claimed to employ 670 looms in London and a further 98 in Ipswich. Changes in fashion forced the dissolution of this company in about 1720, but the significance of the refugees in the London silk manufacture endured. It was moreover from Spitalfields and through Spitalfields connections that the skills introduced by the refugees were later spread, with varying degrees of success, to other parts of Britain like Edinburgh, Macclesfield and Sudbury (Suffolk).[8]

Numerous refugees were engaged in other branches of the textile trades. Lacemaking and tapestry work had been adversely affected by changing European tastes, so Huguenot skills did not rival those of earlier aliens in these fields. Instead they were diverted into different channels. Exeter's Passavant carpets became famous. It is likely too that refugees were involved in the establishment of calico printing at Richmond, Surrey in 1690, and later at Bromley Hall in Essex. Certainly calico printing thrived in later Stuart England, so that by 1711 about a million yards of calico were being printed annually.

One of the most striking instances of refugees developing an English industry from nothing was in hat manufacture. As had been the case a century earlier, the skill of dyeing was important, and use of the river Wandle – which seems to have had special properties for fixing dyes – encouraged a notable centre at Wandsworth. This developed in conjunction with the feltmaking and hatmaking industry that became located, despite acute industrial strife aroused in the process, in London's south-western suburbs of Battersea, Putney, Lambeth and Wandsworth. At Caudebec in Normandy the manufacture of soft, rainproof felt hats made from a mixture of fine vicuna wool and rabbit fur virtually ceased, as the hatmakers removed to Holland and England. France became an importer rather than exporter of this kind of hat, while in England the Feltmakers' Company lamented that 'a French hat called a Cordeback (being *à la mode de France*) . . . being generally worn because of the name both by rich and poor hath almost eaten out the [native] feltmakers'. It is one of the delightful minor ironies of history that thereafter Catholic cardinals at Rome had to have their red hats made by Huguenot refugees at Wandsworth.[9]

Huguenot involvement in the textile industry was of profound importance for the English economy. The trade secrets the refugees brought with them made possible the development of manufactures which would not have been established otherwise. The French agent Bonrepaus was well aware of the disadvantages that might ensue to his country, and in 1686 specified linens, Caudebec hats and chamois leather as of especial concern. The Court Books of the Weavers' Company of London plainly reveal the profound impression made on expert English opinion by the first demonstration of the art of making lustrings and alamodes in 1684:

> John Larquier and John Quet, who lately came from Nîmes in Languedoc, now appeared and declared that they were . . . fully enabled to weave and perfect lutestrings, alamodes, and other fine silks, as well for service and beauty in all respects as they are perfected in France, and praying to be admitted. . . . [Time was allowed for a supervised demonstration of their skills] . . . John Larguier now produced a piece of alamode silk made in England the which piece was shot with a piece of coloured silk given him by Mr. Willaw. *This Court considered thereof, and conceiving the like hath never been made in England and that it will be of great benefit to this nation,* do agree that the said John Larguier be admitted a foreign master gratis, upon this condition: that he employ himself and others of the English nation in making the said alamode and lutestring silks, for one year from this day.

If the expertise for lustrings came from Nîmes, the ability to design the patterns of expensive flowered silks (in the person of Christopher Baudouin) and to give a lustrous sheen to taffeta (in the persons of the Mongeorges, father and son) are likely to have come from the more important French centres of Tours and Lyon respectively. In an allied sphere, Lewis Paul, the son of a refugee, anticipated Arkwright's water-frame by inventing the first machine on which thread was spun by rollers.[10]

Huguenot textile workers took refuge not only in England but in the Netherlands, Ireland, Protestant German states and Zurich. Far more stayed in France than crossed its borders, but those who left inflicted great damage on the French economy. As the Lyons Chamber of Commerce reported in 1753, 'the epoch of 1685 was fatal for our industry not so much because it deprived us of man power as because it occasioned new establishments to arise in England and Holland.' Since France was a commercial as well as political rival of England and Holland, the loss of trade secrets was extremely serious. The techniques the refugees took with them helped the English and Dutch silk industries to flourish; that in England may have increased in size twentyfold during the fifty years before the Treaty of Utrecht (1713). War conditions helped the enemies of France disrupt her foreign markets, and gave merchants in England opportunities of which they took full advantage. By greatly reducing the amount of linen and silk imported from France, Huguenot textile workers crossing the Channel played a profound part in the dramatic reversal of the

English-French balance of trade which occurred in the 1680s and subsequent decades.

They and their descendants contributed to the English silk industry for generations to come, and helped give the manufacture such firm foundations that it persisted into our own century. At the outbreak of the First World War there were still forty-six workshops in the area of Bethnal Green and Spitalfields (plate 10a), and George Dorée was renowned for his weaving of velvet. The peak of the Huguenot contribution to the craft, however, came in the 1740s and 1750s, and is associated with names like Agace, Alavoine, Auber, Cabanell, Cazalet, Dalbiac, Dargent, Delahaize, Desormeaux, Duthoit, Fleury, Gobbée, Godin, Grellier, Lamy, Lardent, Le Keux, Lemaitre, Mazy, Ogier, Ouvry, Pillon, Prevost, Ravenell, Renée, Rocher, Sabatier, Vansommer, Vautier and Willett. Curiously, the best-known Huguenot name in textiles in modern times, Courtauld, entered the silk industry only as it was being deserted by many other families of Huguenot descent during the second half of the eighteenth century.

Other Crafts and Trades

Pride of place must inevitably go to textiles. The industry employed a great many Huguenots, and dominated the East End of London where they were most densely concentrated. Nearly three-fifths of those whose trade is given in the records of the church of La Patente, Spitalfields, between 1689 and 1716 were connected with textile trades, and an astonishing four-fifths of those named in the French Church of London registers between 1698 and 1706. But people need more than clothing to survive. To the other fundamentals of life – food and shelter – the later refugees contributed much less. A significant community of *fishermen* at Rye, settled in the early 1680s, helped feed the capital. Attempts were made to establish Huguenot *farming* communities around Thorpe-le-Soken (Essex) and Boughton Malherbe and Hollingbourne (Kent), and French ploughmen probably reinforced the Bideford community in Devon. But these groups do not amount to much, and plans for agricultural ventures in Somerset and Yorkshire never came to fruition. Besides, no innovations introduced after the Revocation could hope to compare in importance with those of the earlier foreign Protestants who had helped drain the Fens, bringing the French or paring plough with them and popularizing new crops like coleseed and rape in the process. Huguenot farmers evidently preferred to go directly to Germany, Friesland and Zealand, where more and better land may have been available and they would not be subject to the intricacies and insecurity (in foreign eyes) of the English system of renting land. Climate was also relevant; refugees expert in wine production could not be accommodated. Farmers who came to England must frequently have moved on to the emptier lands of Ireland and America.[11]

Of more lasting importance in changing the tastes and face of England (as also of Ireland, where Huguenots formed a Florists' Club in Georgian Dublin) was the popularization of *gardening*. It was Dutch refugees who had first 'advanced the use and reputation of flowers' in Norwich, according to Thomas Fuller in the 1660s, and it was in Norwich that the earliest recorded English florists' feast was held, in 1631. Refugees were also associated with the promotion of market gardening, for instance in sixteenth-century Sandwich, where a census recorded thirteen gardeners in 1582. Amongst other innovations, it has been suggested that they may have introduced hops into Kent. Some Huguenot gardeners settled at Chelsea, where they were befriended by the Anglican rector – to his considerable financial advantage.[12] It is not the number of gardeners or quantity of production that matters, rather the way they popularized the idea of small-scale gardening and created a new demand for cut flowers and for new types of vegetables and other plants. By emphasizing the cultivation of one variety of flower and growing it to perfection, the refugees paved the way for florists' feasts and so for the flower shows of our own day. By such means even the poorer immigrants could influence the living style of Englishmen, for it was noted that the refugee craftsmen decorated their houses with a taste rarely displayed by their English counterparts.

If Huguenot taste made an impression even in the cramped quarters of Spitalfields, it was stamped more deeply on the life of the nation through the work of the refugee settlement in Westminster and Soho. Here was the centre of French *fashion*, cuisine and high society in England, located conveniently near Court and Parliament. The trades mentioned in the registers of the west London churches make a fascinating contrast to those of the eastern suburbs. Rather than weavers, these congregations were notable for tailors, wigmakers and hairdressers, boot and shoemakers (the fashionable centre for these was Newport Court), food and drink merchants, clockmakers and gunmakers, jewellers and goldsmiths, perhaps also the bath-keepers at the end of 'Long-aker', recommended in Colsoni's *Guide to London*. Here lived representatives of other luxury trades catering for high-class English society, such as perfumers, wine-sellers, fanmakers, furriers and sculptors. It was from the western suburbs of the capital, the fashionable centre of the nation, that the influence of French tastes pervaded the whole of England.

Fashion being evanescent, there is little one can say about refugee bootmakers, hairdressers or tailors. The more lasting products of craftsmanship that surrounded the wealthy men of the day, however, bear eloquent testimony to the skills of the Huguenots. For example, according to J. F. Hayward,

> some of the finest English-made fire-arms in existence bear the signature of Huguenot [*gunmakers*. . .who] set a standard with which the indigenous masters found it difficult to compete. They included two of the leading Paris makers, Pierre Monlong and Pierre Gruché, as well as a French-Swiss of exceptional mechanical ingenuity, Jacques Gorgo.

Surviving productions of such men, who nearly all worked in the parishes of St Martin in the Fields, St Giles in the Fields or St Anne's, include a particularly magnificent pair of flint-lock holster pistols made by Monlong, probably for William III in the 1690s, now at the Tower of London (plate 9). While on the subject of firearms, it may also be noted that there was a Huguenot gunpowder mill at Faversham in Kent. In *watch- and clockmaking*, too, Huguenot craftmanship was conspicuous. Refugees prominent in this skill in the west London area included Thomas Amyot and Jacob and Pierre de Beauffre, while in Edinburgh Paul Romieu (Rewmer, Romeau) prospered and became an elder of the French church after being admitted burgess 'in respect he is very skilful and expert in making of watches of which calling there is none at present [1676] within the city'. Some earlier refugees had also been skilled in clockmaking; in 1622 London clockmakers demanded that aliens work only for English masters, and a few years later the Company of Clockmakers was formed to protect native interests.[13]

Foreign *goldsmiths and silversmiths* had been prominent in London since medieval times. Continental persecution swelled their numbers, and the published Returns of Aliens reveal about 150 Dutch and Germans following these crafts in Elizabethan London as well as over 50 lapidaries and diamond-cutters and about 20 jewellers. There were also 63 French goldsmiths working in the capital in the reigns of Elizabeth and James I, together with a pearl-cutter, 4 diamond-cutters, 5 jewellers and a number of Walloon bucklemakers. The great majority of these were Protestants. Foreign workmanship was claimed by Englishmen to be 'in better reputation and request than that of our own nation', and petitions of 1614 spoke of 'drawing, flatting and spinning of gold and silver after the French manner', developed by strangers brought to London for the purpose. It is hard to estimate just how influential these alien goldsmiths were. The Court of Charles I attracted the medallist Nicholas Briot and the enameller Jean Petitot. Undoubtedly, though, it was Louis XIV's actions that presented England with her greatest artistic gifts in this sphere.

It is now half a century since Joan Evans pointed out the overwhelming predominance of Huguenot workmanship in the great Russian imperial collection of English silver, and subsequent work has confirmed her conclusion that 'any history of the craft in England from 1680 to 1775 must chiefly concern itself with Huguenot smiths'. Their number and outstanding ability are indeed remarkable. They include Paul de Lamerie, by general acclaim the finest worker of gold and silver England has seen, Pierre Harache, Pierre Platel, David Willaume, Louis Cuny, Isaac Liger, Jean Chartier, Simon and Esaie Pantin, Louis Mettayer, Pierre Archambaut (father and son), Jacob and Samuel Margas, Paul Crespin, Augustin and Samuel Courtauld, and James Fraillant. Apart from their sheer skill, they brought to England new designs inspired by Daniel Marot and others, and new techniques, using thicker silver with higher relief work and engraved rather than applied ornament (plate 8). They also introduced new forms of silverware: the helmet-shaped ewer, the soup tureen, Mettayer's bowls, their special form of two-handled cup, the pilgrim bottle (a wine bottle, primarily for display purposes) and the *écuelle*, a flat covered bowl with ear-shaped handles. Their achievement reached its peak in the 1730s and 1740s, but waned after de Lamerie's death in 1751.

Because silver endures, many pieces have survived to provide ample evidence of Huguenot artistry. Much less well known is the immigrants' contribution to *architecture and interior decoration, furniture and cabinetmaking*, which will serve as a further example of the Huguenot role in the transformation of English living conditions. At the time of the Restoration, English craftsmanship in furniture was backward by continental standards. Yet by 1700 the move from oak joinery to fully-fledged veneered cabinetmaking was so complete that shortly afterwards Dutch craftsmen at The Hague had to submit an 'English cabinet' as their masterpiece to obtain full guild membership. The transition began in the 1660s, assisted by Dutch craftsmen who had themselves been influenced by French example and technique. It was given powerful impetus by the Huguenots, who evidently formed a number of workshops in London. Two men stand out as of particular importance, Jean Pelletier and Daniel Marot. Pelletier was a carver and gilder active throughout the 1690s. As the Court cabinetmaker, he introduced to England the baroque gilt furniture which distinguished Louis XIV's court, and inspired the work of John Gumley and James Moore for George I. Marot had a more pervasive influence, for he was not only a furniture designer but architect and landscape gardener, Court adviser in both the United Provinces (where he designed Het Loo Palace in Gelderlánd) and England. He is credited with the sudden shift away from chairs with traditional square or rectangular backs towards the 'curvilinear' type with hooped backs, and more generally with the promotion of decorative furnishings in a baroque style with rich tapestries and hangings (plate 6b). An exceptionally versatile man, son of Jean Marot who had been a leading Parisian architect and designer, he fled France in 1684. Careful in his planning of proportions, he was the first in Holland and England to try to co-ordinate architecture and interior decoration, and to design all the furniture and decorative elements in a room. He provided designs for a good deal of work at Kensington Palace and Hampton Court in the 1690s, and the influence of his pattern books was lasting. The many Huguenot craftsmen capable of interpreting Marot's style – as well as Pelletier, the carver Robert Derignée and the upholsterers Francis La Pierre and Philip Guibert are prominent in the 1960s – encouraged its spread and acceptance. In this field, as in silk-weaving, feltmaking, watch- and clockmaking, silver work, gunmaking and other luxury industries and fashionable pursuits, the Huguenots enhanced the unique character of London. In so doing they helped the capital play its immensely important part in national life.[14,15]

Glassmaking is one of several crafts and industries developed by sixteenth-century immigrants but not notably pursued by later Huguenots. Jean Carré, a native of Arras, revived the manufacture of window glass and introduced the production of fine crystal tableware into Elizabethan England. He had lived for some years at Antwerp, a major European glassmaking centre, and had not only the vision, capital and tenacity, but the skill and contacts necessary for success. Arriving in London in 1567, he immediately built three furnaces, one there and two in the Weald near the Surrey-Sussex border. Within a year, he had acquired a grant of a monopoly to make window glass, brought over Huguenots from Lorraine, Normandy and Flanders, and formed a 'fellowship' to give his ventures adequate financial backing. The furnaces in the Weald produced window glass, and Carré was beginning to organize the manufacture there of drinking glasses in green forest-glass at the time of his death in May 1572. His monopoly lapsed after his death, but his vision had not played him false. The London furnace, at Crutched Friars near the Tower, produced crystal glass for fine drinking vessels. Here Carré's most lasting contribution was Jacob Verzelini, another Protestant from Antwerp, attracted to London by Carré's success. Under Verzelini's skilled direction, the London glasshouse prospered, despite the setback of a major fire which in 1575 destroyed everything within its stone walls including 'near forty thousand billets of wood'. The making of both window glass and forest-glass also expanded, assisted by the arrival of more refugees in the 1570s. Glasshouses employing aliens appeared near Rye, Hastings, Buckholt (south of Winchester), Knole House (Kent) and elsewhere in the south of England, while the Weald furnaces continued to operate. Aliens continued to dominate all branches of the English glass industry in the 1580s, and in 1584 a Sussex MP introduced an unsuccessful bill into Parliament to suppress all glasshouses operated by 'divers and sundry Frenchmen and other strangers'.

In the search for appropriate conditions, and especially for fuel – wood and, later, coal – the aliens or their descendants migrated further afield. By the 1580s, they were to be found in Staffordshire; later also in Worcestershire, in Gloucestershire, at Denton near Manchester, and around Newcastle. Among the families concerned were those of de Hennezel (anglicized as Henzell or Hensey), de Thiéry (Tyttery), de Thisac (Tyzack) and de Houx. By the time coal replaced wood as the key fuel, in the second decade of the seventeenth century, the foreigners' dominance of the English glass industry was a thing of the past. The significance of the part they had played is clear, and the authority on the subject, Eleanor Godfrey, concludes that 'the influx of alien glassmakers, whose numbers and skill infused new life into English glassmaking, was unquestionably the greatest single factor contributing to growth in the industry'. Nor is there any doubt about their Protestantism. The three Lorrainers, four Normans and one Fleming at Buckholt in Hampshire in the late 1570s were all attached to the Walloon/French Church of Southampton. All the glassmakers coming to England, except for a few Italians, were Calvinists, and Jean Carré himself established a French-speaking congregation with a resident minister in the Weald, where his brother-in-law was an elder.

Another industry developed by earlier rather than later immigrants is *mining*, but here Protestant persecution played a much smaller part. The early Tudors, like their medieval predecessors, called in foreign expertise from time to time to help in the extraction of precious metals. Later in the century, such speculative ventures were succeeded by serious and successful attempts to establish brassmaking, copper mining, intensive ironworking and coal mining. In all except the last, alien influences were important. German capital as well as skill was sunk in the exploitation of Cumberland copper, lead and silver. Moreover, alien expertise established or revolutionized a number of *crafts dependent on mining*, including mechanical wire-drawing, the making of needles and pins, and copper-beating; it is in these ancillary crafts, rather than in mining itself, that any truly refugee contribution must be sought. As they were developed, new forms of business organization were pioneered; the Mineral and Battery Society's wire-drawing efforts demanded something like a factory at Tintern, for instance, and the Society combined functions of mining, manufacturing and marketing. There was no later Huguenot input to compare in importance with these changes, only some craftsmen fashioning high-quality knives and scissors, locks, surgical instruments, needles and pins, and iron and copper kitchenware.

Printing and bookbinding are further examples of skills developed more notably by the earlier than the later refugees. It is true that from the Le Blon or Le Blond family came Jacques Christophe, the printer in colours, painter and engraver (1670–1741) who is considered the inventor of modern chromo-lithography and similar processes of colour printing; and a Huguenot named Jourdain set up the first newspaper press in Plymouth in 1696. But these achievements cannot compare with the contribution of the earlier immigrants, who had included the highly accomplished printer Thomas Vautrollier; the typefounders Jérôme Haultin, François Guyot and Hubert d'Armillier; Norwich's earliest printer, Antony de Solen or Solempne; and such high-quality bookbinders as John Denys at Cambridge and Jean de Planche in London. All these displayed greater skill in their crafts than the Englishmen around them. Although his patron was the Roman Catholic Earl of Arundel, Vautrollier was a firm Huguenot, and it is appropriate that he is best known for printing Calvin's *Institutes* in Latin and English. In Elizabethan London there were also prominent Huguenot *booksellers*, men like Jean Desserans (de Surre) and Hercules François (Francis). Many Dutchmen, too, were employed in these various aspects of book production and distribution, so here again we have an industry in which refugee craftsmen were of incalculable benefit.[16]

When the first of the Tudors came to the throne in 1485, there were no paper mills in his realm; by the death of Queen Anne in 1714, there were some 200 in England and Wales, supplying perhaps two-thirds of all domestic needs. It was once thought that Huguenots introduced white *papermaking* to England. Not so; it was produced in the country as early as the opening years of the sixteenth century. But their technical skills and entrepreneurial abilities helped establish the manufacture on a sound basis in England and Scotland during the half century from the 1670s to the 1720s. Until the 1670s, perhaps until the reign of James II, France was England's main supplier of paper; thereafter French paper tended to be supplanted by imports from Holland, Italy and Germany. The manufacture of better grades of paper in France declined while English production improved, and the Huguenots were partly responsible.

In 1685 a petition from Nicholas Dupin, Adam de Cardonnel, Elias de Gruchy and others claimed that they had 'set up several new invented mills and engines . . . not heretofore used in England', and had 'brought out of France excellent workmen' to make quality paper. Earlier that year John Briscoe had been given a patent for making white paper, and when the two interests amalgamated the result was an incorporated joint-stock Company of White Paper Makers, which did well during the war years of the early 1690s but collapsed after peace returned. As usual it is hard to assess the precise refugee contribution, or how much weight should be accorded a petition of 1690 which claimed that English papermakers had made white writing and printing paper 'before the French interest took footing' and still could do so given an absence of monopoly legislation. In any event, the Huguenots enjoyed an enduring and profitable connection with the industry through the Portals, the Gaussens and Bosanquets, John Dickinson (whose mother was of Huguenot origin) and the Fourdriniers. The refugee settlement most closely associated with papermaking was the one at Southampton, a sensible location because old cordage and sails were available for use in the paper manufacture and it was easy to communicate with the principal market at London. Various mills developed nearby, including that of Gerard de Vaux (who had come from Castres in Languedoc) at South Stoneham. Among his workmen was Henri Portal, a refugee from Poitiers, who leased his own mill at Laverstoke (also in Hampshire) in 1718 and subsequently acquired a monopoly of making the paper on which Bank of England notes were and are printed.

There are interesting and significant parallels between the papermaking and silk manufacturing industries. In each, the Huguenots had an important role to play. In each, war conditions and economic policy ensured good chances for profitability: high duties levied on French imports assisted the temporary success of the respective joint-stock companies, the White Paper Company and the Royal Lustring Company, and they both suffered in the years after the Peace of Ryswick. Both relieved English anxieties by improving the adverse balance of trade with the national enemy, France. Both encountered determined, if ultimately unsuccessful, efforts by agents of the French government to disrupt the establishment of new techniques by ruses, bribes and threats. Both reveal divisions of interest within the refugee community: the wealthy merchant Etienne Seignoret tried to bypass the Royal Lustring Company, while the equally wealthy Theodore Janssen – a major paper importer – attempted but failed to subvert the White Paper Company in 1687–8.

Seignoret and Janssen may have found themselves excluded because they did not have such close connections as some other Huguenots with descendants of older immigrants. Perhaps they were so rich that they did not at first perceive the need for any such links, but were prepared to 'go it alone'. The relationship between the older and newer Huguenot refugees is a fascinating question which deserves an exploration in depth it has never had. Certainly the organization of Huguenot skills in papermaking in the Southampton region strongly resembles the development of silkweaving in Spitalfields. In each case established office-holders of the local French church put up capital or acted as entrepreneurs. Behind the White Paper Company lay not only Huguenot workmanship but also the active involvement of older immigrants, now well-established in England, like Adam de Cardonnel and Elias de Gruchy. Cardonnel had become a denizen in 1641 and had been naturalized in 1657, and was a Collector of Customs. De Gruchy was a Jersey-born merchant, a local alderman and future mayor. Like Cardonnel, he was an elder of the French Church of Southampton. Behind the utilization of the new techniques in silkweaving, brought by men like Jean Larguier from Nîmes and Christopher Baudouin from Tours, lay the existing London French/Walloon establishment, headed by such elders of the Threadneedle Street church as André Willau, Pierre le Keux, Charles Lanson and Pierre Marescoe.[17]

Between the reign of Edward VI and the industrial revolution of the eighteenth century, the craft scene was transformed as the whole English economy developed. In 1550 England was backward in her industrial techniques by comparison with continental countries like France, Italy, Spain or the Netherlands; by the early eighteenth century she had caught them up or surpassed them. The quality and range of manufactured wares available in the country had greatly increased. There was a far larger domestic market, and a more informed insistence on fashionable products. All these developments had been furthered by the refugee craftsmen whom England had welcomed to her shores. The name they had made for themselves by 1700 was one to conjure clouds of gloom over the heads of native English competitors. 'The English have now so great an esteem for the workmanship of the French refugees', it was then being reported, 'that hardly any thing vends without a gallic name.' At the heart of exaggeration, as so often, lay a core of truth.

5

Professions

Precision in assessing the contribution of refugee craftsmen is difficult; but an evaluation of what the Huguenots offered England intellectually is impossible. How can one estimate the influence of the formidable trio of late seventeenth-century librarians Henri Justel (at the royal library in St James's Palace), Elie Bouhereau (a doctor from La Rochelle who became the first librarian of Marsh's Library in Dublin) and Paul Colomiès (also from La Rochelle, at Lambeth Palace Library), or of their eighteenth-century successors like Matthew Maty and his son Paul Henry Maty at the British Museum? What was the impact of over 65 members of the House of Commons of Huguenot descent between 1734 and 1832?[1] And the numerous Huguenot diplomats? How can one assess journalists and pamphleteers, a wit and dramatist like Tom D'Urfey, writers like Harriet Martineau or Joseph Sheridan Le Fanu? What has been the influence of Peter Mark Roget's *Thesaurus of English Words and Phrases*, beside me as I write?

In some professional fields the refugees contributed only a useful injection of competent trained men. In others, they offered very much more. *Acting* is not a career normally associated with the Huguenots, but it would hardly have attained the respect it came to enjoy in the eighteenth century without David Garrick (1717–79), grandson of his refugee namesake, so largely responsible for the Shakespearean revival of the time (plate 14c). And how much poorer would our own generation have been without the genius of Sir Laurence, now Lord, Olivier. English *law*, too, benefited greatly from descendants of the refugees. The names of Sir John Bernard Bosanquet (1773–1847), Francis Maseres (1731–1824), Sir John Sylvestre and John, first Baron Romilly come to mind. Above them all ranks the law reformer Sir Samuel Romilly (1757–1818), John's father (plate 12d). A man of mercy, reason and eloquence, he tackled with vigour the tendency of contemporary English criminal law to resort to the death penalty for trifling offences.

The stage and the law required firm command of English and were consequently influenced by descendants of refugees. But the *army and navy* (plate 11) were influenced much earlier. When William III landed in England in 1688, his second-in-command was Frederick, Duke of Schomberg, once a Marshal of France and now, thanks to Louis's actions, fighting for the Protestant cause at an age approaching 80. Many of William's key officers were Frenchmen including his chief of artillery (Goulon), his chief of engineers (Cambon), and three of his aides-de-camp (de l'Etang, La Melonière and d'Arsellières). Fifty-four officers in the Blue and Red Guards and thirty-four in the Dutch Life Guards headed the numerous Huguenots in William's army; their presence, as refugees from Catholic tyranny, was in itself a formidable weapon for William in the propaganda war that he had to win if he was to become king of England.[2] Schomberg commanded the royal forces in Ireland until his death at the battle of the Boyne in 1690. Two years later the commander-in-chief in Ireland was Henri de Massue de Ruvigny, first Earl of Galway, who later commanded the English forces in Portugal during the War of the Spanish Succession. (Chapter 9 evaluates the full extent of the Huguenot contribution in the wars against Louis XIV.) Most remarkable among individual first-generation Huguenots was John (Jean Louis) Ligonier, who died as a field-marshal in 1770 at the age of 90. Born at Castres, he reached Britain via Switzerland and served under Marlborough in his major engagements at Blenheim, Ramillies, Oudenarde and Malplaquet between 1704 and 1709. Much later Ligonier commanded the British foot at Fontenoy (1745), but he is best remembered as an outstanding and dashing cavalry officer. He became commander-in-chief, and was created first Earl Ligonier.

There were many army officers of Huguenot descent fighting in the Napoleonic wars, like Colonel Sir William Howe Delancey who was killed at Waterloo, but by that time it is the naval roll-call that is more impressive. Following in the footsteps of his uncle Vice-Admiral James Gambier who had died in 1789, the second James Gambier became a Lord of the Admiralty and full admiral, leading the bombardment of Copenhagen in 1807 and subsequently commanding the Channel fleet. Other distinguished officers of Huguenot descent serving in the Napoleonic wars included the 'gallant and good' Captain Edward Riou, and Sir John Laforey and his son Sir Francis, who both attained the status of full admiral.

Protestants being 'people of the book', the Reformed churches always stressed the need for *education*. It was in the best Calvinist tradition that both Walloons and Huguenots were concerned to educate refugee children and made important contributions to English schooling. Perhaps it was inevitable that they should do so, for there were many men of letters among the refugees. Even the early foreign settlement at Southampton, small though it was, had a school, and one member of the congregation, Adrian de Saravia, became a distinguished headmaster of the local English grammar school in the 1570s. Similarly the first Canterbury settlers brought a teacher, Vincent Primont, with them, and there were no fewer than eight in the French Church of London in 1560. All education in early modern Europe had a strong religious bent, and Protestant refugees were ideal teachers of foreign languages to Englishmen. John Belmain acted as French tutor to Edward VI and Elizabeth. Pierre du Ploiche wrote *A Treatise in English and French righte necessarie and profitable for all yonge children* in 1553, and the preacher John Véron, who died in 1563, produced a Latin-English dictionary. The best known sixteenth-century refugee teacher was Claude de Sainliens or Holyband. In addition to his manuals for improving French grammar and conver-sation, his *French Littleton* and *French Schoolmaster*, Holyband gave England a French-English dictionary and an Italian textbook. His works, appropriately enough, were printed by his fellow-countryman Vautrollier. During the next century a stream of further French textbooks flowed from the pens of Huguenot refugees or their descendants: G. N. de la Mothe's *The French Alphabet* (1592), Peter Erondell's *French Garden* (1605), Jean de Grave's *Path-Way to the Gate of Tongues* (1633), William Herbert's *Sure Guide to the French Tongue* and *French and English Dialogues* (1658 and 1660 respectively), and Guy Miège's *New French Grammar* of 1678. Such works were important, for they helped make available to Englishmen the French styles and ideas that were becoming so fashionable. Also influential were Huguenot works on hand-writing. John de Beauchesne was the author of England's first printed manual on the subject (1570), providing specimens of the various contemporary styles of writing, and Esther Inglis was an exquisite calligrapher. Her 'Argumenta in Librum Geneseos' (1606), is a truly delightful work, with every one of its thirty-seven pages written in a different style and adorned with coloured floral illustrations executed by pen (plate 14).[3]

When refugees began arriving from France in large numbers in 1681, it immediately became apparent that concern for education was as lively as ever. The Threadneedle Street church at once sought premises for a school, and one of its pastors recommended unsuccess-fully to Bishop Compton that French Academies be established in England. Later the Consistory urged the French Committee distribut-ing relief funds to establish schools. Large numbers of refugee ministers were drawn into teaching, for not all could find positions in French churches. As schoolmasters or tutors, either temporarily or permanently, they were able to make use of their knowledge of

French and the education they themselves had received in the French Protestant Academies. Such work might not have been exciting, but at least it was less alarming than pursuing one suggestion made to Compton, that surplus intellectuals could profitably be employed in instructing the North American Indians! And it met a real need, for many English gentlefolk were anxious to employ them as tutors for their offspring. In a few cases this may have been merely an exercise in Christian charity. But the prestige of France under Louis XIV, the 'Sun King', was increasing the demand for some knowledge of French culture and language as a necessary part of the upbringing of any Englishman or Englishwoman who claimed to be educated. The influx of potential tutors was therefore most timely. What it could mean at its best is revealed in the love for France and brilliant mastery of the French language displayed by Philip Dormer Stanhope, fourth Earl of Chesterfield, a pupil of the minister Philippe Jouneau who had come from Barbésieux to London in the 1680s.[4]

For those unable to find or unwilling to accept a safe niche in a gentleman's household there were other opportunities, especially around the capital. 'The French have set up several great schools both at London and in the countries near it', Misson observed in the 1690s. Today the best-remembered French educational institutions in later Stuart England are the private academies like Solomon Foubert's courtly academy with its emphasis on riding and military accomplishment, founded in the early 1680s, Metre's in Long Acre, opened in 1686, and Meure's in Soho, flourishing by 1691. But there was also a full range of schools, both boarding and day, catering for girls as well as boys; it is hard to assess their significance because so little is known about English private schooling of the period. The villages around London made ideal sites, so schools run by Frenchmen sprang up at such places as Chelsea, Greenwich, Islington and Marylebone. Peter Prelleur, who became noted as an organist, harpsichordist and composer, was at first a writing master in Spitalfields. At Chelsea one of the teachers was Jean François Bion, previously Roman Catholic chaplain on board the royal galley *Superbe*, but converted to Protestantism after witnessing the sufferings of Huguenot prisoners. His *Account of the Torments the French Protestants endure aboard the Galleys* was published in London in 1708. Other refugees joined existing English institutions. Thus Jacques Cappel, who had followed in the footsteps of his father Louis as a professor of Hebrew at the important Huguenot seat of learning at Saumur, eventually became professor of Latin at Joshua Oldfield's Nonconformist College, Hoxton Square, in 1708.

We cannot pursue the later educational efforts of the Huguenots and their descendants in any detail. Their French grammars, like one produced by the refugee minister Paul Berault, continued in use. They still taught. It is appropriate, for example, that they should have been largely responsible for the growth in stature of the King's School at Canterbury, where there was such a large Huguenot community. They continued to found schools, such as David Sanxay's at Cheam, destined to have a distinguished future. And their interest in education has persisted to this day. The Westminster French Protestant Charity School was founded in 1747 specifically for descendants of Huguenot refugees, and was so enthusiastically supported in its early years that in 1752 the project had over a hundred regular subscribers. Distinguishing features of the school included its annual sermon on the Revocation, and its holiday on St Bartholomew's day. It aimed to give primary education to about thirty pupils, half boys and half girls, but by the time of the Napoleonic wars it was faced by economic difficulties and restricted itself to the education of girls alone. The school survived into the twentieth century; but with primary education now available to all, its purpose had ceased to exist. It was closed in the 1920s, and from its ashes rose the Westminster French Protestant School Foundation, providing financial assistance where needed towards the secondary and tertiary education of boys and girls of Huguenot descent. This Foundation still exists, as does the Educational Fund of the French Protestant Church of London.

At the close of the seventeenth century, Marylebone was the home of schools established by Denis de la Place and Peter de la Touche, and de la Mare's boarding school for young ladies. At a coffee house in the parish there gathered on occasion an impressive group of Huguenot minds including Abel Boyer (plate 12c), Pierre Antoine Motteux and Pierre Coste. Boyer's miscellaneous writings included *The Political State of Great Britain*, his *Complete Frenchmaster*, which went through twenty-three editions after its publication in 1694, and his popular French-English dictionary. Motteux was a translator and dramatist, who amongst other works completed an edition of Rabelais begun by Sir Thomas Urquhart, and produced a free rendering of *Don Quixote*. Coste translated Isaac Newton's *Opticks*, but is of particular importance because of his active association with John Locke, whom he brought to the attention of the European reading public.

With men of this calibre we reach the interesting question of the Huguenot contribution to what Paul Hazard christened the 'crisis of European thought' during the period from about 1680 to 1715. The 'crisis' revolved around the need to probe the foundations of belief, in the wake of the new material discoveries and the moral, social and economic developments of the sixteenth and seventeenth centuries. In the end it was resolved by the advent of the Enlightenment, the near-deification of human reason which characterised the thought of western and central Europe in the mid-eighteenth century. Eventually, many adopted the position that even the deepest secrets of man and his environment, and of God, should be open to unbiased examination and accepted or rejected purely on the merits of that examination. But before such a consensus could be reached, new questions had to be put and new stances adopted.

The preoccupation of the Enlightenment with the sovereignty of the human mind could hardly be further removed from orthodox Calvinism, which viewed man as but dust when set against the majesty of God. All the same, the international community of Huguenot refugees assisted the *evolution of Enlightenment thought* in a number of important ways. First, the diaspora in itself raised some of the central questions at the heart of the 'crisis'. As E. S. de Beer has put it,

> The refugees had to earn a living and to vindicate their conduct: the latter not to the countries of refuge, but to the country whence they had fled. Most of them by their flight had disobeyed royal edicts; to justify themselves they must examine how far the king had maintained or violated the positive laws of France, and beyond the laws the moral foundations of political life. Closely connected with that were the rights of the individual conscience, the question of principle, uniformity or liberty in religious worship and organization, and the practical question of toleration. Above all, the refugees must state for what cause they had fled: they must state their beliefs; they must determine what they believed in a world of changing beliefs.

Second, among the refugees in the Netherlands was the great dialectician and logical enquirer Pierre Bayle. The use of scepticism as an instrument of study, which he had acquired from Descartes and subsequently greatly developed, was broadcast throughout Europe by his influential *Historical and Critical Dictionary* (1695–7). In religious matters, Bayle himself was a Calvinist and a fideist (that is, one who believes that knowledge depends on an act of faith) rather than a sceptic. But for Voltaire and other thinkers of the Enlightenment, Bayle's methods and caustic style stimulated scepticism. Bayle's advocacy of complete freedom of conscience – he taught that even atheism was to be tolerated by the State – was also influential in the eighteenth century; and his attacks on Catholic clergy and feuds with orthodox Huguenot ministers like Pierre Jurieu provided models for Enlightenment anti-clericalism.

Applied in England, Bayle's scientific method transformed the local history writing and antiquarianism of a Camden or an Aubrey into a sounder, more sceptical historical approach, more determined to be accurate and more interested in assessing motivation. There was a new emphasis on biographical dictionaries and improved textual scholarship. Des Maiseaux's translation of Bayle's *Dictionary* was followed by nationalist calls for an English biographical dictionary; among the works that resulted, and followed Bayle's method, were the *General Dictionary Historical and Critical* and the *Biographia Britannica*. A new interest in European intellectual journals spawned periodicals like the *History of the Works of the Learned*. European interest in turn stimulated the belief that the English had an intellectual history worthy of definitive record, thus encouraging attempts to establish, for example, a critically sound text of Shakespeare. All these developments were aspects of a new burst of systematic and nationalistic scholarship which owed much to Bayle.

The hopes of the Enlightenment rested heavily on English thought, based on observation, and the English constitution. Neither was well-known in Europe before the Revocation, but the assimilation of English philosophical and social opinions by French thinkers was an essential pre-condition of the Enlightenment. It was largely thanks to Huguenot refugees, who acted as abbreviators, commentators, journalists, publishers and translators, that such opinions were transmitted to the Continent. Paul de Rapin (Rapin-Thoyras) (plate 12b) also made English institutions known across the Channel through his *History of England*. At the same time, of course, the refugees diffused French thought in England, facilitating a cross-fertilisation of ideas. Men like Pierre Des Maiseaux, philosopher and literary critic as well as Bayle's English translator, were well acquainted with both English and continental scholars. Bayle's *News of the Republic of Letters* and Jean le Clerc's *Bibliothèque Universelle et Historique* stand out among numerous projects which helped enlarge the horizons of Europeans by familiarising them with a wide range of ideas and sources.

The most important single English contributor to the Enlightenment was John Locke, who believed in religious toleration (within certain limits) and vindicated both English constitutionalism and the rights of the individual. Locke was in almost unbroken contact with French-speaking Protestants either in France or in exile from 1675 until his death in 1704, and the bonds he formed were significant because they ensured the rapid transmission of his ideas to a receptive international audience. Pierre Coste, probably selected for the job by Jean le Clerc, translated the *Essay concerning Human Understanding* under Locke's personal supervision. His translations, which concentrated on the presentation of Locke's ideas rather than mere verbal accuracy, conveyed Locke's thought to early eighteenth-century Europe.

Coste, like many of the men mentioned in connection with both education and the 'crisis', had been trained as a minister, and *pastors* were the most eminent refugee group. Pierre Allix was a doctor of divinity of both Oxford and Cambridge, and René Bertheau and Samuel de L'Angle each had an Oxford DD. Jacques Abbadie, Luke de Beaulieu, Charles Daubuz, Pierre Drelincourt, David Durand, Isaac Dubourdieu, Jean Dubourdieu, Jean-Armand Dubourdieu, John Jortin, Claude Grostête de La Mothe, Michael Malard, Abraham le Moine were all writers as well as ministers, and all are recorded in the *Dictionary of National Biography*. That these were all conformist ministers, closely allied to the Church of England, merely reflects a weakness of the *Dictionary*; an equally imposing list of non-conformist Huguenot ministers could be compiled, starting with the formidable preacher Jacques Saurin.

As time passed, Huguenot descendants became associated with the full range of Christian belief. They were important in early Methodism, and Vincent Perronet, a close associate of the Wesleys, was styled the Methodist 'archbishop'. His son Edward, who wrote the hymn 'All hail the power of Jesu's name', died an independent minister at Canterbury. Anthony Benezet, born in St Quentin, became a Quaker and in 1731 emigrated to America, where he championed the cause of the negroes and the Indians.[5] Francis Maseres was a Unitarian, and James Martineau, Harriet's brother, a Unitarian divine. Most surprisingly, there is a significant connection between the Huguenots and the Oxford Movement; Cardinal Newman's mother was a Fourdrinier, and the name of Edward Bouverie Pusey speaks for itself.

The importance of Huguenot *merchants* to English commerce and early banking at the end of the Stuart era is considered in chapter 9, but the impact of earlier Walloon or French refugee families like the Delmés, Lethieulliers, Lordells and Papillons should not be forgotten. In the eighteenth century, their Huguenot successors helped ensure British political stability through their wealth and support for the Protestant succession. In mid-century, Huguenots held getting on for a fifth of the 'gilt-edged' English securities of the day. Their loyalties and their substance are both shown by a petition of 1745 from the weavers of Spitalfields, in which 137 manufacturers promised specific numbers of men for service against the Young Pretender. Of the 137, no fewer than 81 had foreign names: and the 'foreigners' promised nearly twice as many men as the English firms. The largest contingents offered by those with foreign names were James Dalbiac (80), Daniel Gobbee (70), Louis Chauvet (65), Godin and Ogier (60), Abraham Jeudwine (60), John Rondeau (57), and Peter Auber and Son (52).

Huguenots played a significant part in early English *insurance*, providing 15 per cent of the proprietors and holding 15 per cent of the first public stock issue of the London Assurance Company in 1720. They increased in importance in the field, establishing within it family traditions to compare with those of the Romillys in law, the Gambiers or Laforeys in the navy, or the Dubourdieus in the church. David Bosanquet was a director of the London Assurance, 1729–44; Samuel, William and Richard Bosanquet were all directors of the Royal Exchange Assurance later in the century, William becoming deputy governor in 1791 and sub-governor in 1810; Jacob and Charles Bosanquet were members of Lloyds Insurance (and Charles of its Patriotic Fund committee) during the Napoleonic wars. John Lewis Loubier, John Lewis junior, and Henry Loubier were all directors of the London Assurance between 1732 and 1765, as were William and Hughes Minet between 1747 and 1787. Other eighteenth-century directors of the company include the Huguenot names of Arbouin, Aubert (Alexander Aubert was governor from 1787 to 1805), Aufrère, Bréholt, Cazalet, Fauquier, Gualtier, Jamineau, Langlois, Laprimaudaye, Menet, Molinier, Pigou and La Porte. Huguenot connections with insurance have continued into our own time. Sir Henry Hozier (Winston Churchill's father-in-law) was Clerk to the Committee of Lloyds (1874–1906) and introduced the Lloyds Signal Stations, while Raymond Dumas and John Minet have been eminent Lloyds' brokers this century.[6]

Finally, let us glance at *the arts and sciences*. An early refugee painter of importance is Jacques Le Moyne de Morgues (c.1533–88); a comprehensive catalogue of his work was produced by the British Museum, in association with the Huguenot Society of London, in 1977. He is best known for his record of Laudonnière's expedition, an abortive attempt to establish a Huguenot settlement in Florida in 1564–5; but he was particularly effective in executing detailed watercolour drawings of plants, flowers and fruits, having a deep love of detail and appreciation of their colour. The album of these at the British Museum was produced in the 1580s, after Le Moyne settled in England for religious reasons, and displays skills setting him above any contemporary English competition. Isaac Oliver or Olivier (d.1617), linked by marriage with the Flemish immigrant painting families of Gheeraerts and de Critz, was a notable miniature painter. Together with his master and competitor Nicholas Hilliard, he has preserved for us James I and his court. Both were painters of rare skill and command of realism, 'inferior to none in Christendom for the countenance in small', as Henry Peacham put it in 1612; Oliver had the more sophisticated style, using shadow to provide a three-dimensional effect. In view of his refugee background, it is appropriate that he often worked on religious themes. His contemporaries, the sculptor brothers Jean and Maximilian Poultrain from Arras, who translated their name to Colt in England, were men of lesser genius. Superior to them, and pre-eminent in England from 1625 to 1635, was Hubert Le Sueur, son of a Parisian master-armourer. Le Sueur was commissioned to produce the monumental tombs for the Duke of Richmond and Lennox and the Duke of Buckingham, in Westminster Abbey. He made many representations of Charles I, the best-known being the equestrian bronze now at the bottom of Trafalgar Square.[7]

While prominent in the England of his day, Le Sueur was not a sculptor of the first rank, but the Huguenots provided one the following century. Louis François Roubiliac (c.1705–62), descended from a Lyons family, reached England in the early 1730s, and by 1738 had set up his studio in the fashionable French quarter to the west of London. His style is spirited and refined, if mannered, and he is perhaps the greatest marble sculptor who has worked in England. 'Roubiliac only is a sculptor,' remarked Lord Chesterfield, 'the rest are only stone masons.' His career is of special interest in showing how widespread was the network of contacts established by the descendants of refugees by the middle of the eighteenth century. Roubiliac had probably come to London in search of patronage, and he found it largely within circles influenced by the Huguenot migration. After 1750, he was engaged on a series of major commissions with demonstrable Huguenot links: a statue of Sir John Cass, whose de la Caisse ancestors had settled in London a century and a half earlier; monuments to the second Duke and Duchess of Montagu, whose family had long patronized Huguenot craftsmen and still employed John Poitevin (perrukemaker), Peter Dunoyer (bookseller), Jacques Regnier (printseller) and others; the famous statue of Shakespeare, now in the British Museum, commissioned by David Garrick (who may well have posed for it); busts of Henry St John, Viscount Bolingbroke, and his second Huguenot wife; a portrait bust of that Earl of Chesterfield who had been tutored by Philippe Jouneau; another of Sir Mark Pleydell, connected by his daughter's marriage to the Bouverie family; and a bust of Field Marshal Lord Ligonier. Even after Roubiliac's death, his Huguenot connections did not desert him. The collection of busts by which he is best known was acquired by his friend Dr Matthew Maty, for presentation to the British Museum.[8]

Prominent amongst other post-Revocation artistic talent are: Louis Chéron, who influenced the Academy of Painting in St Martin's Lane; the Gosset family, expert in modelling in wax; David Le Marchand, a masterful carver of sinuous curves and portraits in ivory; the decorative artist Jacques Rousseau; the painter Philip Mercier and the mapmaker John Rocque; the engravers of the Wyon family; and the gatesmith Jean Tijou, responsible for the gates at the entrance to the north choir aisle, the sanctuary screens, and the balustrading of the geometrical staircase at St Paul's Cathedral.

Among the earlier wave of refugees were some notable *doctors*, including Pierre Chamberlen, Théodore Deodati, Baudouin Hamey, Guillaume de Laune and the eminent physician Sir Théodore Turquet de Mayerne. Chamberlen invented the obstetric forceps, a trade secret which (together with the large wooden box containing the instrument) was handed down within his family for generations. Hugh Chamberlen, his brother's grandson, produced the first satisfactory English textbooks on midwifery, translations of François Mauriceau's writings under the titles *The Accomplisht Midwife* (1673) and *The Diseases of Women with Child, and in Child-bed* (1683), taking the opportunity to advertise the forceps in the process. Gideon de Laune, Guillaume's son, and Sir Théodore Turquet de Mayerne were instrumental in the foundation of the Society of Apothecaries, which was granted its charter in 1617; Gideon headed the first court of assistants, and later served as under warden, upper warden and master. Since medicine was one of the professions forbidden to Protestants by Louis XIV shortly before the Revocation, and the writing had been on the wall for some time previously, numerous doctors left France during his reign. However, they advanced medical science in England less than the earlier refugees, although they included the surgeon and anatomical writer Paul Bussière, and may have aided the establishment of the first dispensary in London.[9]

Denis Papin was a medical doctor by training, but a scientist by profession. He became an assistant to Robert Boyle after arriving in London in 1675, and invented the first pressure cooker, his 'Digester of Bones' – Evelyn's Diary records a meal cooked in it for members of the Royal Society in 1682. Later he realized the potentialities of steam power, only to find his experimental boat sunk by jealous German bargemen. Another Huguenot scientist of note was John Theophilus Desaguliers (1683–1744) (plate 12a), designer of the first air conditioning system, for the House of Commons, and inventor of the planetarium. When a child, he is said to have been sent on board a boat from La Rochelle to Guernsey concealed in a barrel, and from the Channel Islands was brought to London. As an adult he proved able to deliver learned lectures to general audiences with particular success. He became a Fellow of the Royal Society and was awarded a Copley gold medal, a double honour later also enjoyed by the inventive optician John Dollond (1706–61), once a Spitalfields weaver, and the chemist Richard Chenevix (1774–1830).

Desaguliers exercised an important influence on early English *Freemasonry*. The first Grand Lodge was founded in 1717, and Desaguliers served as Grand Master in 1719 and as Deputy Grand Master in 1722–4 and 1726. Indeed the evidence suggests that Huguenots played a key role amongst the freemasons. Josias Villeneau, the first named steward in masonry, was a refugee; he became senior grand warden in 1721. Early grand stewards included the Walloon Protestant John James Heidegger in 1725, Claude Champion de Crespigny in 1732 and John Villeneau in 1746. Between 1738 and 1742, named stewards include Barret, Beaumont, Bernard, Carne, Caton, Combrine, De Charmes, De Vaux, Du Mouchel, Faber, Foy, Hemet, Le Bas, Le Maistre, Ruck and Vol – more than a quarter of the total, a minimum estimate since by 1740 some names would be anglicized and hard to recognize.

Contemporaries of Desaguliers who, like him, were Fellows of the Royal Society were Pierre Des Maiseaux (1673–1745), David Durand (1680–1763) and the mathematician Abraham de Moivre (1667–1755), discoverer of the equation for the normal curve of error and intimate friend of Newton. The Huguenots continued to produce creative minds; when, for instance, the first Westminster Bridge was built, it was designed by Charles Labelye, and the engine used to drive the piles was invented by the watchmaker James Vauloué. At a later date, James Six was responsible for an effective thermometer recording the maximum and minimum temperatures attained during the observer's absence; his basic design has changed little since.[10] Later still, the Peter Mark Roget of *Thesaurus* fame, Secretary of the Royal Society from 1827 to 1849, was responsible for a much improved slide rule.

In the armed forces, the arts, crafts, education, religion, science, trade – in short in almost every branch of human endeavour – England's debt to the Huguenots is profound. The extent of their contribution is emphasized by the fact that in two substantial detailed chapters it has been impossible to find space even to mention the names of Beaufort, Blondel, Boileau, Cavalier, Chardin, Demainbray, Denis, Fonnereau, Labouchere, Layard, Lefevre, Majendie, Maturin, Savory, Teulon, Thellusson, Vigne and Vignoles. Yet all, and many more, will be found in biographical dictionaries. Little did the French rulers realize that their actions against their Protestant subjects would bequeath to Britain so rich an inheritance.

6

The Huguenots and their Churches

Although the Huguenots made far-reaching contributions to England's trade, economy, culture and military strength, this was not their prime intention in coming. They came, first and foremost, to obtain freedom of worship, the right to participate in a particular kind of church. For that right, they were prepared to run great risks.

Certainly, there were organized escape routes from France, and a plentiful supply of guides could be found (at a price) to direct the fugitives along little-known paths by night; over 150 guides were arrested between 1685 and 1703. But, as escaping allied servicemen found under similar conditions in the Second World War, the routes could be uncovered by the authorities, and the guides were not always dependable. Even the most experienced could make mistakes. Shepherding Huguenots across the Spanish Netherlands border early in 1701, the professional guide known as 'le Gasconnet' assured them they had reached a place of freedom – only to find that French troops had taken over since his previous visit. Escape was at best a hazardous process, especially in the 1680s when emigration reached its peak. The French authorities might swoop at any time. In 1715 Pierre Sauzeau entrusted his safety and that of his family to the guide Pierre Michaut. Michaut used two routes for getting refugees from Poitou out of the country, one commencing at Parthenay, crossing the Loire near Angers; the other starting from St Maixent, crossing the Loire near its mouth by Nantes, and proceeding by way of Vitré and Avranches. Both routes ended at Granville, where the Huguenots took ship for Jersey and thence made their way to London. But on this occasion the whole party was caught. Sauzeau and his sons were condemned to the galleys, and the female members of his family confined for life; Michaut was hanged.[1]

Refugees unable to locate or afford guides were forced to rely on written routes, provided by friends, based on the past experience of successful escapers. Many such routes were in circulation. Jacques Nadal of Lasalle (Provence) was in possession of no fewer than five escape plans when arrested in 1686, all written in different hands and all suggesting ways of crossing the eastern frontiers. Jean Marteilhe, who left Bergerac at the age of 16 after the dragoons came in 1700, travelled to Paris with his companion Daniel Legras to seek advice. There a friend gave them 'a small written route' which took them to Mézières, where they hoped to cross the frontier to Charleroi. Losing their way in the Ardennes, they were captured, and Marteilhe spent more than a decade in the galleys. His adventures, translated by Oliver Goldsmith, became well-known to Englishmen under the title *The Memoirs of a Protestant Condemned to the Galleys of France for his Religion, written by himself.*

The obstacles and heartbreak faced by the refugees and the determination and perseverance they needed are brought vividly to life in the memoirs of Jacques Fontaine. He belonged to a large family, having five living half-brothers and half-sisters and four brothers and sisters. Taking the half-brothers and half-sisters first, in order of age: Jane seems to have stayed in France, in any event the memoirs give no details of any sacrifices she may have made for Protestanism. Judith was a widow with four children by the time of the persecution, when she was seized and sent to a convent. Released after being compelled to recant, she escaped and reached London successfully with her daughters. James, a Huguenot minister, died before the 1680s, but his wife spent three years in prison – partly in close confinement – before being banished from France. She reached London with three sons, one of whom had become a Protestant pastor in Germany by the time the memoirs were written. Elizabeth left France with her husband (another minister) and their five children, and went to Dublin and thence to America. The whole family was drowned when their ship was wrecked in sight of Boston harbour. Peter was also a pastor. His daughters were not allowed to accompany him when he was banished after being imprisoned in the castle of Oléron for six months, but later successfully escaped and joined him in London.

Table 3	Dispersion of the Fontaine family
Jane	France
Judith	London
James	dead: wife to London, son to Germany
Elizabeth	drowned at Boston
Peter	London
Susan	France
Peter	France
Mary	England
Ann	Plymouth
Jacques	Taunton, Dublin: descendants to America

Of Jacques's full brothers and sisters, Susan stayed in France, as her husband abjured with little resistance on the appearance of the dragoons. Peter did the same, though (being a minister) with much greater reluctance; he had in fact acquired a passport to leave before the dragoons arrived, but delayed too long in order to collect his resources together. Jacques laid the blame for this stain on his family's honour upon 'the fatal influence of a bad wife over a too yielding husband'. His two remaining sisters, however, were determined to preserve their Calvinism. Mary had married a minister named Forestier, and supported him in his tribulations when he was twice arrested in France before eventually escaping to England by sea. Ann could not prevent her husband's abjuration when the dragoons came, but 'gave him no peace until she persuaded him to take her out of France'. She saw her family safely removed to Plymouth, and died shortly afterwards. Jacques himself, the youngest of the family, was training for the ministry in 1684, when he deliberately gave himself up to temporary imprisonment in order to encourage his fellow-Protestants in prison. The following year he eluded dragoons sent to force him to abjure. Narrowly escaping detection by a French frigate searching ships for refugees, he escaped to Devonshire, whence he moved to Taunton and then to Ireland. His career in exile demonstrates Huguenot enterprise and perseverance. French and Latin teacher, shopkeeper and cloth manufacturer in Somerset, he prospered sufficiently to attract the envy of leading Taunton merchants. After moving to Cork so that he could minister to a French congregation, he established a broadcloth manufacture, and later a fishing business at Bere Haven; finally he set up a school at Dublin. His descendants settled in America.

In one sense it was easier for the Fontaines than for other Huguenots to leave their native land; many of them were either ministers or married to them, and pastors were rather ordered to leave than constrained to stay by the state authorities. Even so, the family was impoverished and irreparably scattered, with three of its members remaining in France, two dying on the way to or shortly after reaching their destinations, and the remaining five and their descendants living in various parts of England, Ireland, Germany and America. Many other families suffered a similar fate, with husbands and wives, parents and children, brothers and sisters, separated for years, if indeed they were ever reunited. The force that drove the Huguenots to risk such dislocation, imprisonment, the galleys or death was their religion, their burning desire to worship freely in the way they had chosen. It is not fashionable nowadays to emphasize this fact. But if we cannot at least begin to comprehend the commitment and sense of joy in the Lord that drove on Jean Marteilhe or Jacques Fontaine, and allowed François Rochette to go to his execution proclaiming 'this is the day . . . let us rejoice', then we cannot claim to understand much about the Huguenots.

In some respects, England was a curious choice of haven. For even while the English authorities welcomed French Protestants, they were persecuting native subjects, Presbyterians and other Nonconformists, who did not wish to be part of a church organized by bishops. They were prepared to allow foreigners to worship in their own way, accepting that it was simply the refugees' misfortune that they had never had the chance to experience the benefits of a Protestant episcopacy; indeed one foreign congregation worshipped in the very heart of the Anglican Church, inside Canterbury Cathedral (plate 5b). But they were not prepared to accept any right of Englishmen to worship in similar fashion. By the time of the Revocation, even the Channel Islands, once a fine illustration of Calvinist order and discipline and the one region in England where Presbyterianism had been officially endorsed, had been reduced to reluctant conformity with forms of worship more to the liking of the Court and bench of bishops.

We saw in Chapter 3 that when the monarchy was restored in 1660, the foreign churches in the realm were in a state of disarray, internally divided and with a Parliamentarian past to live down. In London, the Threadneedle Street Consistory tried to take advantage of the recall of the royalist minister Louis Hérault to destroy a congregation which had existed independently at Westminster since the eve of the Civil War, arguing that its continued existence would 'give encouragement to division' and tend towards the ruin of the City church. The Westminster group counter-petitioned King Charles for protection, and the matter was referred to the episcopal authorities. The decision reached in 1661 opened a new chapter in the history of the French churches in England:

> As many of them as shall submit to the Church of England, under the immediate jurisdiction of the Bishop of London . . . and use the book of common prayers by law established in their own French language, according as it is used in the Island of Jersey [may] meet together at God's service in the little chapel of the Savoy.

So a new episcopalian or 'conformist' French church of the Savoy came into being.[2]

John Durel was appointed to order the new congregation, the king promising to provide for his upkeep. He was a royalist who had chosen to follow Charles into exile when Jersey fell to the parliamentarian forces in 1651. In Jersey he had acted as chaplain to Sir George Carteret, the Lieutenant-Governor, and in exile he received episcopal ordination at the chapel of the residency in Paris. He then served briefly in the Reformed churches at St Malo and Caen, and as chaplain to the Duc de la Force, before returning to England. Durel was, therefore, at once a Reformed and an Anglican minister, on good terms with the Court and familiar with both the major varieties of French and English Protestantism. Like his friend, the future Archbishop Sancroft, he possessed both scholarship and tact, and he was an ideal choice to direct the Savoy church. His connections and personal qualities were needed in 1661, for the foundation of the conformist Savoy church directly raised the thorny question of the relationship between the Anglican and French Reformed churches.

Not all the members of the Westminster congregation were happy with the notion of conformity. 'Two or three (for I think there were no more) utterly refused to submit,' Durel explained in his *View of the Government and Publick Worship of God in the Reformed Churches beyond the Seas* (1662), while others sounded out the views of the continental Reformed churches. The letter written to the 'Protestant Rome', Geneva, signed by nine men of whom at least four were elders, is of considerable interest. The picture they painted was one of sharper division than Durel represented. Some members, they wrote, felt it was better to accept the royal offer than to destroy a flourishing church; others, including themselves, disagreed:

> Our Liturgy and Discipline is identical with that of the churches of France as confirmed by 29 National Synods. As such it is recognized as amongst the purest by all the Reformed churches of Europe. We do not pass judgment on the Liturgy and Discipline of the English churches: but we, who are all French-born, should not give a lead to others by lightly consenting to this step.

The continental churches reacted to such a fundamental problem with caution. Durel was able to show that none of them was prepared to condemn the Anglican Church or liturgy, and later writers have followed him in asserting that there was no complaint from the Reformed churches over the foundation of the Savoy. Nevertheless, they were uneasy. Of the three churches approached, neither Paris nor Geneva replied, and the reply from Bordeaux advised reunion with Threadneedle Street. Durel could stress that many individual pastors expressed support for the Church of England – Drelincourt and Gaches of Paris, Chabret of Geneva, Goyon and Rondelet of Bordeaux, du Bosc of Caen, de l'Angle the younger of Rouen; but an element of doubt remained present. That doubt was not about the

Anglican Church itself, nor about episcopal superintendency, nor about the Prayer Book; rather it took the form of fears for the future of the City church, expressed by Bordeaux, or suspicions that a new, subtler form of Laudian attack was implied, as troubled the Consistory at Geneva.

Time alone could eradicate such suspicions, and it was not until the influx of new refugees in the 1680s and the replacement of James II by the Calvinist William III that they were entirely overcome. In 1662, the Act of Uniformity attacked English Nonconformist congregations. Foreign Reformed churches authorized by the Crown were exempted from the Act, but they were still concerned by it, for it raised the question of the reordination of Reformed clergy. The leading Reformed ministers all accepted the Anglican Church as truly Protestant, and had no hesitation in making use of the services of their episcopally ordained brethren. The attitude of the Church of England to the Lutheran and Calvinist churches was more equivocal. Anglicans certainly wished to refer freely to Luther and Calvin as individual theologians, but their support of episcopacy placed them in a difficult position as far as the continental Protestant churches were concerned. Anglican conviction that bishops were vitally important to the church deepened markedly in mid-century. If bishops were not just desirable but essential in a church, then the Reformed confessions were either in error or in sin. In either case, no intercommunion was possible, and many high churchmen in exile during the Interregnum, like the learned John Cosin, followed Charles II in refusing to take Communion in the Huguenot churches. The delicacy of the situation was appreciated long before the mid-seventeenth century, and persisted long after; Archbishop Tenison, for instance, although a friend to Huguenot refugees in England, was said to be 'very much upon the reserve always as to the foreign Reformed churches, and cared not to be giving any opinion either for or against them'.

The Act of Uniformity made one important difference. Before it, some foreign Reformed ministers had been admitted to Anglican benefices without reordination. In the cases of Pierre de Laune and Caesar Calandrinus, it is likely that no mere sinecures, but benefices with cure of souls were involved. After the 1662 Act no such admissions were possible, as later Huguenot writers recognized. The position of the Anglican Church had been firmly asserted as Catholic and Reformed. From the refugees' point of view, the practical result was far from encouraging: pastors who had long ministered in the French Reformed Church had to be reordained if they were to serve in the Church of England, but proselytes – converts from the Roman

Catholic priesthood – could walk straight into English benefices, being already priests.

The second stage of Archbishop Laud's attack on the foreign congregations in England had been the limitation of their privileges to aliens and their first-generation descendants. Such a restrictive approach was still possible under the wording of the Act of Uniformity, and in 1668 was attempted by Bishop Morley of Winchester against the French Church of Southampton. Acting on advice from the Threadneedle Street Consistory, the pastor at Southampton, Couraud, drew the exemption clause in the Act to the bishop's attention. Morley replied that it was irrelevant, since all the members of the congregation were natural subjects of the king. It was then urged that Charles had repeatedly shown his desire to protect strangers and had but recently granted privileges to those of Norwich, 'even to those of them who are born in the kingdom'. Eventually Morley withdrew his threat, but the non-conformist churches were left acutely aware of their vulnerability.

The Crown may have been unwilling to countenance such direct action, but the creation of the Savoy church signalled a new and deliberate policy that henceforth only conformist congregations would be founded for the benefit of foreign Protestants in the British Isles. The year 1662 nearly saw the demise of the important but divided French Church of Canterbury after a faction decided to conform; only with great difficulty was a royal order against the non-conformists eventually reversed. In the following year the Dover congregation, which had been formed in the 1640s and so had no royal warrant for its existence, found itself disturbed by local Anglican and municipal officers. Its petition to the Crown failed to find favour, with the result that no formal foreign church existed at Dover until a conformist one was founded in 1685. While these Kent congregations suffered, new ones were established elsewhere. In 1666, anxious to encourage immigration to Ireland, Charles sanctioned a conformist French church in the Lady Chapel of St Patrick's Cathedral, Dublin. Two years later, Dutchmen living in Westminster were also allowed to set up a conformist place of worship. Should there be any future influx of refugees, the chances that they could preserve genuinely Calvinist practices seemed poor.

Durel had walked a tightrope in 1661, and his creation of the conformist church of the Savoy was not free from either internal dissension or external criticism. Even the royal financial backing which made it viable was a cause of friction, for it restricted the choice of the congregation and divided the loyalties of its ministers, who eyed the wider, greener pastures now available to them and tended to view the Savoy as a route to preferment in the Anglican Church. Durel himself held six benefices in all by 1679; Jerome, who had helped him fashion the new congregation, moved to the conformist church of Dublin and did even better. More significant, however, were enduring tensions inherited from Durel's homeland of Jersey, his model for the Savoy church. For its character was an uneasy mixture of Anglicanism and Calvinism. By this date, the Anglican prayer book (translated into French) was in use in Jersey, but the islanders had shown little enthusiasm for it, and some of their behaviour differed from English practice. Their ministers did not wear surplices – something likely to raise emotions at the time – and did not make the sign of the cross. Moreover, the congregation received Communion standing, which had provoked the Anglican Peter Heylyn to remark that the islanders were 'a strange and stubborn generation, stiffer in the knees than any elephant, who will neither bow the knee to the name of Jesus, nor kneel to Him in His Sacrament'. These divergences were outward signs of a cast of mind that remained Presbyterian rather than Anglican. Since Durel fashioned the Savoy out of his experiences in the Channel Islands, it is not surprising that the new conformist church met criticism not only from Calvinists who wanted to preserve their old organization but, on very different grounds, from Anglicans with High Church tendencies. It was to be described by a hostile observer in the early eighteenth century, Michael Malard, as an 'amphibious church', 'a monstrous composition of an Episcopal face and a Presbyterian heart'.

What exactly was this 'amphibious' institution? It had its own regulations (the earliest extant are dated 1721, by which time they could have been modified in response to new demands), derived from the French Protestant background of the church members but less detailed than would have been the case in France. It had a Consistory after the French fashion, but there were no deacons. By the 1720s the elders, elected annually, were serving in pairs for a month at a time and meeting together in Consistory weekly on Sundays; the English authorities called them 'churchwardens'. The lack of a diaconate meant that the elders had to carry out poor relief duties as well as see to the running of the church. Although they had many of the same practical responsibilities as their non-conformist brethren, it is unlikely that they exercised the same degree of control over individual behaviour, doctrine and preaching.

The outward ceremony of the Savoy church might also be described as 'amphibious'. In the older Reformed churches, services normally opened with psalms (the Marot version was used), and continued with exhortation, prayers and systematic Scripture readings. Communion was celebrated monthly. The central feature of the normal Sunday services was the sermon, delivered without notes by a preacher whose hat and lack of surplice attracted Anglican comment. It was invariably at least an hour long, and sometimes much longer – at Threadneedle Street, Jean de la Marche was accused of frequently continuing for three or four hours until he was left preaching to blank walls, and Samuel Pepys reported one 'tedious long sermon' which dragged on 'till they were fain to light candle to baptise the children by'. At the Savoy, the liturgy of the Anglican Church was used, in translation, rather than French Calvinist forms of worship. Durel's 'translation' was in reality a revision of Pierre de Laune's, prepared in 1616; it was frequently at variance with the English original, or so it was claimed in James II's reign. The traditional Calvinist emphasis was placed on psalm singing; the Savoy probably used the version of Marot and de Bèze, as did the conformist church at Dublin. While the Consistory employed a reader to read the common prayers of the Anglican Church, it followed the French discipline in refusing the use of the pulpit to those training for the ministry. The pastors of the church preached bare-headed as a token of their conformity to the Church of England, and they might on occasion read sermons from notes, contrary to the French habit; but they wore no surplice, and did not make the sign of the cross.

Smaller congregations might be less well organized, but all conformist churches of the later seventeenth century broadly followed the pattern of worship established at the Savoy. Theirs was a half-way house between the French Reformed and Anglican churches. It is unlikely that French ministers in Anglican orders, or their congregations, sympathized with the sacramental teaching of the Book of Common Prayer. At St Martin Orgars in London, the catechism in the Anglican Prayer Book was supplanted in 1702 by Drelincourt's French one. The congregation of St James's Square had to be urged not to bruise English sensibilities by sitting on the altar railings. All in all the evidence suggests that the conformists were Anglicans in name rather than by deep conviction.

But what should be stressed, in the light of the accusation that the Savoy was a 'monstrous composition of an Episcopal face and a Presbyterian heart', is the wide gulf separating all the French churches – both conformist and non-conformist – from English Presbyterianism. They all accepted episcopal superintendency, to a greater or lesser degree; English Nonconformists did not. And they enjoyed a legal existence which English Dissenters did not share. Furthermore English Nonconformists were not officially accepted as members of the French congregations established in England, whether conformist or non-conformist. John-Armand Dubourdieu, a conformist minister, agreed that the French non-conformists could not be called Presbyterian, since 'they neither resemble nor join with them or indeed with any kind of Dissenters in this kingdom'. The French Church of London, acting in its accustomed role as elder statesman, warned Jacques Fontaine when he was minister of the congregation at Cork in 1698 that it was his duty to respect the Anglican Church, 'which should be held in high regard by all true Christians'. One refugee minister, Jean Graverol, called for the reunion of Presbyterianism and Anglicanism, but most kept out of such areas of debate. Generally the Huguenots in exile were only too well aware of the strength of feeling then current on issues insignificant in our own day, and did their best not to antagonize their English hosts needlessly. The ministers of some non-conformist French churches even preached bareheaded because, as Misson commented tongue in cheek in his *Memoirs and Observations in his Travels over England*, a hat on the head of a preacher was

> so unworthy, and so scandalous an object in the eye of a rigid churchman, that he would think a monster from Hell full as pleasing a sight . . . a hat! A hat upon the head of a preacher in his sermon! Bless us! It shocks his eyes, it disturbs his mind, it splits his heart; he sighs, he groans, he laments; a holy fury possesses him, he rushes out, and never sets his foot within the walls again.

Meanwhile, Misson added, those who had kept their hats (including the ministers at the French Church of London) 'pull [them] over their eyes more than ever, for the better resisting this dreadful storm'.

Two consequences resulted from the emergence of conformist congregations after the Restoration. One was the undermining of the structure linking the older non-conformist churches, so painstakingly built up over the previous century. Colloquies were defined as consisting of the representatives of *all* French-speaking churches in the realm, but how could conformist and non-conformist together exercise church discipline? This was a major reason why Colloquies ceased after the foundation of the Savoy, leaving little vestige of hierarchical French Calvinist church order in England. The consistories of the older churches were left to their own independent devices. They were accustomed to greater liberty of action than their continental or Scottish counterparts; now they became more isolated than they had ever been. Yet most of their members believed passionately in the desirability of following the model of continental Calvinism, and they maintained mutual informal links with one another as the 'confederated churches'. In 1689 a meeting was held which was a Colloquy in all but name, but no formal gathering assembled after 1660 – even though an Act of Council of 1662 specifically confirmed Colloquy as their ultimate appeal authority.

The other principal consequence was that when new refugees arrived from Louis XIV's France, they were faced by a choice. History and antiquity favoured the non-conformist churches; they were better known in Europe, and Huguenots naturally found their ways much closer to their French experience. On the other hand, the conformist congregations were held in greater favour by the Court, the Anglican hierarchy, and the ruling English establishment in general. Durel's inaugural sermon at the Savoy was attended by the Duke and Duchess of Ormonde, the Countesses of Derby, Ossory and Atholl, the Earls of Stafford, Newcastle and Devonshire, and 'other persons of great authority'. The Westminster church maintained its connections, being located very close to the Court, and claimed in the early 1680s to be frequently visited and largely maintained by 'Privy Councillors, Secretaries of State, and other great officers of the Kingdom'. It might be thought that poor refugees in need of financial support would have gravitated towards the Savoy in view of these links with high society. In practice this did not happen; the Threadneedle Street congregation remained very much larger, the initial magnet for refugees arriving in London. For one thing, job opportunities for the urban labourer were greater to the east than to the west of London, especially in the weaving trade based on Spitalfields. For another, the City church operated a highly developed relief organization. Moreover, despite all the Savoy's ties with the Court, the older congregation, with its City connections, remained wealthier even though it always had more poor to maintain.

The whole tone of the Huguenot communities in west and east London was certainly very different. We have seen that in the west, in the shadow of the Court and the Savoy, gathered shop-keepers, military personnel, and those connected with luxury trades; by 1690 seven of the ten churches in this area conformed to the Anglican liturgy. In contrast the east London congregations, with their strong weaving element, were without exception non-conformist in the seventeenth century.

Clearly, the refugees' choice of form of worship was influenced by their professional skills, which helped determine where they lived and the circles in which they moved. Yet there is plenty of evidence to show that the majority greatly preferred the pattern of worship to which they were accustomed, and were reluctant to embrace conformity. The peak period of influx into England came only in

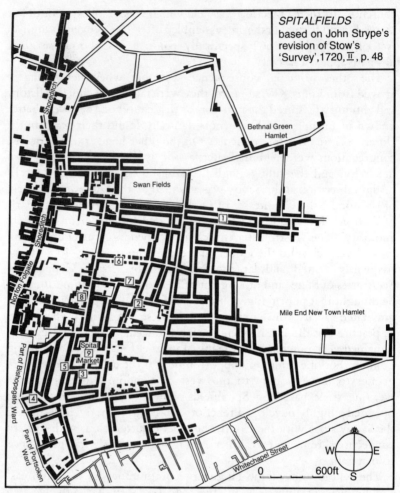

Map 6   French churches in Spitalfields, 1700

Note: locations are approximate. All the Spitalfields congregations were non-conformist.

1 St. Jean	4 Artillery (II)	7 Pearl St.
2 L'Hôpital	5 Crispin St.	8 Wheeler St.
3 La Patente	6 Quaker St.	9 Du Marché

1687, after James II issued his Declaration of Indulgence, tolerating Dissenters. This led to the abandonment of the post-Restoration conformist policy, and the creation of new non-conformist foreign churches. Even though assistance from charity funds was available for the maintenance of the ministry only in conformist churches, it was non-conformist congregations that sprang up when they were able to do so freely in the 1690s. What happened in the west London suburbs is particularly revealing: while in 1690 conformist churches outnumbered non-conformist ones by 7 to 3, by the end of the decade, as the refugees made use of the liberty that came with William's accession and the 1689 Toleration Act, there were as many non-conformist as conformist congregations (see map 7). There could be no clearer demonstration that for most Huguenots, the Anglican liturgy was second best.

In the London area as a whole, there were perhaps two refugees worshipping as conformists to every three non-conformists in the 1680s, after over twenty years of quiet but positive English governmental encouragement of conformity; by the time of William III's death, following a decade of freedom of choice, there were three times as many non-conformists as conformists. The question that has to be asked, although it can never be answered, is: how many Huguenots were discouraged from coming to England between 1681 and the early months of 1687 because of the conformist policy of the authorities? Had the government taken a different line, England rather than the Netherlands might well have become what Pierre Bayle described as the 'great ark' of the refugees.

To many Calvinists leaving France, good ecclesiastical order was a vital matter. If the persecutions from which they had suffered had been permitted by an angry God, they must repent and reform their ways. But alas, the poverty, overcrowding and dejection in which some refugees lived could open the door to blasphemy, quarrels, recriminations, and irreligion; or so it appeared to the Consistory of the Threadneedle Street church, which found it impossible to carry out its church discipline, or even to follow the movements of church members because of their sheer number and the proliferation of new congregations. Other Consistories must have been even worse off, for they had a much less refined organization and structure of government. None of the new refugee congregations had deacons. All had elders, but elections were often held irregularly, and Consistory meetings sometimes proved hard to arrange. The minutes and registers they kept were usually less neat, less substantial, more haphazard than the records maintained by the old-established churches. The detailed procedure of the Threadneedle Street Consistory room could hardly have been matched when the accounts of the church of St James's Square were examined at Richard's Coffee House.

During the 1690s, the Threadneedle Street and Savoy Consistories and those of the larger and more responsible new churches came to agree that the multiplicity of congregations in the London area was

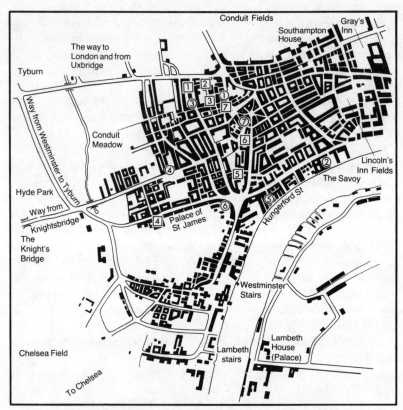

WESTMINSTER AND THE WESTERN SUBURBS OF LONDON 1700
Based on N.G. Brett-James 'The growth of Stuart London' (1935) opposite p. 366

FRENCH CHURCHES 1700 (14)

○ Conformist (7)
☐ Non-conformist (7)

① Des Grecs
② Savoy
③ Le Carré (Berwick St.)
④ Swallow St.
⑤ Hungerford Market
⑥ Spring Gardens
⑦ West St.

1 L'Ancienne Patente
2 La Patente, Soho
3 Milk Alley (II)
4 St. James
5 Leicester Fields
6 St. Martin's Lane
7 'The Church near the Greek Church'

Map 7 French churches in the western suburbs of London, 1700

creating problems for which some solution had to be found. Another area of concern, besides good order, was the maintenance of sound doctrine. In the middle of the seventeenth century, the Protestant churches in France had been rent by divisions over the issues of grace and predestination raised by Moïse Amyraut. Those divisions had been submerged under the wave of persecution, but doctrinal differences emerged once more in the comparative freedom of exile. Orthodox ministers felt that matters were becoming serious when Socinianism infiltrated Huguenot ranks on a significant scale in the 1690s, and again when meetings of the Cévennes 'prophets' created a major stir in London in 1706–7.[3]

Socinianism was in origin a continental heresy, which had reached England via Holland earlier in the century. It denied the orthodox view of the Trinity, stressed the desirability of free enquiry and affirmed the supremacy of private judgment. Its anti-Trinitarian stance led in England towards Unitarianism, its concern for toleration and rationalization towards latitudinarianism. It was possible for some Socinians, like Thomas Firmin, to remain communicant members of the Anglican Church all their adult lives, and indeed no less a person than Archbishop Tillotson was accused of Socinianism because of his rational approach to religion. The official Anglican line, however, was the one expressed by Isaac Barrow: the mysteries of the Trinity were not to be laid bare by the exercise of human reason, 'no competent or capable judge concerning propositions of this nature'.

The Unitarian tendencies of Socinianism offended both the Thirty-nine Articles and the Confession of Faith of the French Reformed Church; but French Protestant authorities felt more strongly than their Anglican counterparts about the heresy, since its emphasis on individual judgment undermined the whole disciplinary structure so carefully created by continental Calvinism to safeguard pure doctrine and good order. They felt that its poison was all the more deadly because it could spread almost undetectably from within. Therefore in the early 1690s both conformists and non-conformists crusaded fiercely against those of their brethren tainted with Socinianism, so fiercely indeed that they were rebuked for a 'most horrible breach of charity' in assembling 'in a perfect Court of Inquisition' and drawing up 'formularies and tests to choke all that have not so wide a swallow as themselves'. The nature of Socinianism was such that it could not be eradicated, and the problem remained. But from the meetings to deal with it, and out of growing fears of disciplinary confusion, there emerged in London a body which had no continental equivalent: the General Assembly of French Churches. Its minutes date only from 1720, but it came into existence in the closing years of the previous century. While preserving the independence of each individual member church, the General Assembly helped to keep order among the thousands of refugees in the capital by providing coherence and a channel of communication between congregations. It was not a Classis or Colloquy or Synod, and its status was curious. There was no appeal to it from individual consistories, and it was not an integral part of the discipline of any church. It consisted of both conformist and non-conformist congregations, but was local rather than national in scope, being confined to London. Its existence meant that the old Threadneedle Street church was a member simultaneously of three different groupings, Coetus (still binding it to the Dutch Church of London), the 'confederated churches' and the General Assembly. Newer conformist churches acknowledged loose Anglican supervision and were attached to the General Assembly, while newer non-conformist ones were linked to the latter alone.

Such ties did not provide the structure required for effective church government. Few Huguenots brought up in the old Calvinist tradition can have been satisfied with the situation, for church discipline had meant so much. Just how strongly individuals felt about its maintenance is suggested by the action of Daniel Fervaques in London in 1665. That was the dire plague year recorded for posterity by Pepys, and many rich people hurried to leave the city for places of safety. Fervaques was wealthy enough to have followed suit, having served as Upper Bailiff of the Weavers' Company the previous year, but he stayed. Plague hit the French Church of London hard, three elders and two deacons dying during the year. Seeing the members of the Blackfriars area unsupervised after the death of their elder, David Bouquet, Fervaques's response was to volunteer to distribute the tokens for the monthly Communion; and this at the height of summer, when plague was at its most deadly, in an overcrowded and dangerous district, when Fervaques had no duty to feel responsible since he held no church office at the time. The same notable determination to see that their church functioned smoothly was shown by the Consistory and congregation as a whole in the years immediately after the plague, for in 1666 the building in Threadneedle Street was burnt to the ground during the Great Fire of London. There were difficulties in getting permission to rebuild, difficulties in negotiating the site, and obvious financial problems for a congregation reduced in numbers by the plague. A special effort towards extraordinary repairs had raised £890 in 1650, but after the Fire the elders expected rebuilding to cost over twice that sum, and their own estimate had to be doubled before work was completed. Yet, while the general rebuilding of burnt churches in the city did not begin until

1670 and over half had not been started at the beginning of 1676, the French congregation was worshipping in its own handsome new church by 22 August 1669 (plate 5a).

Much of the church discipline cherished by the Huguenots of the sixteenth and seventeenth centuries seems rigid to our modern western world, insistent on the virtues of free expression of individual personality. Yet the impassioned and effective response of the City congregation to the difficulties besetting it in the 1660s – not only to plague and fire, but to a more subtle threat presented by its minister Louis Hérault, who used his connections at Court to try to dictate to the Consistory – show that the old church order could evoke devoted support. It provided a connecting thread holding together the experiences of refugees in their old lands and their new, and it possessed powerful merits. One of these, of vital importance to many refugees, was its attention to poor relief. It was the proud boast of the old French/Walloon churches, conceded with admiration by their English hosts, that they maintained the large numbers of their own poor even at times of dire economic hardship, abolishing begging in the streets. Dr Campbell's comparison of French and English efforts at poor relief in early Stuart Canterbury greatly favours the French; they gave more money, relieved far more poor, and paid much higher sums in relief. The best example of the organization, and workload, involved is found in the French Church of London in the 1690s, at the time and place where the problem was most acute.

The Consistory divided the area in which its congregation lived into eighteen *quartiers* or districts, each supervised by an elder and a deacon. The elder dealt with matters of church membership and finance, supervised behaviour, signed authorizations for baptisms, kept an eye on members' marriages, and distributed tokens (cf plate 4a) before the monthly Communion. Poor relief fell on the shoulders of the deacons, drawn from the same superior social class as the elders (with whom they sat at the front of the church), but younger men, serving what might be termed their apprenticeship in church work. They had to house, clothe and support the poor in their care, help them find work, and see that their children were educated and their sick cared for. The church maintained almshouses and rooms where clothes and movables for distribution were stored, and employed teachers, a doctor and a surgeon. Each deacon kept a register of those assisted in his *quartier*, and handed in monthly accounts to the treasurer. Once a year, all the ministers joined the diaconate in making a survey of the state of the poor.

The deacons visited and paid their charges weekly. Two illustrations will suffice to show the detailed nature of the relief they supervised.

Jean Tessier was visited on 18 January 1693, and sent into hospital eleven days later; while there, he was given two shillings a week. In May he was given a pair of shoes and a pair of breeches, and the following February, two shirts. His shoes were mended in November 1694. In March 1695 he received two more shirts, and in December more clothing, hose and shoes. Each week, of course, he was being given his pension. When he was finally removed from hospital and put in the church's old people's home in April 1697, he was given another pair of shoes. Tessier was one of the poor whom the church had in permanent care. By contrast, Jacob Marmoy or Marmois, a weaver, was granted special assistance in 1698 for as long as he and his family were ill. The family was large, consisting of Jacob and his wife, and nine children. It was given four shillings a week from Christmas 1698 to the late spring of 1699, thereafter two shillings and sixpence weekly until March 1700. Such admirable and systematic care of the poor appears particularly impressive when judged by contemporary English standards.

The Threadneedle Street church on its own could not begin to cope with the entire refugee problem, although it continued to be burdened with a high proportion of those who arrived in England before 1685, who were excluded from the terms of reference of public collections and royal grants made after the Revocation. In the early 1680s, the City church and the Savoy had in effect acted as national centres of refugee relief, but by the end of the decade the French Committee had taken over the distribution of public charity, and the other London churches were beginning to take an active role in the local organization of relief. The new London churches also partially made up for their lack of deacons through their support for the *Maisons de Charité*, established in Soho and Spitalfields to distribute bread, meat and soup, sometimes also cheap vegetables and small beer. The scale of the problem made it impossible to satisfy everyone, but the existence of the General Assembly helped co-ordinate relief in the capital.

The old methods of charity administration – like all other aspects of church government – were undermined during the eighteenth century by new alternatives and approaches, although concern to educate the young and care for the old and sick remained very much alive. New Friendly Societies prospered and multiplied, and a French Protestant Hospital and a French Protestant School Foundation came into existence, none as closely linked to churches as would have been the case a hundred years before. Secular state aid, the 'Royal Bounty', came to seem more and more essential; indeed the numbers receiving financial aid from the government shot upwards from 2,412 in 1696 to over 7,000 in 1721.[4] To obtain funds for the ministry, churches had to conform, and so growing reliance on state assistance involved persistent pressure on the refugees to give up their Calvinist ways. Various non-conformist congregations therefore became Anglican, usually with reluctance, such as those at Wapping (1705), Southampton (1712) and Canterbury (1812). Others, however, resisted the pressure, and it cannot be assumed that the majority of refugee descendants were ever drawn into the Anglican orbit.

Despite all the changes that took place in the organization of the French churches in England between the sixteenth and eighteenth centuries, the desire to worship God remained unaltered. The refugees who left France were devoted to the Huguenot cause. Unusually determined and principled men and women, they believed that to serve God was to give meaning to life. This belief engendered a strong sense of personal accountability for their actions, and both in turn fostered the virtues which have marked out the Huguenots and so many of their descendants: frugality, hard work, upright behaviour, responsibility, sobriety. The key to understanding them, their willingness to abandon their homeland, their frequent eventual prosperity in the places to which they went, the time they were prepared to devote to their churches, is one and the same: their concept of, and commitment to serve, a God infinitely greater than themselves.

7

Opposition

Shortly before May Day 1670, a small group of London apprentices and journeymen gathered at the 'Red Cow' and discussed their grievances while downing their ale. The outcome was a paper. 'Feare God', it read,

> To all Gentlemen Apprentices and Journimen inhabitants of London and suburbs this is to acquaint you that by forraigne nations wee are impoverished by them tradinge within our Nation espetially by the French that is not all we may be fearfull of our lives first by theyr Rebellion in their owne land secondly by the fire and now thirdly by our tradinge but truly gentlemen now we are otherwise resolved for we will not suffer it noe longer for by your assistance, we are resolved to meet in Morefields betwixt eight and nine of the clocke in the afternoone on Mayday next therefore faile not for wee your brethren Apprentices and Journimen will not faile you for wee will not have them raigne in our Kingdom.
> Soe God save the King: and all the royall family procure what armes you can for wee are resolved to doe it.[1]

The arguments in the paper are as weak as its punctuation, and this particular effort merely alarmed the authorities for a short time. All the same, it shows that the refugees' environment was not always welcoming. Some of the forms of opposition they encountered are considered elsewhere: Archbishop Laud's attack in chapter 3, other Anglican reservations in chapter 6 and James II's less than generous welcome in chapter 8. But hostility was more widespread, for the different classes in English society could not all be expected to welcome the newcomers.

The weaving and other craft skills, which enabled the refugees to earn a livelihood and in some cases eventually to prosper, also exposed them to attack. Such skills threatened the livelihood of the *menu peuple* – the poorer elements of society, from small shopkeepers, master craftsmen and journeymen downwards. Consequently, wherever the Walloons or Huguenots went, they were liable to encounter opposition. The Elizabethan Privy Council, with its desire that 'special regard' be had for those 'repaired hither for the cause of Religion', was kept busy trying to ensure that its policy was put into practice. There were always particular problems in London, which because of its size and potential opportunities already acted as a magnet to landless Englishmen from all parts of the country. Even during the reign of Edward VI, 'five or six hundred men waited on the mayor and aldermen of London complaining of the late influx of strangers, and that by reason of the late dearth they cannot live for these strangers, whom they were determined to kill up through the realm if they found no remedy.' Complaints about aliens, inspired by those practising manual trades and crafts, continued, especially in the years 1571–5, 1585–7, 1592–3, 1604, 1606–7, 1615–23 and the period of the Interregnum. Without such complaints, we would know much less than we do about the foreigners of late Tudor and early Stuart England, for the unrest encouraged the government to demand information about the numbers, density, occupations and religion of aliens, particularly in London and its suburbs. (Such returns were to be compiled discreetly, the Privy Council insisted in 1592, so that no commotion was caused by Englishmen believing they had government support for hostile action.)

One answer to the problem of overcrowding in London, supported both by the Privy Council and the leaders of the foreign churches in the capital, was the dispersal of groups of aliens around the country. But though such settlements were planted in centres far smaller than London, they still ran into trouble from similar quarters. We have noted the rather unhelpful local responses to the petitions of the first refugees coming to Southampton. An attempt was made to re-establish the Dutch community at Halstead, Essex, in 1590, after 'discourtesies offered them by the townsmen' caused the original settlers to move on to Colchester; judicial protection was considered necessary. The Canterbury refugees were invited by local civic authorities, but threats of arson and other expressions of discontent from artisans forced the Privy Council in 1587 to urge foreigners there to be discreet in their commercial activities.[2] Eventually special officers, known as 'politic men', had to be recruited to help maintain civil order between natives and foreigners.

'Politic men' had already made their appearance further north. 'The Book of Orders for Dutch and Walloon Strangers in Norwich', now in the Norwich civic records, gives a clear picture of the hostile environment often faced by first generation refugees as a result of petty local trade jealousies. Although the earliest settlers were invited to the city, where the traditional mainstay of worsted weaving was in decline, trouble arose at once. Because a general assembly of citizens would not admit any strangers under its common seal, the mayoral seal had to be applied to each licence permitting an alien, his family and servants to settle. With a new mayor, Thomas Whalle, 'diverse complaints of the city artisans against the strangers' were renewed; Whalle supported these complaints and moved to eject the aliens, but was defeated by a majority of aldermen. It was as a result of these troubles that the 'politic men' (or 'political elders', or 'arbitrators') came into being. As 'governors to the whole company' of foreigners, their job was to ensure that agreements made between them and the city authorities were kept.

The Norwich refugees found themselves hedged about with commercial and social restrictions. They could not sell their products retail, except to their own countrymen, but only wholesale. They could not walk in the streets after 8 p.m., a provision described as intended to avoid drunkenness and disorder. They were not allowed to buy the skins of sheep, lambs or calves, after a complaint from local English glovers and tanners. They were ordered to restrict themselves to one loom, or two if they had more at the time the order was made. They were not to transport their yarn without mayoral permission, and were to buy it only at their houses, not in the market or by the roadside. Dutch and Walloon tailors, bodgers, shoemakers and cobblers were not allowed to keep shop but only to have 'a lattice of a yard deep before the windows', and could sell only to their fellow-countrymen. No alien visitor was to be harboured or lodged for more than one night without the mayor being informed. And so forth: regulation after regulation, each liable to frequent redefinition or extension, each backed up by punishments of forfeitures or fines.

No wonder the strangers at Norwich soon felt driven to petition the Queen for leave to buy wool, employ their own dyers and sell their products freely. The Privy Council responded by urging Christian charity on the civic authorities, especially for 'them, who do suffer affliction and exile for the Gospels sake'. But the authorities did not feel charitably disposed; on the contrary, they felt betrayed by the appeal above their heads, and resented the 'lusty stomach' of the aliens. (The copy of the petition to the Privy Council in the *Book of Orders* is endorsed 'an untruth . . . an other untruth . . . most unprofitable and unreasonable requests to the impoverishing of the whole city'.) The Mayor ordered the doors of the sealing hall shut so that no textiles could be authenticated and released. Eventually, in 1571, the Privy Council arbitrated, improving the aliens' situation, and gradually the rules agreed were accepted by both sides. Such teething problems may have been inevitable, but they show how exposed the foreigners were, how jealous were local townsmen. The refugees remained a scapegoat ready to hand. In 1575 they were accused of driving up the price of timber and ordered to use sea coal in their houses. In 1579 their 'corrupt keeping of their houses and necessaries' and their pollution of the river was blamed for the spread of the plague.

Accusations of this sort imply barriers of understanding between Englishmen and the aliens in their midst. Because their habits were different, foreigners were to be distrusted. This did not, of course, apply only to the Huguenots: 'Taffy was a Welshman, Taffy was a thief.' The stereotypes of the various foreign nationalities to be found in late Tudor and Stuart England make an interesting study. Increasing numbers of poor Irish were arriving, and were isolated from English society by their accent and Catholicism perhaps even more than were French-speaking Protestants by their language. Like the Huguenots, the Irish tended to be drawn to London, where they congregated especially in the parish of St Giles; they were far more likely than the Frenchmen to be viewed as disposed towards crime and drunkenness. The Jews, who were readmitted to England in the seventeenth century and grew in numbers from the 1650s onwards, remained a much smaller community than the Huguenots. Jews and Huguenots had something in common: circumstances compelled both groups to learn English; both had ties with Dutch investors, and there were big Jewish, as well as Huguenot, investors in Bank stock in the 1690s and early eighteenth century. But the Jews were involved in a far more limited range of economic activities than the Huguenots, largely confined to specialized trade in such high-risk areas as diamonds and coral. There were no Jewish artisans to compare with the Walloon and Huguenot weavers. Nor did there exist any religious bond between the Jews and the host community. On the contrary, even a man like Roger Williams, who championed both religious toleration and the Jewish cause, could speak of 'Jews or Antichristians' in one breath. The stereotype immortalized in Shylock stood firm.

When his son visited the Continent in 1610, Sir Henry Slingsby urged him to 'take heed what company he keeps in too familiar a fashion, for the French are of an ill conversation and full of many loathsome diseases'.[3] Most preconceptions about the French held in the seventeenth century would be more familiar to modern Englishmen. They were considered fashion-conscious, and their clothing distinctive (see plate 16). Their gesticulations drew comment: 'the French, like the sea, are perpetually in motion,' wrote the author of *A Satyr against the French* (1691). Sexual prowess was already seen as a French national trait, but could not readily be associated with the

Huguenots with their sober ecclesiastical discipline. It was the eating habits of the refugees that made the greatest impression: their consumption of snails, garlic and onions attracted attention, and they were reported to be 'living much upon cabbage and roots'. As usual, such stereotypes were based on exaggerations of genuine traits. The remarks about diet, for example, were founded on the sheer poverty of many Huguenots which drove them to survive in any way they could. In the process, they made one notable contribution to English menus, oxtail soup. Previously the tails had been left on bullocks' hides when London butchers sold them to fellmongers. When the fellmongers in turn threw them out, scavenging refugees put them to good use, turning this reject into a delicacy.

Stereotypes were made possible by the concentration of aliens in particular areas and occupations, and flourished because of fear – in the case of the French Protestants, fear that they would undercut the wages and destroy the employment prospects of poor native Englishmen. The opposition from the *menu peuple* that we have illustrated from the records of Elizabethan Norwich continued throughout the seventeenth century and beyond in all the areas where the refugees were clustered. In some respects, indeed, it worsened. Under Queen Elizabeth the national enemy was Spain, but by the time of the Restoration Spain was no longer a threat and a much older adversary, France, had taken her place. 'We do naturally all love the Spanish and hate the French,' recorded Pepys in his diary, and 'French dog' was a common cry of abuse in the streets. This anti-French bias was intensified in the later 1660s by the popular belief that foreigners were responsible for the Great Fire of London. As a contemporary Dutch report explained, rumour had it that

> the conflagration was begun by a Dutch baker, who was bribed to do this work, and that the French went about scattering fireballs in the houses. All foreigners alike were held to be guilty, no discrimination being shown. . . . It will be a long time before the people of London forget their wild rage against the foreigners.

Fears were not confined to London, and were increased by exaggerated reports of the numbers of Frenchmen. In 1668 it was believed in Yarmouth, quite without foundation, that a house-to-house enquiry had revealed 18,000 foreign lodgers in the two London parishes of St Giles and St Martin's alone, while letters reached Coventry giving – so an agent reported to Secretary of State Williamson –

> a very terrifying account of great numbers of French lately landed in several parts, and of a more than ordinary confluence of French

to London, and of great apprehensions of I know not what danger from them, and several such like reports which being improved by disaffected and discontented spirits very much distract and affright the country hereabout.

Anti-French feeling had political, religious and economic roots. Englishmen feared Louis XIV's increasing power in Europe and the Catholic advance that accompanied it, and in the 1660s and 1670s they were more and more disturbed by the false but growing belief in an unfavourable trade balance with France of nearly a million pounds a year. As Protestants and refugees, the Huguenots should not have been adversely affected by such fears, but heightened anti-French feeling meant that everything French became suspect. The near-hysterical opposition from some quarters to the admission of any Frenchmen to England is displayed in verse in a document subscribed 'Fire is past but blood is to come':

> The nation it is allmost quit undone
> by French men that doe it dayly overrune. . . .
>   . . . beware tak heed
> least when they com they mak you for to bled
> and when you see them doe not cry pecany
> for they are French these have no mercy on you
> they care for none but for themselves alone
> they have made our nation grevously to groane
> under a burthen of great miserey.

This same poem, if it can be dignified with that title, introduces a further problem met by the refugees: that they were frequently mistaken for papists, or rumoured to be papists in disguise. The verses accuse the French of being papists come to 'destroy both nation, king and state', and such a feeling was sometimes encountered by the Huguenots, for instance in London in 1681, in Rye the following year and in Norwich in 1683. On this last occasion the minister appealed for Court protection after the rabble rushed through the streets, dragging Frenchmen from their homes, sacking their houses and killing a woman.

There was, then, a general dislike of Frenchmen, reinforced by political, religious and economic fears and inflamed by exaggerations and rumours regarding both their numbers and their evil intentions. The events of the 1670s leading to the Exclusion crisis of 1679–81 encouraged an atmosphere of unease and tension, in which it was easy to believe that some of the French in London must indeed have come to 'destroy both nation, king and state'. Moreover, mixing with these currents of suspicion were the very reasonable fears of the English poor that the refugees must inevitably worsen their chances of employment, undermine their meagre wages and drain away the supply of domestic charity. Their economic situation had already worsened in the generation before the 1680s; 'a general poverty seems to have invaded the whole nation,' Richard Haines wrote in *The Prevention of Poverty* in 1674, 'and labourers generally, if they have families, are ready to run a begging.' The married labourer with family responsibilities was badly off throughout the country, but the situation was worst in the very area where the Huguenots settled in greatest numbers, in the suburbs of London, and especially in Spitalfields. Here was the home of the silk industry, into which so many refugees were drawn: a pauper industry even before their arrival, as the author of *The Trade of England Revived* (1681) explained,

> because there hath not been for a long time any other but this to place forth poor men's children, and parish boys unto, by which means the poor of this trade have been very numerous who can do nothing else almost having been bred up to it from their youth.

Social as well as economic and political pressure was at its most acute in London, with its size – huge by the standards of the day – and its unparalleled concentration of population in a confined area. It is, therefore, no surprise to find that action by the *menu peuple* posed its greatest threat to the Huguenots in the East End. The quotation with which this chapter opened reveals the muddled arguments that appealed to the journeymen and apprentices, who joined with lesser master weavers in a series of riots in August 1675. The riots had a number of causes. The relative status of small masters and journeymen had been deteriorating, and the use of engine looms threatened jobs. The charge of unfair trade practices had long been laid against foreigners. The Company of Silkweavers had protested in James I's reign about the 'multitude of aliens' engaged in their trade in England, and urged that new 'engines' devised by immigrants to work tape, ribbon, laces and other narrow pieces threatened Englishmen with wholesale unemployment. 'That devilish invention of looms brought in by strangers . . . with looms of 12 to 24 shuttles', they claimed, caused 'the destruction of many poor'.[4] This longstanding connection in the popular mind between engine looms and foreigners was echoed in 1675. Having mounted concerted attacks on the looms, the rioters turned on the aliens in their midst, as a newsletter reported:

The weavers of London seem [to] be encouraged also against the French for yesterday a great company of them fell upon the French weavers, broke all their materials, and defaced several of their houses and greatly disturbed the city.

Although the government took prompt action to protect them, Frenchmen living in London cannot have enjoyed the experience. It was never in their interest to be in the limelight, to have their existence exposed to public comment, and it is significant that the author of the newsletter added, 'I like not the beginning, I dread the issue of such attempts. May our governors be wise and encourage our natives, more than foreigners.'

Even the sympathy aroused by the *dragonnades* could not save the refugees from fears of further such disorders. Thomas Atterbury reported to Secretary Jenkins that the apprentice weavers in Spitalfields in August 1683

> do cabal, and intend a petition to his Majesty the purport of which
> is in opposition to the French weavers in their neighbourhood.
> Others say that if they can get a sufficient number together they
> will rise and knock them on the head.

He urged the quartering of a troop of horse at Whitechapel, as 'a means to awe the rabble'. London was not the only place where such designs of 'knocking them on the head' were mooted. In 1682 the Earl of Arran needed a squadron of the king's guard in Dublin to disperse a gathering of some 300 would-be rioters who had managed to assemble for a May Day attack on the refugees there, even though both the Watch and the masters of the apprentices had previously been alerted.

While such physical assaults were alarming, opposition to alien weavers was not as continuously threatening as it had been in the 1640s and 1650s. Then the Weavers' Company had been more democratic, and violent threats by the *menu peuple* were not necessary; foreigners could be attacked through Company regulations. By the 1670s the richer master weavers held the upper hand, and for them the Huguenots created a desirable pool of cheap skilled labour; it was journeymen and apprentices, not the wealthier masters who employed them, who thought in 1685 that

> weavers all may curse their fates
> because the French work under-rates.

The currents and cross-currents influencing the acceptance or rejection of the refugees were indeed complex, and the same ambivalence is to be found in the attitudes of civic authorities. By accepting skilled aliens into their towns they could boost flagging local economies without incurring any burden of poor relief. All too often, though, the Norwich story of subsequent conflict was repeated, as town rulers sought to extract the last ounce of economic advantage, and the refugees for their part strove to avoid being exploited. The range of responses from towns to suggestions that they should house Walloons or Huguenots varied from a reasonable degree of enthusiasm to point-blank refusal. When Sir Thomas Meres, MP for Lincoln for over twenty years, asked whether that corporation would allow French Protestants to live in the city and provide them with a stock and lodgings, he was informed that there was no suitable housing available, the town was in no condition to support them, and moreover 'that it is the opinion of this Common Council that it will be no advantage to this city but a prejudice to them and all others'. And that was in 1681, when public opinion against the *dragonnades* should have been at its height. Clearly the rosy picture of welcome, painted by Samuel Smiles over a century ago and still widely accepted, was overdrawn:

> They received a cordial welcome . . . the people crowded round the venerable sufferers with indignant and pitying hearts; they received them into their dwellings, and hospitably relieved their wants . . . the sight of so much distress borne so patiently and uncomplainingly, deeply stirred the heart of the nation; and every effort was made to succour and help the poor exiles.

Parliament was also divided as to the merits of assisting the refugees, with the House of Commons showing itself less farsighted and more reluctant than the Lords. In 1593 Sir Walter Raleigh argued that

> it is no matter of charity to relieve [refugees]. For first, such as fly hither have forsaken their own king; and religion is no pretext for them, for we have no Dutchmen here, but such as came from those princes where the Gospel is preached, and here they live disliking our church. . . . The nature of the Dutchman is to fly to no man for his profit, and they will obey no man long. . . . I see no matter of honour, no matter of charity, no profit in relieving them.

Exactly a century later Sir John Knight, MP for Bristol, echoed Raleigh's sentiments in the best-known of all attacks on the Huguenots. As printed, his speech in response to a Bill for the general naturalization of Protestants included these observations:

> A fourth pretence for this Bill is, a want of husbandmen to till the ground. I shall say little on this head, but request the honourable

person below me, to tell me, of the 40,000 French, which he confesseth are come into England; how many does he know, that, at this time, follow the plow-tail? For it is my firm opinion, that not only the French, but any other nation this bill shall let in upon us, will never transplant themselves for the benefit of going to plow; they will contentedly leave the English the sole monopoly of that slavery . . . should this Bill pass, it will bring as great afflictions on this nation, as ever fell upon the Egyptians, and one of their plagues we have at this time very severe upon us; I mean, that of the land bringing forth Frogs in abundance, even in the chambers of their kings: for there is no entering . . . the palaces of our hereditary kings, for the great noise and croaking of the Frog-landers.

It concluded with the resounding motion that 'the serjeant be commanded to open the doors, and let us first kick this Bill out of the house, and then foreigners out of the kingdom'.

The House of Commons was not impressed, and ordered the printed speech to be burnt by the common hangman. Nevertheless it repeatedly rejected or set aside or smothered Bills aiming at the general naturalization which would have secured for the refugees the right to bequeath landed property to their heirs and made them Englishmen in the fullest sense. Such an Act was first advocated around the middle decades of the seventeenth century. No general naturalization act covering the sixteenth-century immigrants had been proposed, but by the time of the Restoration the situation had changed. The earlier refugees, now largely integrated into English society, had developed contacts through whom the needs of the new arrivals could be expressed. Well-established foreign churches in England could emphasize that Protestants who had been persecuted abroad deserved sympathy and support. Moreover England was no longer considered overpopulated, as in Elizabethan days, but under-populated. And the skills brought into the country by the earlier wave of Dutch and Walloon refugees were widely recognized. Now it was pointed out that the Huguenots also brought new skills and financial assets. In the light of the *dragonnades* and the Revocation, it could not be argued successfully that the refugees had come simply to denude England of her wealth before retiring home at the first opportunity, although a few tried to make such accusations.

However, arguments for and against a general naturalization act raged fiercely for half a century after 1664. From the refugee point of view, the advantage was obvious; naturalization under a general act would cost a matter of shillings, whereas a private bill could cost £50 or £60, and was therefore a practical possibility only for the rich. The advantage to the country was affirmed by the Committee of Trade. The House of Lords had little difficulty in agreeing upon an Act in 1670 and again in 1673, and Charles II evidently supported the proposed 1670 Act and certainly publicly urged such a bill in 1681. But the Commons repeatedly dodged the issue. In 1667 debate dragged on until the House adjourned. The Act sent down by the Lords in 1670 was deliberately delayed and did not get beyond a first reading; this was also the fate of a bill in 1689. Acts in 1673, 1685 and 1693–4 reached second readings and committal, but no further. In 1680 leave was given to introduce a bill but no progress was made, while in 1690 and again in 1696 such leave was actually refused. The last bill of the century was rejected outright in 1697. Not until 1709 was an Act of General Naturalization eventually passed, and then it was soon repealed. The House of Commons was not always to blame for these delays, sometimes being adjourned unexpectedly, but the chequered history of the bills shows the low priority placed on general naturalization. This was not the warm welcome to refugees *en masse* that was continually and strongly urged by those well acquainted with the situation in France, like Henry Savile, the English Ambassador in Paris between 1679 and 1681.

Economic objections lay at the root of Parliamentary reluctance to grant general naturalization, just as they were the major cause of mob opposition to the refugees. It was, above all, the mercantile jealousy of the trading companies and London authorities that was expressed in the delaying tactics of the Commons. Their representatives, anxious to preserve their privileges, argued that competition might ruin industrious English families, that royal customs revenues would diminish if a general naturalization bill was passed, and that London and other cities would lose profitable revenues. The capital, indeed, was always a loud voice crying out against excessive naturalization and urging restrictions on the number of aliens entering England. In 1580 the Mayor represented to Lord Treasurer Burghley that so many foreigners thronged London that 'they eat out the Queen's subjects, retailers and artificers that bear charge in the City'. Thirteen years later the capital's representatives in the Commons spoke strongly and successfully against a bill that would have allowed aliens to retail any foreign commodities, arguing that foreigners exported English wealth and undersold Englishmen overseas because of their network of contacts, and asserting that royal taxes would be diminished if English retailers were impoverished. 'I beseech you have respect unto this City, upon whose flourishing estate the whole realm dependeth,' one of the London burgesses implored on this occasion.

The City Companies were quick to complain if the many rules limiting the economic activities of aliens were broken, or at other times when hardship threatened and competition was especially to be feared. Foreigners were frequently accused of sending English gold and silver overseas, of keeping their skills to themselves instead of teaching them to Englishmen, of ignoring regulations governing the numbers of apprentices they might have, and so forth. At some times the complaints were voiced more loudly than others – in 1622, for example, there was an outcry from many trades simultaneously – but the city fathers advanced a consistent policy throughout the seventeenth century and beyond. Their stand may have been short-sighted, but it certainly supported the immediate economic interests of Londoners. Proceeds from the packing and transporting of all alien merchants' goods entering or leaving London, plus a tax on goods offered for sale there, helped swell the city coffers. Aliens paid double parish dues as well as increased national and local customs; they had long been taxed more heavily than natives; they could become free of the city only with difficulty, and even then with restrictions; and they were subject to greater limitations than Englishmen as to the number of workmen and apprentices they could employ. If they became full Englishmen through naturalization, all these disadvantages would be waived, and they would be able to compete with Londoners on equal or, in view of their foreign connections, superior terms.

Even before the general naturalization of aliens was proposed, their competition was widely feared and the privileges of individual trading companies jealously guarded. The mob action we have discussed was infrequent, occurring only when rumbling discontent finally erupted. Ever-present rumour and constant niggling complaint can be discerned in the more routine actions of individuals and companies seeking to preserve their rights. Take for instance the closing decades of the seventeenth century. The shopkeepers of London protested, shortly after the Restoration, about the 'multitude of aliens' who had 'taken upon them to exercise their several vocations'. The Company of Bakers forbade Samuel Caron and Adrian Porck to work in 1668, while the Company of Barbers imposed a £100 bond on Louis Saunier should he work longer than four years in London. French cabinet-makers were molested in the exercise of their trade in 1673, as was the buttonmaker Noel de Launay between 1674 and 1676. The Company of Goldsmiths resisted an order from the Court of Aldermen to admit John Louis into its number in 1682–3. The closing years of the century witnessed action by glaziers, founders and bakers against French Protestants. In short, insecurity ever haunted the refugees. Even their ministers could not all secure employment because they were so numerous, while many of the Huguenot soldiers who had fought for William III in Ireland and on the Continent found themselves out of work when Parliament reduced the army to 7,000 men in 1698.

The opposition they encountered in the exercise of their crafts helped force the refugees into the suburbs around London. Other factors encouraged this. Food may have been cheaper in the outskirts, and accommodation certainly was; in 1730 the Savoy church in Westminster informed the Bishop of London that as the western part of the capital had grown, 'the French refugees have retired to the extremities of it . . . where the houses are cheaper'. But the desire to evade over-attentive guild supervision must have been a powerful incentive. True, the Companies were successful in increasing their area of search and control, but effective supervision of work conditions and quality of goods became harder as that area grew. Norman Brett-James has shown how bad relations between Huguenot hatmakers and the Feltmakers Company encouraged the newcomers to settle and work (and seek to evade the Company's regulations) in such areas as Wandsworth, Battersea and Lambeth. For similar reasons alien weavers and cordwainers settled in the suburbs of Elizabethan London, and silversmiths in sanctuary areas. The many sums spent prosecuting 'unlawful weavers, Frenchmen etc' entered in the Renter Bailiff's accounts for the Weaver's Company indicate how widespread was the evasion of its rules.

Trade opposition also strengthened the refugees' inclination to cling to their churches, especially those that were well established. At Canterbury and Norwich the 'politic men' worked closely alongside the elders of the foreign congregations. In London, Coetus helped defend members of its constituent churches against excessive claims and unreasonable actions on the part of the City Companies. After the Restoration the French Church of the Savoy also became involved in defending the cause of the refugees, and when the Companies sought to enforce a seven-year apprenticeship on them in 1682 it represented their plight in no uncertain terms:

> The coming and continuing of Protestants into this kingdom can so little prejudice, as it must needs be of advantage to it . . . yet we find so great an aversion in [the people here] from us, as to envy us the bread we get by our honest and hard labours, and would compel us to return under the persecution we fled, or which is little (if at all) better to dwell here as once the Jews did in Egypt, a kind of slaves to take all the pains, and they reap all the fruits: a sad choice and a hard usage, which cannot be believed by our brethren abroad, who look upon this land as a sanctuary and refuge of Protestants.

Backed by the Savoy with its Court and Anglican ties and the Threadneedle Street church with its City and mercantile connections, the Huguenots could hope to find protection.

However, appeals from the churches could only be effective for as long as government support for the refugees endured. Fortunately for them, it rarely wavered. Excluding the Laudian regime and the first two years of James II's reign, there was continuing solid support – all the more surprising in view of the unmistakable political inclinations of the descendants of the Walloon refugees. During the Civil War, the great majority had been parliamentarian. When political parties first emerged at the time of the Exclusion crisis in 1679–81, they were prominent in support of the Whigs, who were antagonizing the Court by exploiting anti-Catholic feeling and the fears aroused by the 'Popish Plot' and by seeking the exclusion of James, Duke of York, the future James II, from the succession to the throne. This was a critical period for the new refugees from France, because the *dragonnades* began in 1681. An influential government minister used Sir John Chardin, himself a recent arrival, as his mouthpiece to warn the French Church of London that Charles II's goodwill towards the Huguenots might not survive political action contrary to his wishes. Nevertheless Thomas Papillon and John Dubois, both past lay officers of the congregation, stood as Whig candidates for the positions of sheriffs of London and Middlesex in the disputed elections of 1682. Swept into office by popular vote over the heads of the Court candidates Dudley North and Ralph Box, they thereby roused the ire of the Tories to its fullest pitch. When, in April 1683, they were called before the Lord Mayor and reproached for their part in thwarting the Court over the previous two years, their foreign ancestry was thrown in their teeth:

> Sir James Smith said . . . they were French or Walloon Protestants that came into this nation for refuge, and had got estates, and would overthrow the government and cut our throats. . . . Sir James Smith said again, addressing himself to my Lord Mayor, 'It is true these are French or Walloon Protestants, and now there is come over a great many more of late, and in a little time they will be the same as these are'. To which my Lord Mayor replied, 'I hope the king will take a course to send them back again to their country'.

Such statements showed that foreign ancestry might still be held against the grandchildren of refugees, yet in the event government support for the Huguenots continued during Charles's reign. Under

William III, an obvious and unequivocal ally, the new refugees felt able to take an active political role much earlier than the Walloons had done a century before. Englishmen noted that large numbers of Huguenots voted in parliamentary elections. The great majority were natural supporters of the Whigs, who were enthusiastic about pursuing the war against Louis and supported developments such as the Bank of England, which the Huguenots helped sustain with expertise, capital and their foreign connections. Partly as a result, partly because they disliked William III's Dutch entourage, Tories increasingly laid stress on their Englishness as a matter of policy. By the time over 10,000 German Protestant refugees from the Palatinate arrived in the summer of 1709, there was an almost complete division of opinion along party lines about the desirability or otherwise of alien immigration. It was, therefore, fortunate for the Huguenots that the Tories were left in disarray, their influence eclipsed, after the second decade of the eighteenth century. By the time the Tory party recovered strength, the process of assimilation of the refugees was irreversible.

Enough has been said to show that the popular picture of a uniform welcome for the Huguenots is naive. The manners, the eating habits, the very poverty of the refugees were targets of criticism. They encountered opposition at one time or another from all elements of English society: from the Crown, from some quarters of Parliament and of the Anglican establishment, from civic authorities, from the Trading Companies, from the Tories, from the *menu peuple*. 'There are some here', the Abbé le Blanc wrote in the 1730s, 'who cannot bear the sight of a Frenchman with tranquillity.' It was with good cause that the leaders of the French Protestants in England urged them to maintain a low profile, as when the Consistory of the Threadneedle Street church advised its congregation in 1697 to lay aside 'all those proud and haughty airs' alienating English opinion. That said, it remains true that the Huguenots were, generally, well received in England, especially when their substantial numbers are borne in mind. Aliens crossing the Channel had always encountered hostility, and no previous group had ever been so widely welcomed. Their treatment can best be put into perspective by comparing it with the reception accorded the poor Palatines in 1709. Both the Protestantism and the destitution of the Palatines were questioned, and they were accused of everything from introducing smallpox to stealing bread from the mouths of the English poor. Most were despatched to the American colonies and to Ireland; disorder broke out when an attempt was made to settle some of them in Sundridge, Kent; and popular hatred of them provided a theme for the Sacheverell rioters. In short, they provoked a

9   Pair of flintlock holster pistols by Pierre Monlong, probably for William III

10 (a)   A silkweaver at work in the 1880s

10 (b)   Original building of the French Protestant Hospital, Bath Street

(a)

(b)

(c)

(d)

11   The Huguenot military contribution: (a) Schomberg (his death at the Boyne is
depicted below), (b) Ligonier, (c) Galway, (d) Admiral Gambier

(a)

(b)

(c)

(d)

12   The Huguenot literary and professional contribution: (a) Desaguliers, (b) Rapin-
Thoyras, (c) Boyer, (d) Sir Samuel Romilly

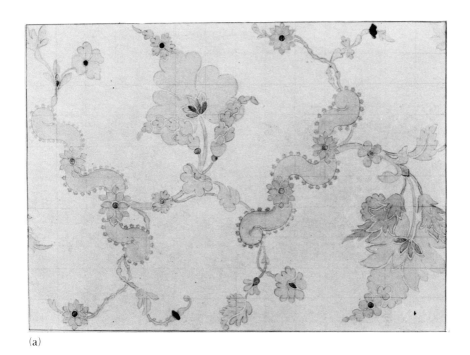

(a)

(b)

13 Silk (a) design, by Anna Maria Garthwaite, and (b) finished product, woven for
Captain Peter le Keux (d. 1743)

(a)

(b)

14 (a and b)   Calligraphy by Esther Inglis, reproduced *original size*

14 (c)   David Garrick in one of his favourite Shakespearean roles, as Richard III

15   Inaugural certificate of the Huguenot Society of London, signed by Sir Austen Henry Layard (Layard of Nineveh), the first President, and Arthur Giraud Browning, the driving force behind the Society's foundation in 1885

16 Hogarth's *Noon*, set at the door of the church 'des Grecs' in Hog Lane, Soho, the most fashionable conformist French church in England after the Savoy was closed in the early 1730s. Note Hogarth's satirical comment on French dress and French habits, and the pastor in the doorway austerely dressed in Geneva bands. The kite caught in the gutter represents flight, and is an allusion to the refugee origins of the congregation

reaction far more hostile than did those who fled the Low Countries in Elizabethan times or France in the 1680s.

Indeed, of all the many groups who over the centuries have sought safety, profit, employment or religious freedom in England, the Huguenots enjoyed the best reception. Their willingness to make sacrifices for the Protestant cause opened doors which otherwise might have remained tight shut. Fortunately for them, both during the middle decades of Elizabeth's reign and in the 1680s and 1690s, Protestantism was equated with national survival. The second period of immigration brought a greater number of refugees to England, and therefore offered greater scope for opposition: but against the normal wave of resentment and economic self-interest could be set the prevailing political passion of the day, anti-popery, considered in the next chapter. One important reason why the forces friendly to the Huguenots proved stronger than the hostile elements was that English public opinion had long been prepared for the possibility of a major inrush of refugees, and conditioned to be sympathetic to them.

As early as 1667, English newsletters were reporting Louis XIV's hostility to the Protestants in France, and the following year the French author of *A Brief Relation of the Persecution and Sufferings of the Reformed Churches of France*, translated 'for more general information', claimed that were he to undertake a full history of the persecutions of French Protestants by the Roman Catholic clergy, 'he should be engaged to write a volume, they are so numerous'. He correctly predicted the Revocation, concluding that should the French clergy prevail on Louis to drive the Protestants out of his dominions,

> we hope God will give us such strength and courage, as, without
> regret, to abandon our native land, that we may serve him
> wherever his providence shall call us.

Others had seen the dangers ahead by 1671, when newsletters reported increasing oppression, 'the [Roman Catholic] clergy there endeavouring by degrees to rout them quite out'. Fears for the existence of the Protestant church in France were reinforced during the 1670s by the publication of a number of inflammatory tracts emphasizing the persecuting nature of Catholicism. Some of these marked the centenary of the Massacre of St Bartholomew. Others underlined the cruelty of Catholic practices in parts of Germany and Hungary. All such reports helped to keep the theme of the inveterate evil of Catholicism in the consciousness of Englishmen, and to prepare them for the still more poignant complaints of the Huguenots in the 1680s. Adults alive in England in that decade had been brought up on descriptions like this account of the massacre of Protestants in

Piedmont in 1654, written by the Cromwellian agent Jean-Baptiste Stouppe (who was also a minister of the Threadneedle Street church):

> My pen falls from my hand in describing these things; yea, the very thoughts of them makes my whole body to tremble, my hair to stand up; a heart of adamant, a hand of steel, and a pen of iron, could not express half the horrid prodigies of cruelty and lamentable spectacles which were seen . . . here the leg of a woman, there the head of a child, sometimes the privy members of a man, the entrails of another, and sometimes the pieces of another, whom the beasts had not yet made an end of eating.

How could they fail to respond to the new tales of terror that would come with the *dragonnades*?

As the dangers faced by French Protestants increased from 1679 onwards, so too did the number of accounts of the persecutions reaching Englishmen. Week by week in August and October 1679, the *Domestick Intelligence, or News both from City and Country* brought home their plight. From its opening number in December 1680, *The True Protestant Mercury* made a particular point of reporting 'the intolerable pressures, under which those of the reformed religion groan, and which daily are multiplied upon them'. Other papers like *The Currant Intelligence* followed suit. No literate Englishman in the early 1680s could have been ignorant of what was happening in France, for accounts of events there filled not only newsletters and papers but also pamphlets. Pierre Jurieu's *The Policy of the Clergy of France, to destroy the Protestants of that Kingdom*, printed in 1681, summarized what had taken place during the previous twenty years, while *The Great Pressures and Grievances of the Protestants in France* commented on the laws oppressing Huguenots. *Animadversions upon the French King's Declaration . . . of June 1681* lamented Louis's decree authorizing the conversion of Protestant children to Catholicism after the age of seven. *The Deplorable State and Condition of the Poor French Protestants Commiserated*, also printed in 1681, referred to the Huguenots being 'reduced even to the extremity of want and misery, expecting every hour in the night to be allarm'd with another St Bartholomew's massacre'. During 1682, sermons urging congregations to give money for the refugees were published: Samuel Bolde's *Sermon against Persecution* and George Hickes's *The True Notion of Persecution stated*. Perhaps most widely read of these pamphlets was *The Present State of the Protestants in France. In Three Letters*, first published in 1681 and reprinted as part of *An Apology for the Protestants of France. . .* in 1683, which both described events in France and defended the refugees in England against their enemies.

The sympathy for the Huguenots engendered by the *dragonnades* was kept alive by a continuing supply of pamphlets. James II sought to ensure that little reaction to the Revocation was publicly expressed in England in 1685–6; but Jean Claude's *Account of the Persecutions and Oppressions of the Protestants in France* made a significant impact before it was suppressed, and other works discussing the persecutions circulated in England after being printed abroad. 'Here is every 15 or 30 days a French sheet comes forth of the sufferings of those people, with reflections, printed at Rotterdam,' it was reported from London to Viscount Hatton in November 1686. In the last year of James's reign and the first years of William and Mary's, there was a great outpouring of literature concerned with Louis's actions against Protestants in France, Orange and Piedmont, and another group of pamphlets burst on the scene at the close of the century, when persecution was renewed in France following the Peace of Ryswick, and English indignation was aroused by the treatment meted out to Huguenot slaves on the French king's galleys.

At all times, then, English public opinion was kept informed about events across the Channel and sympathetic to the cause of French Protestants through a barrage of newsletters, papers, books and pamphlets. Englishmen who were not literate were confronted by the reality of refugee sufferings through public collections, normally though not always supported by persuasive arguments from the clergy. At Litlington, Cambridgeshire, the curate and churchwarden who carried out a house-to-house collection failed to impress those they visited; but then they did not provide leadership by example, making out the required return to the archdeacon for £0. 0s. 0d! On the other hand, influential London clergy lent their full weight to such appeals. William Smythies went far beyond the bounds of duty, visiting refugees in their homes, writing and preaching on their behalf, and taking such pains in caring for poor Frenchmen lodged at the Pesthouse that he embarrassed himself financially.

Many bishops urged support for the Huguenots, often contributing generously themselves. Barlow of Lincoln, Burnet of Salisbury, Ken of Bath and Wells, Dolben of York, William Lloyd of St Asaph, the other William Lloyd of Peterborough and Norwich, Turner of Ely, Trelawney of Bristol and probably Lamplugh of Exeter all showed marked kindness to them. If Archbishop Sancroft was a little lethargic in the 1680s by comparison with Compton of London, he was none the less a friend to the refugees. His successors at Canterbury – Tillotson (1691–4), Tenison (1695–1715) and Wake (1716–36) – were notable protectors of foreign Protestants in England, genuinely concerned to relieve their plight. Episcopal efforts encouraged a generous response to the briefs that were issued. Bishop Compton's circular commending the 1686 collection to his clergy (plate 7) is especially eloquent:

> You have such an object of charity before you, as it may be, no case could more deserve your pity. It is not a flight to save their lives, but what is ten thousand times more dear, their consciences. They are not fled by permission (except the ministers, who are banished,) but with the greatest difficulty and hardship imaginable. And therefore it will be an act of the highest compassion to comfort and relieve them. . . . When we reflect upon that desolation that has been made before their eyes, of all their goods and stores, the barbarity of usage, both to their bodies and estates, and their quitting their whole subsistence with their native soil, through all sorts of peril, one would imagine it the greatest hardship. But when we come to examine that anguish which is brought upon their minds, it is incomparably greater; their wives, children, and relations imprisoned, clapped into monasteries, put down into dungeons, inhumanly tormented and afflicted, till they renounce their faith, or perish in the trial. All men are not required to be wise enough to judge of the secular consequences of this accident in the peopling our country, increasing manufactures, industry, trading, and the like: but God excuses no man from being good and charitable. They who have no mite to give, have hearts to pray; and this occasion requires, with an equal necessity, our prayers for those who still lie in misery and irons, as it does our benevolence for such as are escaped. Exhort then your people whilst they have time, to do good.

Confronted by such appeals, enveloped in an ideology of anti-popery, and convinced by the stream of print that the sufferings of the French Protestants were real, most Englishmen suppressed their normal suspicion of aliens and accepted the Huguenots into their midst. Their welcome grew warmer during the 1680s, as the policies of Charles II and particularly James II led to growing fears that Englishmen too might have to choose between abandoning their religion or going into exile.

8

The Huguenots and the Later Stuarts

Modern scholars tend to criticize Charles II and show sympathy for James II. Indeed Charles has been a monarch scorned ever since the days of that gossipy diarist Samuel Pepys, a severe critic of his inattention to the business of government and his profligate Court. Few contemporaries rated Charles highly. Bishop Burnet accused him of 'mocking God, and deceiving the world' and urged that 'the greatest kindness that could be shewn to his memory' was oblivion. Modern historians might not go so far, but with the exception of Sir Arthur Bryant they have found little to say in his favour. Charles is seen as holding no principles beyond a wish for an easy life and a loyalty to his dynasty. His Declaration of Indulgence, designed to protect Roman Catholics and Dissenters from the rigours of laws passed by an Anglican Parliament, caused him endless political trouble, but Charles is rarely viewed as a genuine advocate of religious toleration. Yet his treatment of the Huguenots suggests otherwise.

The timing of his actions on their behalf shows that Charles was not motivated merely by desire to serve his own political ends by supporting the refugees, and the warmth and speed of his responses may indicate a genuine generosity of heart. In 1666, even as he was declaring war on France, Charles chose to welcome French Protestants into his country. And when the *dragonnades* began in 1681, he acted with speed and decisiveness in offering the Huguenots both a home and significant privileges, so that those who came to British shores were well treated for the four years before his death in 1685. This gives the lie to Burnet's assertion that the king 'seemed to have no bowels nor tenderness in his nature; and in the end of his life he became cruel.' There was no political need for Charles to lend the Huguenots his support, although he may have perceived trade advantages for the country in so doing. There were those at Court who would have argued that the refugees were opposed to monarchy; certainly the Huguenot congregations in the country were rightly considered sympathetic to the Whigs whom Charles had recently outmanoeuvred, rather than the Tories who were just entering, thirsting for revenge, on what was to be a five-year period of overwhelming influence and power. Nor was it to Charles's advantage to flaunt his independence before Louis XIV – on the contrary, he had just completed a reconciliation with that monarch and consequently would have been anxious not to offend him. A judicious modern analyst of the king's actions and motives, Professor Haley, reached the conclusion that 'there is no evidence that Charles II believed in toleration as an abstract principle'.[1] Perhaps his treatment of the Huguenots provides such evidence. Charles may have been lazy, francophile and ultimately Catholic, but he obviously disliked persecution. He was notably prompt in welcoming refugees when the *dragonnades* started, and in encouraging charitable support for them once they had arrived. If this was not a genuine desire for toleration, the king must have felt a deep fellow-feeling for refugees. He had, after all, spent bitter years in exile himself, and the best-known cliché of the reign recalls his determination 'never to go on his travels again'.

Unlike his idle though more intelligent brother, James has been treated indulgently by modern historians.[2] He is described as honest, plain speaking, consistent and sincere. Alas, his treatment of the Huguenot refugees scarcely justifies such a favourable opinion. It is certainly true that James disapproved of the *dragonnades*; he spoke against the measures employed in France to the Dutch and Spanish ambassadors, and informed Sir William Trumbull

> that though he did not like the Huguenots (for he thought they were of anti-monarchical principles) yet he thought the persecution of them was unchristian, and not to be equalled in any history since Christianity: That they might be no good men, yet might be used worse than they deserved, and it was a proceeding he could not approve of.

It is also true that on coming to the throne he promised representatives of the foreign churches of London the same protection and support that they had received from Charles. Moreover he issued a brief for a public collection on their behalf as had been done in 1681, and continued to grant letters of denization. By such means some otherwise hostile contemporaries like Burnet or White Kennett were convinced of James's kindness to the Huguenots.

The refugees themselves were less convinced – and with good reason. They found James shifty and untrustworthy, his actions but a front to placate English public opinion. In 1685, for example, a bill for the general naturalization of French Protestants currently residing in England 'and such others as shall come over within a limited time' appeared before the House of Commons, probably prompted by the French congregation at Thorpe-le-Soken. Court opposition ensured that a clause was added to the bill ordering all French churches and congregations to use only the Anglican liturgy translated into French. Such a clause would have destroyed all the non-conformist foreign churches in England at one stroke, and was scarcely an encouragement to persecuted Protestants in France to cross the Channel. Fortunately the bill lapsed when Monmouth's rebellion made it necessary for Parliament to be prorogued; but the all-important French Church of London found its existence challenged in other ways over subsequent years, and its elders were kept uneasy for the rest of the reign.

Two Frenchmen who emphasized James's dislike of the Huguenots in their reports to Louis XIV were the ambassador Barrillon and the agent sent to encourage refugees to return to France, Bonrepaus. Barrillon was sufficiently sure of his ground to urge Bonrepaus to inform James openly of his mission, and Bonrepaus related that the king's reaction was one of delight; James said that he viewed all Protestants, especially those fleeing from France, as republicans. Moreover the agent repeatedly assured Louis that James gave him all possible support. Since it was in Bonrepaus's interest to emphasize the difficulties in his way, not to stress the freedom of action he was given, this is powerful testimony that the fears of the refugees in England were well-founded. Bonrepaus did act cautiously when he sought to dismember the Ipswich silk-weaving settlement by bribery, for both king and Parliament saw its value to the economy. Yet even in this case he later reported to France that James was ignoring warnings about his activities because he considered the refugees to be his enemies. In similar vein, James assisted the formation of a refugee corps under the Marquis de Miremont when it was intended for service well away from England, in Hungary in the war against the Turks. He also sought to restrict the number of refugees reaching English shores. At the time of the Revocation, he prohibited the captains and officers of English ships from taking French subjects on board unless they had passports – which they could not obtain – and punished at least one captain for disobeying this injunction. Given the aroused state of English public opinion, he could scarcely have done more.

That same public opinion forced James to issue a brief for a collection for the refugees, but again it was done unwillingly and with an ill grace, with none of the prompt generosity that had marked the actions of his brother in 1681. Ordered in council on 6 November 1685, the brief was not actually issued until four months later on 5 March 1686 – and even then its reading in the London churches was delayed several weeks. Such procrastination troubled Englishmen as well as the Huguenots themselves, so that one finds even such a staunch Tory as Sir John Reresby commenting on the way in which it 'after a long stop did pass the great seal at last'. What had caused the 'stop'? The diarist John Evelyn blamed it on 'the interest of the French ambassador and cruel papists'. Lady Russell, who had contacts in the refugee community, wrote that the Lord Chancellor, Judge Jeffreys, 'bid [the brief] be laid by, when it was offered him to seal'. Bonrepaus stated categorically that James hindered the passage of the brief as long as possible. Government action, in short, was what delayed relief, action for which the king was responsible.

When the brief eventually appeared, it was still far from being all the refugees would have desired. For one thing, its wording was less forceful than that of 1681. The 1681 document referred to 'the great hardships and persecutions' undergone by the Huguenots for the sake of their religion, and to their present need, 'being forced to abandon their native abodes . . . in haste and confusion'. The 1686 brief said nothing about conditions in France, nor about persecution, merely stating that the destitute French Protestants currently in England needed relief. In 1681 Charles had urged compassion because, he said, he looked upon them 'not only as distressed strangers, but chiefly as persecuted Protestants'; now James simply asserted in a negative and general way that public acts of charity were 'the highest prerogative, and most desirable advantage of kings'. He took care not to abuse his 'advantage' by any excessive generosity, and the 1686 brief limited the duration of the Letters Patent to one year, so that further action had to be taken later in the reign. The 1681 brief had been issued for two years.

Archbishop Sancroft prepared a circular letter to the clergy, to be sent out with the brief. This was carefully censored by James and his Lord Chancellor, Jeffreys explaining to Sancroft that he had altered his draft 'to humour the Letters Patents, and to obviate the inconveniences his Majesty apprehends may attend his service by any though but seeming, reflections.' What he had done was remove anything that might underline the troubles and need of the refugees. Where Sancroft wrote they still arrived daily in England, 'daily' was deleted. No mention was allowed of 'the great rigours and severities used towards them at home' for religious reasons, nor of their 'not being permitted to bring over their estates with them'. This was of particular significance because Sancroft's circular ordered the clergy to encourage charity towards the refugees 'by such motives, and inducements only, as in the [brief] and in this present order are contained'. The archbishop would, therefore, have allowed the Anglican clergy to preach on the sufferings of the exiles. James and Jeffreys did not. The clergy were just to read the brief and use the weak incitements to charity in it and it alone, or to replace the sermon of the day by the standard homily on almsgiving and mercy, which would not have mentioned the Huguenots at all.

Concern was also felt by Englishmen and Frenchmen alike about the distribution of the proceeds of the brief. Because it named no fewer than sixty people – mostly lords, bishops, government officials and clergy – of whom any five were empowered to allocate the money donated, there was a dangerous possibility of government control of the collection. But by far the most significant feature of the brief from the point of view of the refugees was the statement that it was to benefit only those who lived 'in entire conformity and orderly submission to our government established both in church and state'. No such phrase had appeared in the 1681 brief. How was it to be interpreted? It could have been taken to mean that only those refugees who attended conformist French congregations or worshipped in the Anglican Church were to be offered relief. This seems to be what the government intended and what Jeffreys announced, but English public opinion would not allow it. Instead, it was interpreted as meaning that all recipients of assistance had to provide a certificate that they had received Communion according to the usage of the Church of England. In Macaulay's words, James thus 'gave orders that none should receive a crust of bread or a basket of coals who did not first take the sacrament according to the Anglican ritual.' Since the continental Reformed churches accepted the Anglican Church as a true Protestant church, most refugees felt able to comply with this condition, but only after considerable heart-searching; they were, after all, refugees for the sake of religion, and had left their native land to be free to worship in their own way. Macaulay was wrong to claim that James defrauded them of the alms contributed by the nation, yet they had reason for alarm. Jeffreys speedily informed his fellow-commissioners named in the brief that the king considered the refugees to be enemies of monarchy and episcopacy. Likewise in Scotland the Chancellor, the Earl of Perth, the principal royal minister and a recent convert to Catholicism, agreed with suggestions that people supporting the ministry of the French Church of Edinburgh had evidently nothing better to do with their money than give it to rebels and vagabonds.

Attempts have been made to absolve James from any share in all these dealings with regard to the brief, to blame the delays on Jeffreys and Barrillon, the insistence on conformity on the Anglican authorities, the prohibition of preaching about the suffering of the Huguenots on the demands of Anglo-French relations. Such pleading cannot be admitted. The need to preserve good relations with France had been just as real for Charles in 1681, but had not stopped him acting with far greater determination and speed. Since James was quite prepared to ignore the French king's advice and desires on other matters, there is no good reason to suppose that his treatment of the Huguenots reflects a simple desire to please Louis. Barrillon may have influenced James, and Jeffreys helped him carry through what he wanted, but it was the king himself who was responsible for his failure to make fuller use of his 'highest prerogative' of charity. Under the circumstances the exceptionally generous English reaction to the brief, which produced over £42,000 in all after being extended by an order in council in March 1687, was little short of a slap in the royal face – as James well realized.

Early in 1687, his insistent desire to see Catholicism tolerated led James to develop a new policy involving a close alliance with the Dissenters, and his defenders then tried to blame the Anglican establishment for insisting on conformity in the 1686 brief. They were wrong. Anglican authorities had not sought this in 1681, and neither Sancroft of Canterbury nor Compton of London, the bishops most concerned by the move, would have initiated such a step. In 1686 Compton had been instructed to bring the conformist French Church of the Savoy to a stricter adherence to Anglican ways. (James was angry because it was always willing to receive converts from Catholicism.) The instructions that Compton received came from Sancroft, but Compton's reply makes plain that the source of pressure was the Court:

> I humbly conceive, that it would be an insolent demand in me, to require more of the French church in the Savoy, than . . . King [Charles II] himself did in his constitution of them. Which only requires their conformity according to the usage of Guernsey and Jersey, where never surplice or sign of the cross were ever used or required: and where they have always taken care of their churches by way of Consistory. Therefore I hope it will no longer [be] reflected upon me. . .and I hope your Grace, will do me the favour to acquaint the king, and my Lord Chancellor with thus much.

Not content with such a reply, James saw that further instructions were speedily despatched. Remarking that the French translation of the Anglican liturgy 'is not so exactly done as it ought to be, and in many particular offices differs very much from the English', he ordered that it be revised, corrected and reprinted. So it was not the Anglican hierarchy but James and Jeffreys who were seeking so strenuously to urge more Anglican ways on the refugees.

Equally irritating to the Huguenots, and much more alarming to the English public, was the king's use of his powers of censorship. How could *The London Gazette*, the official newspaper, maintain silence about events in France in 1685? As Evelyn recorded in his diary,

> One thing was much taken notice of, that the *Gazettes* which were still constantly printed twice a week, and informing us what was done all Europe over etc.: never all this time, spake one syllable of this wonderful proceeding in France, nor was any relation of it published by any, save what private letters etc. the persecuted fugitives brought: Whence this silence, I list not to conjecture, but it appeared very extraordinary in a Protestant country, that we should know nothing of what Protestants suffered.

Bonrepaus was quite open about the source of the strange silence, informing his superiors in France that it was due to James's orders. The same royal policy led to the suppression of such works as *An Edict of the French King, Prohibiting all Publick Exercise of the Pretended Reformed Religion in his Kingdom* and Jean Claude's *Account of the Persecutions and Oppressions of the Protestants in France*. Claude's book (in both French and English) was publicly burnt by the hangman at the London Exchange and elsewhere, and its translator arrested. Public discontent was further intensified by the knowledge that James had been prompted by Barrillon, and concern was expressed that the French Ambassador should have, as Evelyn put it, 'so mighty a power and ascendant here'. James's actions merely increased public sympathy for the Huguenots, especially when he willingly licensed the publication of French Catholic works like the Bishop of Meaux's *Pastoral Letter . . . to the New Catholics of his Diocess*.

To sum up this analysis of James's behaviour: while the king never endorsed violent persecution, he probably approved of the Revocation and certainly disliked the Huguenots. When the Catholic poet John Dryden came to write *The Hind and the Panther* in 1687, he praised the king:

> Behold! how [James] protects your Friends opprest,
> Receives the Banish'd, succours the Distress'd:
> Behold, for you may read an honest open Breast.

The evidence set out in this chapter presents a very different portrait. While in public he posed as the protector of the refugees, James deliberately shut his eyes to the violence practised against them in France and did what he could to discourage them from coming to England and to unsettle those who had sought asylum in his kingdoms. Moreover the two-faced policy he pursued was his own, not something urged on him by an intolerant Anglican establishment, although concocted with the aid of Barrillon and Jeffreys. Perhaps James never turned out to be 'Queen Mary in breeches' as had been forecast in 1681, but his behaviour showed the Huguenots that, like the king from whose land they had fled, his royal word was not to be trusted. That is why comparatively few new refugees crossed the Channel in the early part of his reign, before the Declaration of Indulgence offered legal guarantees in 1687. It is also why the French Protestants in England supported William almost to a man in 1688. Indeed their distrust was so strong that even in 1715 it could still be claimed that they formed the single most 'desperate' and disciplined body in England opposed to the restoration of the Stuarts.

It was because he was so deeply committed to Catholicism and his quest for toleration for fellow Catholics that James II eventually lost his throne. Christopher Hill describes the king's behaviour as 'anachronistic', but the anachronism lies in the historian's vision, not the royal concern for religion. Deep religious commitment like that of the Huguenots, involving a willingness to take risks and, if need be, to suffer, was widespread in the 1680s; the forces stirred by the Reformation and Counter-Reformation still acted powerfully in hearts and minds. Indeed it is precisely because the king was touching a vital nerve that he succeeded in uniting the whole 'political nation' against him despite its many deep internal dissensions and splits. James's downfall demonstrates not only his own folly and incompetence, but also the power of anti-popery as an ideology capable of reglazing the shattered glasshouse of English politics. We need to examine this ideology, because the Huguenots were so closely connected with its appeal in the 1680s that they played a significant part in James's enforced departure and the 'Glorious Revolution' of 1688.

Anti-popery was an emotional and political driving force of great strength in later Stuart England.[3] Its origins stretched back to the persecution of Queen Mary's reign as viewed by Elizabethan and seventeenth-century Englishmen through the blood-stained pages of John Foxe's *Acts and Monuments*, his 'Book of Martyrs'. It was based on fear, but not on fear of individual Catholics in England, who were few in number (Dr Miller estimates some 50–60,000, little more than 1 per cent of the total population), generally politically docile, rurally based, and constantly in the sights of a formidable armament of penal laws. Rather the fear was of popery in general. Roman Catholics were viewed as obedient slaves of the pope, who was thought to wish to uproot Protestantism with the maximum amount of violence, cruelty and bloodshed, and to be especially keen to regain England, which had once been a papal fief. In pursuit of this end, it was believed, Catholics would lie and break any oath.

Seventeenth-century Englishmen looked on history as cyclical rather than progressive, and regarded their past experience as of great value in understanding their present situation and interpreting their future prospects. Hence their fear of popery. Their fright was founded largely on continental examples of the terrors of Catholicism. They thought of the Massacre of St Bartholomew in France in 1572, of the Armada sent against England by Philip II of Spain, of the 1641 massacres in Ireland, of the persecutions of the Vaudois in Piedmont in the 1650s – all events kept before their minds by pamphleteers. They reflected, too, on the 1605 Gunpowder Plot, brought to mind each year by fast days and church services of thanksgiving for its failure. When the *dragonnades* began in France in 1681, they became even more convinced that Catholicism was cruel, tyrannical and persecuting.

Since the time of Philip II, moreover, Catholicism had been firmly identified in the public eye with absolutism. This identification was confirmed for most Englishmen by the events of the 1630s (when Archbishop Laud, one of the architects of the policy of 'Thorough' government without Parliament, had twice been offered a Cardinal's hat) and the 1640s (when Charles I had been prepared to include Irish Catholics in his army). It was not logical, for Laud and Charles I were both firm Anglicans. Nor was the fear of popery soundly based; strained relations between Louis XIV and Pope Innocent XI clearly show that European Catholicism was not monolithic. But to debate the foundations of anti-Catholicism is to obscure its vital force for the generation of Englishmen living after the appearance of Andrew Marvell's *Account of the Growth of Popery and Arbitrary Government* in 1677–8. This influential pamphlet drew on the deep springs of anti-Catholic feeling and at the same time refreshed and replenished them. Marvell reproduced the equation of 1641. He pointed to signs of Catholicism at Court, where James as heir apparent aroused fears of renewed persecution, and to arbitrary tendencies in the government, in which the Earl of Danby's activities during the 1670s were evoking some fears of a repetition of 'Thorough'. To these he added an Anglicanism prepared to persecute Dissenters, and the sum, he found, amounted to a plot to introduce popery and absolutism. Such fears were reinforced by Danby's demand for a sizeable army, and later by the Popish Plot invented by Titus Oates. The result of the hysteria of 1678–81 was that three fears coalesced into one. Fear of a standing army and arbitrary government created by the actions of Danby and Charles II, fear of Popish treason and massacres inspired by Oates, and fear of possible persecution under a future Roman Catholic king, James, joined together to produce one common apprehension. As Sir Henry Capel put it in the House of Commons in April 1679, anti-Catholicism lay at the very heart of that general fear:

> From popery came the notion of a standing army and arbitrary
> power. . . . Formerly the crown of Spain, and now France,
> ³ supports this root of popery amongst us; but lay popery flat, and
> there's an end of arbitrary government and power. It is a mere
> chimera, or notion, without popery.

Superficially, the hysteria surrounding Oates's Popish Plot had dissipated by the time James came to the throne in 1685, but the latent potency of anti-Catholicism remained. Almost from the beginning of the reign, the credibility of James's government was undermined simply because he was a Catholic. If papists could lie freely, how could they be trusted? Even a king's word was to be doubted. Had not Charles died a Catholic after making many declarations of his Protestantism? Was not Louis ignoring his own promises of protection for the Huguenots in France? The attitude of English Protestants to James throughout his reign reflected less what he had done than what it was assumed he would do. The question of credibility assumed particular importance when James began to introduce a policy of general toleration in 1686–7, but it was in Englishmen's minds long before; even circles well-disposed to monarchy were already debating his integrity by the end of 1685.

The strength of anti-Catholicism in England was such that it would have been politic for James to have kept his religion as far as possible in the background. However, he was determined to improve the position of Catholicism, and if English Catholics were to have security, then the penal laws against them had to be either removed by Parliament or annulled through the exercise of the royal prerogative. James never hid his intention nor relaxed his efforts to put it into practice, and his endeavours eventually cost him his throne. In the words of the royalist Sir John Bramston's autobiography,

> though King James his reign was short, not full four years; yet was
> his design very apparent, – the Roman religion he resolved to
> establish, maugre all the laws, and what averseness soever in the
> nobility, gentry, and the common people also. . . . [His] furious
> hasty driving ruined him, and all his.

The importance of the refugees in the England of James II can only be appreciated against this background of anti-Catholicism, the king's lack of credibility and his utter determination to forward the cause of his religion at any cost. They were living proof of Roman Catholic tyranny; what seemed to contemporaries like White Kennett to be their 'vast numbers' and their state of destitution provided irrefutable evidence of the horrors of popery and arbitrary government. As such, their psychological effect on English public opinion was profound. Presumably it was greatest where the Huguenots landed and settled, especially in the south and east of the country. But Members of Parliament and other visitors to Westminster and London could not fail to take back to their shires reports of their numbers and condition, and the briefs for charitable collections on their behalf were read throughout England. Moreover, because of the risks they ran and the sacrifices they made to escape from France, the refugees attracted the attention of newsletter writers, especially when a sizeable number – like the 800 recorded in Narcissus Luttrell's *Brief Historical Relation* in May 1687 – arrived as a group.

It is evident from a wide range of sources – amongst them Luttrell, Evelyn, the Lyme letters, Bramston's *Autobiography*, Roger Morrice's Entering Book and Lady Russell's letters – that James's attempts to suppress news from France and the Continent about the treatment of the Huguenots were singularly unsuccessful. It is also clear that the refugees themselves believed implicitly in the tales of persecution that reached England, and spread them among their new hosts. Their stories and their presence deepened the already strong English aversion to Louis XIV; people of every shade of political and religious opinion, from the Tory Bramston to the Whig Lady Russell and from the Catholic Dryden to the Quaker William Penn, combined in expressing abhorrence of the man and his policies. The almost hysterical tone of the comments on Louis in Evelyn's Diary and the Verney papers ('I hear he stinks alive, and his carcass will stink worse when he is dead, and so will his memory to all eternity') seems truly representative of English opinion.

The refugees drew attention to events in France and Savoy which could only further encourage anti-Catholicism and support the identification of popery with cruelty and tyranny. As the Huguenot refugee Jurieu and the Whig exile Burnet both observed from across the Channel in the Netherlands, the persecution of the Protestants in France alerted Englishmen to the dangers of popery. Burnet also wrote that it was not Louis personally so much as Catholicism itself which 'obligeth him to extirpate heretics, and not to keep his faith to them'. Quite apart from the persecution, moreover, the French king's military successes on the Continent were bound to bring home to Englishmen that Protestantism was everywhere on the defensive, that its prospects seemed grim. Of the three most important Protestant powers, Sweden was appreciably less strong than a generation earlier, England seemed to be becoming a French client, and the weakness of the Netherlands in the face of French arms had been made all too apparent in 1667 and 1672.

One of the effects of having many new refugees settled in England was that news and rumours from France spread across the Channel quickly and doubtless attained greater credibility through being repeated by more voices than previously. In 1682, Louis Maimbourg had prophesied that Louis XIV's assistance would ensure the disappearance of Protestantism in France and England simultaneously. This belief, or hopes akin to it, often found expression in France later in the decade. Thus in January 1686 reports were current that Louis had offered James fifty ships and 50,000 men, and these reports can only have assumed greater significance when French dragoons assisted in the massacre of Protestants in Savoy, of which news reached England early in May. More concrete than rumour was a speech of the Bishop of Valence in July 1685, widely circulated in England, urging Louis to join James in extirpating heresy in England by force of arms.[4]

A further way in which the refugees (both in and out of England) helped to undermine James's government was through their contribution to Dutch propaganda organized by William of Orange. William's agents had long been accustomed to stress the dangers of popery in the English Court, and William had long used Huguenots or men of Huguenot descent as his propagandists. Now they reported James as asking Louis for French forces to reduce Anglicans to the same state as Huguenots, making use of such 'evidence' as the speech by the Bishop of Valence to bring their point home. Whig exiles in Holland, also in contact with Huguenot refugees, added to the writings smuggled into England describing Catholic atrocities such as intended massacres of Protestants organized by Jesuits. James, almost certainly, never had any thought or intention of asking for or using French troops in England; but the readiness to believe he would do so provided fertile soil for the seeds of alarm and discontent sown by these various exiles in Holland.

At every stage of the reign, then, the Huguenot refugees dispersed around Europe undermined James's hopes. They helped to harden public opinion against the one cause for which the king would risk anything, Catholicism. Since mid-century France had been allied with Protestant European powers. The Revocation and the plight of the refugees helped to unite them and to bring that alliance to an end. When James sought an accord with the Dissenters, Huguenots abroad urged both the refugees in England and English society in general not to accept the proffered toleration. Works such as François de

Gaultier's *A Letter of Several French Ministers fled into Germany . . .*, promptly translated (by the future Archbishop Wake) and published in English in 1688, argued that James's Declaration of Indulgence was illegal and endangered Protestantism in England. As the Revolution approached, refugees united factions in Holland, co-ordinated diplomatic support for William and swelled the ranks of his armed forces. Moreover, they underlined the contrast between James and William, greatly to the advantage of the latter. James's foreign policy was essentially independent and isolationist, but he was no obvious enemy to Louis as was William, and he could readily be seen as a French client. Whether or not James was averse to oppression, his liking for toleration was easy to question, whereas William was renowned as a lifelong opponent of persecution. And while James had burnt Claude's *Account of the Persecutions*, William – as was known in England – had given Claude a pension.[5]

Most important of all, England was prepared to accept William and Mary more readily because Huguenot refugees evoked parallels between the state of Protestants in France and England. Separated as we are from the events of James's reign by a gap of three centuries, we find it inconceivable that Englishmen could have taken seriously the thought that they might have to face anything equivalent to the Revocation and the *dragonnades*. Nevertheless, the possibility certainly exercised their minds. The Presbyterian minister Roger Morrice often mulled over events in France, comparing them with what was happening in England. Others shared his fears, like the author of these satirical lines from 'Hounslow-Heath, 1686', a poem on James's standing army:

> Now pause, and view the Army Royal,
> Compos'd of valiant souls and loyal;
> Not rais'd (as ill men say) to hurt ye,
> But to defend, or to convert ye:
> For that's the method now in use,
> The faith Tridentine to diffuse.
> Time was, the Word was powerful;
> But now, 'tis thought remiss and dull:
> Has not that energy and force,
> Which is in well-arm'd foot and horse.

Fears of *dragonnades* were heightened as James expanded his army with Roman Catholic recruits from Ireland, and the expression 'to dragoon' came into the English language at this time.

The immediate reaction to the Revocation of the Edict of Nantes was strong and, as Barrillon pointed out, those most opposed to it foresaw a similar action taking place in England. Once the Edict had been revoked, James's credibility as a Catholic sovereign was questioned more than ever, especially as he developed his policy of toleration towards the Dissenters. It cannot have helped him that the most prominent elements of English Catholicism, the Court Jesuits and especially Father Petre, had close connections with the French Catholic Church. If the Catholic king of France could so cavalierly ignore and repeal a 'perpetual and irrevocable' grant, how could the promises of the Catholic king of England be trusted? When James overrode the Test Act by granting commissions to Roman Catholics, and thus breached what was to Englishmen a fundamental law of the greatest importance, it was inevitable that his actions should be compared to those of Louis. When James proceeded against the Fellows of Magdalen College, Oxford, for refusing to accept a Catholic as President, and yet repeated his promises to maintain the Church of England, it was observed by Burnet

> that the king of France, even after he had resolved to break the Edict of Nantes, yet repeated in above an hundred Edicts, that were real and visible violations of that Edict, a clause confirmatory of the Edict of Nantes, declaring that 'he would never violate it'.

The fears of most Englishmen were summed up by one John Westbrown of Harwich, who queried in a 'libellous paper' of 1688[6]

> whether the usage of the Protestants in France and Savoy for these three years past be not a sufficient warning not to trust to the declarations, promises or oaths in matters of religion of any papist whatsoever.

The Huguenots made a substantial contribution to James's downfall. Their presence in England confirmed the existing English belief that Catholicism, absolutism and cruelty were indissolubly bound together, and also refuelled the fires of anti-popery which had been temporarily damped down since the collapse of the Popish Plot scare. They helped to undermine the credibility of James's policies. In England and more particularly overseas, they actively promoted the cause of William of Orange. Above all, the refugees excited public attention because Anglicans feared that they might share the same fate of recantation or exile at some future date; as Samuel Bolde had warned his English congregation in a sermon against persecution preached and printed in 1682, 'you know not how soon your own condition may be the same with theirs'. This ability of Englishmen to empathize with the refugees made James's policies in their regard – the silencing of the *Gazette*, for instance, or the burning of Claude's book (just when news of the Savoy massacres was reaching England) – nothing less than sheer folly. Moreover, it was not the king's rash and illegal acts alone that undermined his subjects' loyalty, but those acts when viewed in the light of Louis XIV's cruelty and tyranny. Once again we return to the fact that the refugees were the living – and frightening – proof of that tyranny.

Because of this, Huguenots were assured of a sympathetic welcome and generous response from Englishmen even at the time of maximum immigration; and after the Revolution they had nothing to fear from monarchs who had every reason to reward them for their assistance. In any case, William came from a Calvinist background and had always been deeply sympathetic to the plight of the Huguenots, while his wife Mary was charitable by nature; and his successor Anne was as committed to the long struggle against Louis XIV as he was himself. All three rulers made generous provision for the refugees, and from this time on the relations of the Huguenots with the English monarchy become of less interest than the part they played in the wider European struggle.

9

The Huguenots and the Defeat of Louis XIV's France

Between 1689 and 1713, with a short respite from 1697 to 1702, England was at war with the France of Louis XIV. Did the Huguenot refugees in England make any substantial contribution to the defeat of the country from which they had fled? It seems an obvious and worthwhile question to ask, but the Huguenots tend to be either ignored altogether by modern British historians or mentioned only for the crafts they brought with them. The implication of many recent surveys of Stuart England, such as those by Professors Kenyon and J. R. Jones, is that the arrival of the refugees was significant mainly because it fomented growing English hatred of foreigners. Economic historians are more likely to acknowledge the weaving skills of the refugees or their input to the early funds of the Bank of England, but cannot tackle the wider question with which this chapter is concerned. No one would maintain that the Huguenots won the war for their adopted country, but it would have been extremely difficult, perhaps impossible, for England to have defeated France without their contribution.

The loss of rather fewer than quarter of a million refugees was not in itself disastrous for France, a country of some eighteen million people. Nor could they have taken with them enough wealth to impoverish France permanently. Some sectors of the French economy did indeed suffer severely. Reports from *intendants* and other royal officers frequently minimized the economic dislocation caused by the persecution, so as not to be seen to be opposing the Court; yet it is plain that there was a significant lessening of productivity. All the same, making full allowance for the state of the evidence, French sources on their own do not lead to the conclusion that the loss of the refugees was crippling. However, the true significance of the Huguenot emigration can only be evaluated when it is remembered that the great majority of the refugees joined Louis XIV's enemies:

144

their contribution in the Dutch Republic, England and elsewhere must be studied. France's loss was immediately doubled because it became her enemies' gain. But the contribution of the Huguenots cannot be quantified in such simple terms: it was out of all proportion to their number. The very nature of their lives as refugees imbued them with greater zeal and energy, forced them into extra efforts to ensure their survival and establishment in their new homes. Some could offer craft skills or military professionalism, with consequences in their countries of adoption which could never have been foreseen in France. Others, fortunate enough to be able to bring with them substantial assets, came to hold a position of great importance in the financial life of their new homelands. As their assets were not tied to land-holding and offices, they were possessed of liquid capital which could be directed comparatively readily into war finance or privateering ventures. The damage done to France by the persecution of her Protestant offspring cannot therefore be calculated by any mere profit and loss measurement of numbers, wealth or even skills. It was indeed one of the weaknesses of Louis XIV's government that it too often thought in such simplistic terms.

Of major importance to the allied cause was the defection of trained French Protestant soldiers. In 1689 the English army was no match for the best forces in Europe, yet at Blenheim (1704) and thereafter the French suffered decisive defeat at its hands. Marshal Vauban estimated the military loss of refugees to enemy forces as 500 or 600 army officers and 10,000 or 12,000 soldiers. Those figures are small by comparison with the total French military establishment, which may have reached some 300,000 at its peak under Louis XIV, but they were sufficient to concern the Marshal – and with good reason. This was no simple loss of trained fighting men but a double one, since the soldiers in question had enlisted with Louis' enemies. Moreover, the factor of motivation must be taken into account.

Consider the case of Samuel de Péchels, Sieur de la Boissonade, who served for a time as a lieutenant in Schomberg's cavalry regiment in Ireland. He was not himself an outstanding soldier, although he founded a military dynasty which gave great service to England – he was the father of Lieutenant-Colonel Jacob de Péchels, grandfather of Lieutenant-Colonel Sir Paul Pechell, great-grandfather of Major-General Sir Thomas Brooke Pechell and great-great-grandfather of Rear-Admiral Sir Samuel and Admiral Sir George Richard Brooke Pechell. In the case of the founder of the line, though, it is his motivation that is of particular interest. In August 1685 he had been at Montauban when his family was afflicted by the *dragonnades*. He, his wife (who was very close to confinement) and their young children were thrown out, drenched by the troopers for sport, later ordered back to their house. In any case they had nowhere to go; both his mother's and his sister's houses had long been filled with soldiers. By the end of the winter of 1685–6, his property had been dispersed; as well as paying for the maintenance of large numbers of soldiers quartered in his house (apparently thirty or more), he had been made responsible for the payment of others quartered in a tavern. Since the family still held to its Protestantism, Samuel's mother and youngest sister were dragged off to a local convent. His wife escaped, and was hidden by a local weaver, but his children were seized. He himself was imprisoned, sent to Aigues-Mortes and later Marseilles, and transported to America in 1687. After a most unpleasant journey during which shipwreck and slavery were narrowly averted, he reached San Domingo. The following year he managed to escape to Jamaica in an English boat, and thence reached London. There he hoped to be reunited with his family, but the reality did not match his expectations. He found instead that his wife, with one boy, was at Geneva, which they had reached, separately, thanks to the help of a guide. His youngest son had died at Montauban, and his daughters were still there, the eldest in a convent. His mother and youngest sister remained imprisoned. This was the background against which he joined his regiment.

Huguenot soldiers who had suffered such experiences could be expected to fight with extra zeal and determination when confronted by French dragoons and their allies. Again and again, in Ireland and Flanders and the Spanish peninsula, at Carrickfergus and Limerick and the Boyne, at Landen and Neerwinden, at Almanza and Alicante, refugee soldiers displayed conspicuous gallantry. After the first siege of Limerick in 1690, Cambon's regiment of foot was left with only six officers able to serve out of seventy-seven. At the battle of the Boyne, when Field-Marshal Schomberg was struck down, he was rallying Caillemotte's Foot, after its commander had been mortally wounded, by pointing at the dragoons and papists on the southern bank of the river and shouting 'there are your persecutors: forward, lads, forward'. While the refugees helped win the battle of the Boyne, and the dash of Ruvigny's Horse carried the day at Aughrim, it was often in defeat that Huguenot courage shone most brightly. The Huguenot cavalry charged with desperate valour to cover the army's retreat at Neerwinden. Galway's Horse at Landen, La Fabrèque's dragoons at Almanza, showed the same mettle. Many Huguenots, including Colonel Frederick Sibourg and Major Francis La Balme Vignoles, displayed courage of an even higher order when they stood fast and died with Major-General John Richards at Alicante in 1709, blown up

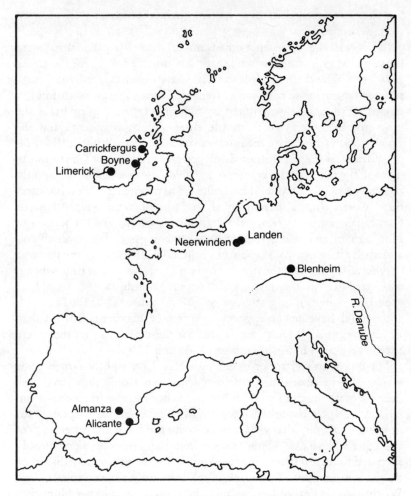

Map 8   Some battles in which refugees opposed Louis XIV

by the 1,200 barrels of French gunpowder (previously inspected by the allies) exploded in a mine. The most extraordinary example of refugee motivation was provided by the regiment raised for the allies by Jean Cavalier in 1706. Shortly afterwards it fought at Almanza, where the regiment found itself facing troops its members had known only too well in their homeland. The result of the confrontation was electrifying on both sides. Disdaining to fire, they rushed at one another with bayonets. A carnage occurred on that part of the battlefield which the experienced Duke of Berwick, the victorious French commander on the day, remembered as long as he lived.

Cavalier's regiment lost over half its men; the French they charged were decimated.

However, the Huguenots had much more to offer than mere bravery. Many of those who had accompanied William when he invaded England were almost immediately reorganized into three refugee regiments for service in Ireland. Their superiority to English troops there in 1689 was noted by Schomberg; he reported that the king got better service from the three French regiments and the cavalry 'than from twice the number of any others'. William III – who was furious at the ingratitude displayed by the House of Commons in disbanding the French regiments in 1698–9 – used them to the full, convinced of their value. The Duke of Marlborough likewise knew their worth. (He also employed the son of a refugee, Adam de Cardonnel, as his secretary throughout his campaigns.) The Earl of Nottingham, too, was certain of their advantages to the government, and spelt these out to Marlborough in 1703: French regiments were easy to raise, lessened the need to call on Englishmen at a time when it was hard to fill the ranks of existing English forces, would be especially suited to any attempt on the French coast from Portugal, and would have fewer expectations and be easier to disband than English regiments. Doubtless it was for these reasons that they were extensively used in Spain between 1706 and 1710.[1]

Marlborough's victories over Louis XIV have rightly earned pride of place in the annals of the British army, but would they have been possible without the French refugees? Schomberg's despatches from Ireland in 1689 remarked, 'we English have stomach enough for fighting: it is a pity that we are not equally fond of some other parts of a soldier's business.' This shows that the refugees were already prepared to regard themselves as English, but that they were disturbed by the amateurishness of English soldiers and military organization. Writing to the Earl of Shrewsbury the same year, another Huguenot officer in Ireland, Colonel La Caillemotte, observed in precisely the same vein that his men were slandered by the suggestion that they were French 'since we have nothing in France but the liberty to breathe the air', but also complained that the English soldiers disliked their different manner of warfare and superior attention to duty.[2] English troops could not hope to be effective against Louis XIV's far more experienced armies until the need for a professional approach was recognized. The French refugee soldiers provided an example of this professionalism throughout the army. Apart from the regiments specifically composed of refugees, C. E. Lart estimated that there were nearly 800 Huguenot officers alone – we have no records of ordinary soldiers – who served in the rest of the British army against

Louis XIV. Very commonly they were specialists in engineering and artillery, as was the case in the other allied armies of the United Provinces and Brandenburg.

Contemporaries concurred with Daniel Defoe's estimate that to make a new army from scratch took three years and 30,000 lives. The time England required was largely bought by Huguenot blood shed in Ireland and Flanders in the Williamite wars. No trained, permanent force had existed in England before Cromwell's New Model army. After the Restoration a new type of standing army had emerged, neutral in politics and concerned solely to carry out the wishes of the civil government, but its achievements in the reigns of Charles II and James II hardly suggested it was likely to prove a major thorn in Louis XIV's side. Discipline and sobriety in the ranks had declined since the days of the New Model. While many of the senior officers were professional in their approach, often having continental experience, perhaps two-thirds of them defected from the army after James's departure out of loyalty to their former commander-in-chief.[3] The majority of the regular officers on the peacetime establishment were not trained soldiers. Regimental traditions were not yet formed; drill and training were inadequate, despite substantial improvement during the reign of James II; no notable strategist or tactician had appeared before the Revolution. The army was traditionally and widely hated and feared within England. The best available English troops were those who had been hired out to foreign states and seen active service abroad, especially in France and the United Provinces; but there were not enough of them. Although they had shown their courage at Tangier and in the Netherlands, bravery alone would not suffice. It was therefore of critical significance that just when her troops would be asked to fight from the Boyne to the Danube and from the Dutch estuaries to the barren hills of the Iberian peninsula, England was presented with a substantial body of veterans who had received their training in the armies of Turenne and Vauban, and whose skill and experience were matched by their motivation. They produced no single outstanding commander. There was little glamour in the professionalism of the refugee troops or engineers like Harcourt or Louis Pettit to attract a historian's attention. But the meteoric rise of the army to European predominance owed much to the Huguenots.

There were other ways in which the Huguenots assisted the war effort. One of William's difficulties was his need to hold together an anti-French alliance through years of uncertainty and often failure. Louis XIV did his best to disrupt that alliance by intimidation or by exploiting sectional interests and national differences. The refugees, with their network of contacts, helped immeasurably with propaganda, diplomacy and intelligence. The part they played in James's downfall, in hardening opinion against Catholicism, in short in making a firm alliance against Louis viable, has already been discussed. During William's reign the British diplomatic service was permeated by foreign Protestants: the Huguenots Henri de Massue de Ruvigny (Earl of Galway), Philibert de Herwarth and Gasper Perrinet d'Arsellières, for example, were envoys in Piedmont and Switzerland. Useful naval intelligence might be gained from refugees newly arrived in England, who were often questioned about ships in the ports from which they had come. Some became spies, employed as far afield as Canada. Others urged plans for fomenting discord in France by stirring up the Protestants remaining there, and Louis always had to watch out for internal attacks which helped divert his troops and attention – witness the Camisard insurrection of the first decade of the eighteenth century, which tied up a complete French army under Marshal de Montrevel even though the Camisards received little external assistance. And refugees surely strengthened the English navy, although their value to it has never been assessed.[4]

Another substantial contribution by the refugees in England to the defeat of Louis XIV brings us into the realm of economics and international trade: their assistance in funding the war effort. England was faced in the 1690s by a war burden that was massive by comparison with the nation's past experience and existing taxation. A generation earlier, at the time of the Restoration, it had been accepted that the Crown needed an ordinary revenue of some £1,200,000 a year. In practice Charles II had to make do for most of his reign with considerably less than this, although under James II the Crown's ordinary revenue attained an average of £1,600,000 p.a. But the demands of the wars waged between 1689 and 1713 (with a precarious peace between 1697 and 1702) were of a different order of magnitude altogether. Those of William's reign cost over £5,000,000 a year, those of Anne's nearly £8,000,000. The experience of the past century – military failures in the 1620s, for instance, or the state of near-bankruptcy brought about by the second and third Anglo-Dutch wars – augured ill for England's chances of survival. That she not only survived but conquered was in large part due to a transformation that took place in the 1690s, the decade of the 'financial revolution', which witnessed the birth of a new world of banks, of stocks and shares, of new credit instruments and a public debt. At the same time the trade of the capital was becoming increasingly cosmopolitan. This transformation was significantly assisted by the refugees – especially those based in the City and the east London suburbs.

The Huguenots took with them into exile 'immense sums, which

Table 4   *Wartime government expenditure levels*[5]

War years	Average expenditure (£million p.a.)
1585–1604	0.5 – 0.6
1651–3	2.8 (+)
1665–7	2.2
1672 and 1674	2.53
1678	2.71
1688–99	5.26
1702–13	7.77

have drawn dry the fountain of commerce' in France, claimed Michel Levassor in 1689 in *The Sighs of France in Slavery, breathing after Liberty*. This cannot be accepted; but the refugees did make a major contribution to Louis's enemies, while in the short term undermining the morale and overseas credit of French traders by their departure. The wealthiest refugees mostly sought asylum in Holland and, to a lesser extent, England. The exiles in London were sharply divided into extremes of prosperity and great poverty, but even so the wealth of the Huguenot leaders remains formidable. Merchants were numerous in proportion to their total company, as was the case in New York and other centres of refugee settlement. Take, as an example, the eldership of the Threadneedle Street congregation at the close of the seventeenth century. The normal pattern in that church was for elders to serve only three or three and a half years, and there was a substantial pool of men of similar status from which replacements could be drawn.

Included in the Consistory[6] between 1698 and 1700 were the wine merchant Pierre Albert, who contributed £7,000 to the New East India loan of 1698; Daniel Brulon, who had been granted the freedom of the city in 1682 for conveying the total catch of French fishermen at Rye to London; Jean Esselbroun, with a turnover of cloth exports to Near Europe in the financial year 1695/6 amounting to £6,900; Jacques du Fay, who had invested £5,000 in government securities in 1692–3 and subscribed £2,800 to the Bank of England in 1694; Louis Gervaise the younger, probably the inspiration behind the foundation of the Royal Lustring Company in 1692, who had subscribed £800 to the Bank of England in 1694 and £3,000 to the Million Bank the following year; Daniel Jamineau, a merchant with worldwide connections whose 1695/6 turnover included nearly £3,000 in imports of currants, sugar and ginger, and over £1,000 in exports of drapery and leather gloves to Europe; and Elie du Puy, contributor of £3,000 to the 1698 East India loan. All these were first-generation refugees, born outside the country.

They were far from being the only wealthy refugee members of the church. René Baudouin was estimated to be worth £15,000 in the mid-1690s. David Bosanquet's turnover in 1695/6 was £13,457; his assets amounted to some £100,000 on his death in 1732. Robert Caillé was a substantial stock dealer, holding £2,450 of Bank stock on his own account in June 1697 and contributing £2,500 to the Bank subscription of 1709. Daniel Hays in that year owned £4,000 Bank stock, over £20,000 East India Company stock and £7,700 in the loan to the Emperor of Germany. Jean du Maistre imported over £5,500 worth of predominantly Italian silk in 1695/6. The prosperous merchant Herman Olmius purchased the manor of Waltham Bury (Essex) from the Earl of Manchester in 1701, and was a prominent Bank stock proprietor and one of the commissioners of the Bank subscription of 1709. Pierre Reneu subscribed £600 to the Tontine of 1693, £2,000 to the Bank of England the following year and £4,000 to the East India loan of 1698, and held £3,425 in the Million Bank by 1701. Other merchants and stock dealers who at one time or other held office in the church include Jean le Platrier, Jean Girardot du Tilleul, Charles Trinquand and Humfroy Willet, all accustomed to thinking in terms of thousands of pounds.

Wealthiest of all may have been Etienne Seignoret, a silk merchant from Lyons who established himself in Lombard Street in partnership with René Baudouin. Twice convicted of trading with France during wartime, he was on the second occasion fined £10,000. The basis for the fine was an official valuation that he was worth between £80,000 and £100,000, although Hilaire Reneu put it at only £50,000. Certainly payment of the fine left him still a very rich man. His turnover in 1695/6 consisted of over £9,000 drapery exports and £7,000 silk and cochineal imports; he was the largest individual holder (£6,581) in the Million Bank in 1701; and in 1709 he subscribed £6,800 to the doubling of the Bank of England's capital, while also holding £14,187 of East India stock.

Such a barrage of figures does not make for easy reading, but does give some indication of the scale on which the wealthier Huguenots could operate. When one considers the many well-known refugee names not to be found in the last paragraph because they were never officers of the Threadneedle Street church in the later seventeenth century – the names of Amyand, Aufrère, Chamier, le Coq, Herwarth, Huguetan, Janssen (Sir Theodore declared an estate of nearly quarter of a million pounds at the time of the 'South Sea

Bubble'), Monginot de Salle, Ruvigny and the like – it becomes possible to see some justification for the computation that the exiles brought with them an average of at least £100 sterling per head. This figure was put forward by Hilaire Reneu or Renu in 1707 in his introduction to a translation of Jean Claude's *Short Account of the Complaints, and Cruel Persecutions of the Protestants in . . . France*. Reneu was as well placed to make a sensible 'guesstimate' as anyone could be, and was considered a balanced and responsible person. Although himself a wealthy man, well connected with Huguenot high society in London, he was deeply involved in refugee relief work and consequently aware of the great poverty of many exiles. He was, moreover, an experienced valuer, whose assessment of the wealth of some refugee silk smugglers in the 1690s seems to have been preferred by the House of Lords to the results of an official enquiry. The figure of not less than £100 per head was a French estimate, but Reneu was prepared to enshrine it in print and therefore must have regarded it as reasonable. If 40–50,000 refugees arrived and settled, this would provide a total of four or five million pounds entering later Stuart England. It is not possible to offer any more reliable assessment, but whatever the true figure, it was obviously substantial. From 1679 onwards informed contemporaries like Halifax and Savile had foreseen the advantages England would reap from the refugee exodus. Their optimism was well justified.

Other distinctive qualities besides their precise assets made the Huguenots valuable to their new country. Pride of place in this respect goes to their network of connections with refugees in other countries and especially the Dutch Republic, with relatives and newly 'converted' Protestants who had stayed in France, and with the descendants of previous Walloon refugees in England. This was, after all, a period when confidence and personal ties and knowledge, the seine of kinship and clientage that bound person to person, was a particularly important factor in international commerce. The Huguenots in exile were ideally placed for trade: they often lived by the sea, they had overseas contacts and fostered close links with other refugee communities. It might seem surprising that they were willing to maintain ties with their previous co-religionists in France, who had abjured Calvinism rather than run the risks they had taken, but they certainly did so. Perhaps, initially at least, such ties multiplied rather than contracted. The 31 elders of the Threadneedle Street church between 1698 and 1700 include four born in London, three in Bordeaux and in Valenciennes, two each in Amiens, Canterbury, Paris and Rouen, and one each in Alzey in the Palatinate, Blois, Boulogne, Chinon, Dieppe, Guernsey, Ile de Ré, Loudun, Montélimar, Nérac, Pittenweem (Fife),

Saintes and Vitry-le-François. So much wealth, so many chains of personal contacts ending in one Consistory room may well have given rise to new trade links. That is speculation. What is certain is that old direct ties persisted. Pierre Albert traded with his family at Bordeaux; Baudouin, Seignoret and François Gruber were fined for persisting in trading with France during wartime, and one of Seignoret's relatives set up a silk smuggling route between London and Lyons; Jacques du Fay was accused of remitting large sums of bullion to France. Scholars have demonstrated that in France itself the new financial empires of *nouveaux convertis* like Thomas Le Gendre or Samuel Bernard were partly founded on contacts with their fellow-countrymen in exile. The international connections of the French Protestant merchants in England, particularly in certain trades like wine and silk, played a significant role in the reorientation and worldwide development of English commerce.

New Huguenot refugees and the descendants of earlier Walloon or French ones frequently worshipped in the same French churches and shared very similar mercantile interests. The two groups influenced one another considerably. Often they are hard for the historian to distinguish, and the older-established elements may be regarded as intermediaries between the newcomers and their host society. Thus in 1681 Thomas Papillon and John Dubois served on the 'English Committee' supervising charity distribution to French refugees, and in 1705 this committee included Sir John Houblon, John Lordell, Charles du Bois, James Denew and Peter Delmé – all descendants of old refugee families that had 'made good' in England. One wonders how far new ideas were transmitted from the Huguenots through more anglicized members of the foreign congregations to the English merchant community at large. This channel of communication was certainly perceived by contemporaries. In 1686 a newsletter reported royal moves against the Threadneedle Street church, and its author was concerned that this might cause the removal not only of many substantial Huguenot merchants 'but many other of our merchants dissenters, who resorted to the said church, and discourage all the rest'. The 'other merchants dissenters' attending the French Church of London were anglicized descendants of earlier refugees, the families of Delmé, Papillon, Houblon, Denew and the like. 'The rest' indicates the bulk of English merchants who were Dissenters; and the newsletter author believed that between them these three groups possessed 'six parts of ten of the moving cash that drives the trade of the whole nation'.[7]

What was the effect of the arrival of the new refugees on the motivation of the older French/Walloon group? Did it become more willing to hazard its resources during the financial revolution? How far did the newly available expertise and capital backing increase its confidence? Motivation cannot be measured. However, descendants of earlier refugees did play an important role in the developments of the 1690s. Of the twenty-four initial Directors of the Bank of England in 1694, seven came from the Huguenot-Walloon camp although only one (Janssen) was a new arrival: Sir John Houblon, the first Governor of the Bank, Sir James Houblon, Abraham Houblon, John Lordell, James Denew, Theodore Janssen and Samuel Lethieullier.

These men believed the new financial ventures would work, and they transmitted their confidence to the London commercial scene at large. Behind that confidence lay their contacts with the Huguenot community, and the refugee experience of their own families which assured them of the significance of liquid capital assets available for investment. Uncommitted ready cash gave the more fortunate and wealthy among the new arrivals a great start in the foreign mercantile world to which they came, particularly when combined with the refugee's determination to secure a favourable position in society. No wonder it was commonly said later that a drop of Huguenot blood in the veins was worth a thousand pounds a year. In 1744, 542 London merchants signed a loyal address to the king. Over a hundred bore French names, the great majority Huguenot, and many of them were of formidable substance.[8] When the descendants of the old Walloons and the English merchants of the last decade of the seventeenth century perceived in the new refugees in their midst a source of strength for the English economy, their vision was sound. They noted, too, something else about them: a financial expertise developed in dealing with *rentes* in France, described by Mrs Alice Clare Carter as 'a technical skill which acted on our financial developments as their industrial skills acted on our trade'. It is significant that a Huguenot, John Castaing, was responsible for the early list of market prices in government loans, 'The Course of the Exchange', from which evolved the Stock Exchange Official List, and that the officers of the French Church of London felt confident enough to invest surplus charitable funds in the Bank of England even as early as 1695.

The Huguenots played a significant role in the financial revolution. The liquidity of their assets and their preparedness to invest, the confidence they encouraged in the London money market, their technical financial skills, their superior motivation and especially their connections were all important. But these considerations are impossible to measure, whereas thanks to the researches of Mrs Carter and Professor P. G. M. Dickson the actual contribution of the refugees to Bank stock and similar investments is known. Of the £1,200,000 subscribed to the Bank of England in 1694, 123 newly arrived Huguenots provided £104,000; this may be taken as a minimum figure, since Professor Dickson seems to have identified Huguenot names solely from published denization and naturalization records, which may not be wholly adequate as a basis for identification. By the time the fourth dividend list for Bank Stock was drawn up in 1697, just over £190,000 out of a total of some £2,200,000 was held by Huguenots; if the investments of the older Walloon immigrant families like the Houblons are included the figure rises to around £330,000 or 15% of the total. Huguenots were less prominent in the Tontine loan of 1693 but more prominent in the Million Bank. Overall Mrs Carter summarizes the cash contribution of the new generation of refugees to the early English Funds as being 'of the order of 10%', a percentage which increased during the early eighteenth century.

A tenth of the Funds is a good deal less than many contemporaries believed the refugees supplied, but it remains significant. It is evident that refugee resources helped the London mercantile community survive the pressures of the 1690s and the War of the Spanish Succession, and thus assisted the country at large to continue the fight against Louis XIV. Another contribution to be mentioned in this regard involves privateering. Dr D. W. Jones has recently drawn attention to the way in which the war conditions of the 1690s affected some groups of London merchants much more seriously than others. Baltic merchants, for instance, were kept fully occupied by the demand for naval supplies, and the export trade to Dutch and German ports boomed; but Iberian trade contracted and wine merchants were particularly badly hit. The desire to reallocate resources as trade contracted, Jones argues, made the wine merchants 'the common denominator . . . in both the great [stock] flotations of 1694 and 1698'. While most may have redeployed their assets in this way, some preferred to launch themselves into the task of outfitting ships for systematic privateering operations against the French; these included Jean de Grave, an officer of the Threadneedle Street church and a member of a particularly successful syndicate with over sixty captures to its credit, who did not invest in either of the great joint stock flotations of the decade. Other Iberian and wine merchants who were elders of the City church and part owners of privateers were David Garrick (whose ship was called *The Protestant Cause*) and Jacques Denew; but the latter also subscribed £2,000 to the Bank of England in 1694, and clearly did not put all his eggs into one basket as Jean de Grave seems to have done. Perhaps de Grave was so incensed by the treatment he had received in France, where many dragoons had been quartered upon him and he had been forced into hiding at Rouen, that he found the outfitting of privateers a pleasingly direct, as well as profitable, form of contribution to the war effort.

All in all, the significance of the refugees in enabling England to sustain her war effort was very great. Huguenot soldiers won time in which to remodel the English army, and gave it a disciplined backbone when it was inexperienced and vulnerable in the 1690s. Huguenot connections assisted diplomatic ties, the dissemination of anti-French propaganda, and the expansion and reorientation of English trade. Huguenot money helped fund the war. The Revocation of the Edict of Nantes was therefore a major factor in Louis's defeat.

This is not the conclusion of the one serious modern attempt to evaluate the significance of the loss of the refugees to France, Professor W. C. Scoville's *The Persecution of Huguenots and French Economic Development*, published in 1960. Based on a formidable study of French archives, this book asks whether the Revocation was the principal cause of the French economic decline. It concludes that it was not, but that the decline was due rather to extensive and costly involvement in warfare, bad harvests, changes in consumer taste and decreased demand for luxury goods, and growing prosperity in other countries such as England and the Dutch Republic. The book is packed with valuable information, but its conclusions and chapter summaries too often seem to defy the evidence that has been so carefully assembled. In his determination to argue that the Revocation was not the principal, but merely one, cause of French economic decline, Scoville tends to undervalue the evidence for disruption caused by the persecutions in France. French losses in terms of sailors will serve as one illustration of the problems inherent in his approach.

It is clear that the prospect of losing trained sailors worried Louis XIV's government and that the prospect of attracting skilled seafarers appealed to Englishmen. Henry Savile noted in 1681 that many French seamen were Protestants, and seven years later the Venetian ambassador at Paris reported that the majority of sailors along the western coast of France had departed. The loss deeply concerned Louis's ministers Seignelay and Louvois, and repatriation of refugee sailors was a high priority for Bonrepaus, the French envoy extraordinary sent to the Netherlands and England specifically to entice skilled refugees to return to France. The envoy, indeed, believed that the majority of the refugees were 'gens de mer'. In the early 1690s the French Marshal Vauban estimated the naval loss of refugees to enemy forces as 8,000 or 9,000 able seamen.

Scoville suggests that Vauban's estimate of numbers and the Venetian ambassador's report were both exaggerated, but offers no reliable evidence with which to support his contention. The obvious concern of the French government, the opinion of the Venetian ambassador and the estimate made by Vauban all indicate substantial losses. The sole evidence cited to the contrary comes from Bonrepaus, who wrote in 1686 that the number of French seamen serving in England and Holland was probably only some 800. But Bonrepaus, as Scoville himself points out in a different context, had important reasons for underestimating the effects of the Revocation: by so doing he emphasized his own successes and minimized the general failure of his mission. Not a shred of evidence is provided to support Scoville's own suggestion that 2,000 or 3,000 sailors and captains might have left France because of religion, and the percentages and fractions that Scoville proceeds to offer based on that estimate are, therefore, quite spurious. In short, the evidence adduced in Scoville's book is inadequate to substantiate his conclusion 'that religious persecution was not the paramount depressant of French shipping'. A similar observation could be made in other fields. Moreover, Scoville's time-span for studying the effect of the persecutions is often too short. In the case of the French marine he asks 'whether the situation anywhere was appreciably different after the Revocation from what it had been shortly before', and then compares figures for Bordeaux for 1682 and 1686–8; but many French Protestants – and, significantly, many *wealthy* French Protestants – had already fled their homeland before and during 1681 (cf. table 2).

Scoville argues that French economic decline was due less to the exodus of the refugees than to extensive warfare, changes in taste and declining demand for luxury products, bad harvests, and greater prosperity in the countries that were France's competitors and enemies. The point, surely, is that all those areas except the quality of the harvests were affected by the Huguenot dispersion. Without the support of refugee troops, William's obstinate resistance to French domination in the 1690s could well have been pre-empted by defeat on the battlefields of Ireland at the start of the decade, and England would certainly have found it far harder to come to terms with the initial superiority of the French army. Without the exodus of skilled men able to meet demands for French fashions in the areas where they settled, the market for luxury French exports would have remained stable. The development of industries such as linen, silk or paper, for which Stuart England had previously been largely dependent on French imports, strengthened English self-reliance, improved England's balance of trade and provided France with stiff competition in other markets. The emergence of financial institutions such as the Bank of England enabled the country to carry the massive burden of war, and to keep pressure on the French economy in so doing. It is therefore not possible, as Scoville attempts, to assess the damage done to the French economy by the Huguenot exodus primarily by examining industries within France itself. A broader canvas is needed, extending to the transformation of England taking place around 1700 in which the refugees played such a significant role.

This is not to belittle the native English contribution to the changes that took place. It is self-evident that the battles of Blenheim and Ramillies could not have been won without the genius of Marlborough and trained English soldiers, that the Bank of England would never have been viable but for the knowledge and skills of well-established London merchants, or that London would have been one of the wonders of the early eighteenth-century world even if its growth and range of fashions had not been assisted by the Huguenots. But the refugees cannot with justice be ignored or confined to the obscurity of specialist monographs. While precise quantification is impossible, their influence on England was much greater than the mere number of 40,000–50,000 immigrants would suggest, and substantial enough in every sphere we have examined for historians to neglect at their peril.

No wonder that suggestions that Louis XIV should be forced to re-enact the Edict of Nantes were speedily abandoned during peace negotiations; as Lord Portland explained in 1709, people in England and the Netherlands simply would not countenance the thought of the return to France of so much industry, ability and wealth. It is not as mischievous as might at first appear that the English *Dictionary of National Biography* should open with the Huguenot Jacques Abbadie and close with the Dutch military and political family of Zuylestein. Both came in the train of William of Orange, and the national transformation which took place in later Stuart England in things political, military, commercial, financial, cultural and fashionable owes much to the foreigners to whom, reluctantly or enthusiastically, the country opened its doors.

10

The Process of Assimilation

'I'll make you laugh', wrote an elderly Plymouth resident, Pentecost Barker, in 1762. 'A gentleman employed a gardener to pick snails from the walls, and then, coming into the garden behind his back, heard him, in killing the snails, say "—— take the French! When they came here first, they would not suffer a snail to live; but they are now grown so proud, that we are overrun with them".' Clearly the Huguenots were from early days associated in the eyes of Englishmen with strange foreign ways. Equally clearly, to the writer of the letter those ways had been left behind and the descendants of the refugees assimilated into English society. He looked back through the window of his memory:

> Those, of whom I remember many scores, who came from France
> in 1685–6, etc., are mostly dead; and their offspring are more
> English than French, and will go to the English Church, though
> some few may come to us. What an alteration Time makes! There
> was . . . a French Calvinist Church, and a Church of England
> French Church here, besides a Church at Stonehouse. Many
> women in wooden shoes – very poor, but very industrious – living
> on limpets, snails, garlick and mushrooms. . . . When I went to
> Rochelle, in the year 1713, I brought over several pair of *sabot de
> bois* (so they call them) for some at Stonehouse. But they are all
> dead and gone.[1]

In 1950 a United Nations sub-committee on the prevention of discrimination defined minorities as 'those non-dominant groups in a population which possess and wish to preserve ethnic, religious or linguistic traditions or characteristics markedly different from those of the rest of the population.' There are other sorts of minorities, for instance those which would like to be fully assimilated into the majority, yet find themselves resisted; but this United Nations definition best fits the Huguenots, who possessed and sought to preserve their own ecclesiastical organization and their own language.

Sociologists suggest that for such a minority, a substantial degree of assimilation takes three generations. Pentecost Barker's letter, written 77 years after the Revocation, agrees with this estimate. Certainly the Walloons were well ensconced in English society by the time Huguenots began flooding in from Louis XIV's France, while the Englishness of the refugees of the later seventeenth century could hardly be questioned by the time of the Napoleonic wars.

The process of assimilation cannot, however, be categorized simply. Movement in that direction could take place very soon after the arrival of a refugee, perhaps by the translation of a name (Wood for Dubois, for instance, Inglishe for Langlois, or White for Blanc). Fontaine's *Memoirs* show that his wife's name, de Boursaquotte, had been anglicized to Bursicott as early as 1686. Unfortunately, it is normally impossible for a historian working on English records to know whether a rendering was approved by the refugee himself, or was merely the product of the thought processes of an English scribe. At the other extreme, there remain to this day a few families or individuals so acutely conscious of their Huguenot background that it is hard to insist that they have been fully assimilated even yet. Sometimes this consciousness appears as an exceptional degree of attachment to British ways. R. V. Jones's account of Scientific Intelligence in the Second World War, *Most Secret War*, recalls how Sir Henry Tizard, on hearing his family of Huguenot descent described as 'more English than the English', replied 'with a name like mine, you have to be!' (Perhaps he would have been less touchy had he known that King George VI, President Roosevelt and Winston Churchill were also of Huguenot descent, Churchill through the American Jeromes who came originally from La Rochelle.) In the same vein Tizard's contemporary August Courtauld is described by his biographer Nicholas Wollaston as 'peculiarly English'.

A modern English member of a distinguished Huguenot family like Le Fanu or Lefroy, Minet or Ouvry might well act in a particular way or within a particular framework as the conscious or subconscious result of an acute awareness of his family's past. Of especial interest are the works of the New Zealand novelist Yvonne du Fresne, who inhabits a world fashioned and given meaning by her refugee forefathers. The preface to her recent novel *The Book of Ester* (1982) depicts her early recollections of 'the Huguenot women' sitting in their New Zealand homes earlier this century and surveying 'their lands and their history': 'the fires of the Reformation still reach out their long fingers to us in New Zealand'. This could hardly be said to be true for most modern New Zealanders, even the small minority of them with obvious Huguenot connections, but no reader of her writings could question the vivid reality of her vision for the novelist herself.

The refugees reached England the possessors of a particular language and style, but few groups can – even if they wish – live permanently between two cultures. And it is far from certain that the Walloons and Huguenots did so wish. True, they were attached to their own background and customs, above all to their Calvinism. Initially they may have hoped to return to their homelands. But after the Duke of Parma's advances in the Netherlands during the 1580s, and after the later failure of William and Anne to incorporate clauses for the re-establishment of Protestantism in their peace treaties with France, it became clear that any such hopes were doomed to disappointment. Both Walloons and Huguenots (the former perhaps the more reluctantly) faced reality and accepted eventual assimilation. Even before that, unlike other Frenchmen of their day who came into contact with England, they had mastered spoken English on a colloquial level; however attached they were to their native ways, they simply could not afford to do otherwise.

Various indices of the degree and rate of assimilation can be used. Free intermarriage is probably the best criterion of full assimilation, but it is hard to establish reliable figures. English scribes in English churches naturally tended to write French names in an English way, while French scribes in French churches similarly wrote English names in a French manner. Place of birth is helpful only with first-generation refugees. Consequently the only satisfactory basis for generalizations would be a large-scale effort at the reconstitution of individual families. As is indicated in the appendix, which should be read in conjunction with this chapter, major difficulties stand in the way of such an undertaking. Without it, one can but offer impressions. Curiously, the impressions are likely to be more reliable for the Walloons than for the later Huguenots, because their records are more satisfactory. The marriage acts of the 1690s, described in the appendix, are largely responsible: so great was their impact that despite a much increased congregation, the French Church of London in the early eighteenth century celebrated less than a quarter of the marriages of the early seventeenth century.

Most new arrivals married other refugees, although there were always some exceptions, as in 1682 when a poor Huguenot Jacques Duqua, 'having recently come from France for the sake of religion, or so he says', shocked the Consistory of the Threadneedle Street church by marrying an English girl (to whom he could not speak) within a fortnight of the burial of his former wife. Second-generation marriages were also frequently contracted within the refugee orbit, and one of the things that annoyed Archbishop Laud in the 1630s was that the children of strangers did not inter-marry with the English. However, their offspring were much more likely to marry members of the host society, although a few families continued aloof for a further generation. The situation is confused by marriages between Huguenots and foreigners from other nations, brought together by psychological, religious and mercantile ties: thus the German immigrant Melchior Wagner, who was naturalized in 1709, married Mary Ann Teulon, the daughter of one Huguenot refugee, while their son George married the granddaughter of another.[2]

Another criterion for assimilation is the degree of adherence to their church discipline achieved by the Walloon congregations. The records show that the sixteenth-century refugee churches sought to prevent members marrying English folk. They had ecclesiastical reasons for the stand they took, since they viewed their churches as closer to apostolic purity than the Anglican Church with its episcopacy, and wished to see them maintained as 'candles to the world'. Time was to show that practical considerations were also relevant. In some parts of the country, Norwich for instance, the Walloons paid contributions towards the maintenance of the English parochial ministry and (probably) poor relief, as well as to their own church, from the early days of their settlement; in other cases this double assessment came later, as at Canterbury, where contributions to English poor relief funds were introduced in the middle of the seventeenth century. Strangers could not escape the burden by becoming denizens, nor were their children freed from it although they had been born in England. Where such a state of affairs existed, there was a strong financial inducement to members – especially those born in England, who were likely to feel less need of protection – to try to claim that they were Anglicans.[3]

Fortunately for the continued existence of the foreign churches, there was an equally strong inducement to city councils to resist any such claim, since it would inevitably transfer a greater share of the burden of poor relief to the local English authorities. The case of the English-born Denis Lermyte (or Lermitt or L'Hermite) of Norwich, who fought a long battle to avoid paying double dues in the second decade of the seventeenth century, assumed sufficient importance to reach the Privy Council. The local and central government officials who heard the case were as insistent as the Walloon church that Lermyte and two other principal members of the congregation, Joel Desormeaux and Samuel Camby, 'rich in means and refractory in condition', should be forced to submit. In the 1620s that was still practicable, but fifty years later it was not. Until 1665 the Consistory of the French Church of London suspended members who married 'aux Anglois', ignoring the ecclesiastical discipline which required them to publish their banns in due form in their foreign church as well. Thereafter it increasingly recognized its powerlessness, and in 1683 it conceded that those marrying in English churches without publishing banns in the French one should not even be cited to appear before it. Meanwhile it had become the turn of Anglican officials to be concerned when descendants of refugee ancestors long dead were married in their foreign church without banns being published in their English parishes. In one such case in 1676 the ecclesiastical court at Canterbury suspended Vital de Lon, the minister who celebrated the marriage, and the two he married, John Six and Mary Le Hook, both of whom (and their parents before them) were said to be English born.[4]

The history of the French-speaking congregations offers a sound guide to the rate of the assimilation process. Between the sixteenth and late seventeenth centuries, churches of early foundation changed from being predominantly Walloon with a minority French element to 'anglicized Walloon' and finally became unequivocally French. Take for example the officers of the French Church of London. At the end of Elizabeth's reign they were largely Walloon, but by the 1640s over 45 per cent had been born in England, while the remainder born overseas were as often from France as from the Spanish Low Countries. Half a century later, after the Huguenot influx of the 1680s, the Walloon element had become insignificant, and those born in England were greatly outnumbered by those born in France. Maps 9 and 10 contrast the birthplaces of the elders alone, without the deacons, for the 1650s and the 1690s.

A similar picture can be painted for the other congregations of early foundation. Those at Norwich and Southampton both contained more English than Walloon or French families at the time of Laud's attack in the 1630s. The situation was slightly different at Canterbury, where – as in London – the congregation had recently been increased by renewed immigration from the Continent, but there too about a third of the heads of families had been born in England.

It has been observed that the careful maintenance of their church discipline assisted the survival of the earlier refugee communities. The Huguenots of the later seventeenth century found themselves in an environment less ecclesiastically strict. The very number of their congregations, the development of new churches conforming to the Anglican liturgy alongside the non-conformist ones, and a widespread English and international trend towards greater freedom of expression for individual conscience combined to place insuperable difficulties in

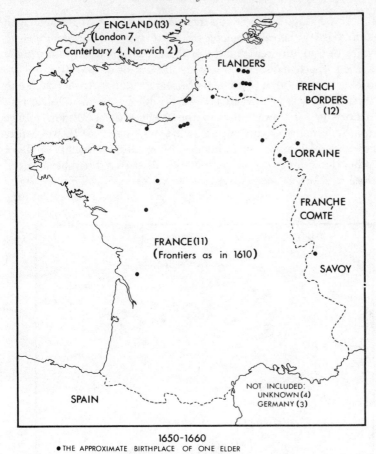

Map 9 Birthplaces of the 43 elders of the French Church of London, 1650–60

the way of Consistories that wished to enforce the old ways. Moreover, while the churches of sixteenth-century foundation had been constantly reinforced and reinvigorated during the Stuart period by a stream of new refugees, the stream diminished to a trickle during the eighteenth century. The result was that the Huguenots tended to be absorbed by the host community rather more speedily than the Walloons had been. To judge from baptismal entries the largest French congregation, at Threadneedle Street in London, probably numbered just over 7,000 between the 1680s and the first decade of the eighteenth century. By the 1710s and 1720s it had decreased to some 5,000. A generation later that figure had been halved; in the 1740s and 1750s it numbered around 2,500. The loss in the next generation was still more striking, and between the 1770s and 1790s its size averaged around 900. By the early nineteenth century the figure had fallen to only one or two hundred, and the process of assimilation was virtually completed.[5] Such statistics substantiate the lament of Jacob Bourdillon, whose sermon marking fifty years of service to the Artillery Church in Spitalfields was printed in 1782. Bourdillon was then 78, having been born in 1704 and called to the Artillery in 1731. His jubilee sermon reflected the experience of what must have been a frequently disheartening lifetime of ministry. Nine of the twenty refugee churches flourishing in London when he had arrived had been forced to close, and others seemed set to follow suit. (Bourdillon was right: by 1800 only eight remained, and by 1900, only three.) Worse, the

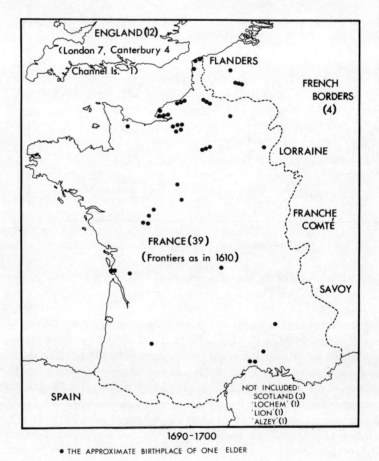

ENGLAND (12)
(London 7, Canterbury 4
Channel Is. 1)
FLANDERS
FRENCH
BORDERS
(4)
LORRAINE
FRANCHE
COMTÉ
FRANCE (39)
(Frontiers as in 1610)
SAVOY
SPAIN
NOT INCLUDED:
SCOTLAND (3)
'LOCHEM' (1)
'LION' (1)
'ALZEY' (1)

1690-1700

● THE APPROXIMATE BIRTHPLACE OF ONE ELDER

Map 10   Birthplaces of 61 elders of the French Church of London, 1690–1700

French language was neglected, the descendants of refugees appeared ashamed of their ancestors, and the zeal of those who had fled from France seemed to have died with them.

While the strictest possible adherence to church discipline could not prevent the eventual assimilation of the Huguenots, it could slow down the process. It is not mere accident that while all the conformist congregations in London have vanished, the one French church still surviving today has always maintained its Calvinist way of doing things. Another factor retarding assimilation was the clustering of refugees in certain areas. Ghettos have always been characteristic of refugee settlements, and just as the English Protestant exiles of Queen Mary's reign headed for a mere handful of continental cities, so both Walloons and Huguenots preferred the company of their fellows. The thickest concentrations were at Canterbury and in the western and eastern suburbs of London. At Canterbury, Francis Cross wrote at the close of the last century, the aliens on arriving in Elizabeth's reign

> had for the most part been domiciled in the parishes of St Alphege, St Mary Northgate, St Peter, Holy Cross, and St Mildred, within easy access to the river; and in these parts of the city the foreign element continued for more than a century exceedingly large. Even now the old houses by the narrow water-ways are strikingly suggestive of Flanders; strange names are common on the signboards; and many of the people bear in their features traces of their descent from Netherland or French ancestors.

The settlers at Norwich were likewise concentrated in certain areas, nearly half of the 4,000 aliens present in 1571 living in two of the twelve city wards, Westwymer and Mydlewymer. While the communities at Canterbury, Norwich and Spitalfields were deeply involved in the weaving trade, the settlement in the west London suburbs around Leicester Fields and Soho was not. Lacking ties of craft organization, frequently brushing shoulders with the English high society which provided the principal market for their fashionable products, and divided between conformist and non-conformist congregations, the refugees in this area merged into an English environment comparatively quickly. But in the eastern suburbs, under the watchful eye of the Threadneedle Street church with its annexe in Spitalfields, the situation was different. Here the Huguenots were almost all non-conformist, and the majority were initially employed in one trade; and here, perhaps longer than anywhere else in England, they maintained their own identity.

It was well understood by contemporaries that there was a connection between the clustering of refugees and the maintenance of their language. For example *A Letter to the French Refugees concerning their Behaviour to the Government*, published in 1710, complained that they seemed 'to make as it were a separate body in the nation' by persisting in using French and living together rather than dispersing. Language had always been of special importance to Protestants; in the south of France during the sixteenth century the Calvinists had been instrumental in spreading one universal French language in order to replace the Latin used in the Roman Catholic worship they rejected. The desire to retain their mother tongue was particularly strong amongst the Walloons, and the churches established in Elizabeth's reign long sought to ensure that French, not English, was spoken at meetings of church officials. Thus the rules governing the company of deacons drawn up by the French Church of London in 1648 laid down that special permission from the President was necessary before English could be used, on penalty of payment of a fine. The decree of the 1658 Colloquy that only French was to be used during its deliberations also indicates that a problem existed. Nevertheless in their larger congregations the French/Walloon community managed to maintain its language for over a century.[6]

Jacob Bourdillon's jubilee sermon shows that even where they were most densely concentrated, in Spitalfields, the Huguenots were not so successful. Perhaps they did not wish to be. Frenchmen of their time, even those who found themselves across the Channel for long periods, were not normally interested in learning English; the classic case is that of the diplomat and *littérateur* Charles de St Evremond, who finally came to understand English only after a lengthy stay in later Stuart England, and never spoke it. Undoubtedly very few refugees were in the fortunate position of the minister André Lortie from La Rochelle, destined to become rector of Barton, Nottinghamshire, who claimed to have spoken English since childhood. Most, both ministers and laity, had little or no English when they arrived. If as intelligent and literate a person as St Evremond was so slow in mastering the language of his adopted country, why should the Huguenots have fared any better? Yet they seem to have done so. Some indeed had difficulty, like another highly educated man, Abraham Tessereau, who attributed his problems to his advanced years, or Henry Pujolas, Anglican minister at Parson Drove in the Cambridgeshire Fenland from 1692 to 1749, who was described as having an imperfect command of English even at the age of 83. And some had no inclination to make the effort: reporting to Archbishop Sancroft his wish to confer Anglican orders on a French minister, the Bishop of St Asaph added that he 'does not intend to continue here, and therefore he will not learn to speak English, but reserves himself for the first opportunity of returning into his own country . . . as soon as ever he sees an abatement of this present persecution'. But it is known that other refugees like Paul Girardot in 1686 were determined to master English quickly. *Forms of Prayer used in the Reformed Churches in France. . .* was published in London in 1699 'for the use of such of the French nation as do desire to learn English'.[7] The needs of commerce demanded that skill. And there are indications in the French church registers that English was early adopted on a significant scale. The records of the diaconate of the Threadneedle Street church for the 1690s include frequent references to the 'Flemish church' (rather than *temple*) and to 'communion' (rather than *cène*). *Ouvrier en soye*, used in the registers of the French Church of London and La Patente, Spitalfields before 1700, was thereafter replaced by the English 'weaver', although that was such a hard word for Frenchmen to spell that William Minet noted no fewer than thirty-eight variations in the records of the two churches.

The more disillusioned migrants feel about the environment from which they have come, the speedier the process of assimilation is likely to be. Years of cynical manipulation of loopholes in already oppressive legislation, the violence of the *dragonnades* and finally the repeal of a 'perpetual and irrevocable' guarantee combined to convince most later seventeenth-century refugees that they had little immediate chance of returning to France. After 1685 such expectations as they retained depended on divine intervention, or on William's ability to force a reversal of policy on Louis XIV by diplomatic and military means, which never seemed very likely although the subject was raised during the negotiations before the Peace of Ryswick. By the time of the first of Marlborough's great victories at Blenheim in 1704 nearly twenty years had elapsed since the Revocation, and any lingering hopes were dashed when the Treaty of Utrecht (1713) failed to incorporate clauses benefiting French Protestants. It was not until 1787 that Louis XVI granted them the *droit d'Indigènat*. By then the passage of time, coupled with repeated Anglo-French wars which encouraged descendants of refugees to emphasize their loyalty to England, meant that assimilation of the refugees was virtually complete.

Their hopes of return to their homeland bleak, the Huguenots in England had scant choice. A very few did retreat unobtrusively back to France, but most were faced with the prospect of establishing themselves permanently where they were or migrating again, to Ireland, perhaps, or to the New World. (Examples of such multi-migration, which was common, will be found in the appendix). In any event, they were confronted by the need to accept an English-speaking environment. The alternatives had not been so clear-cut for the earlier wave of refugees, largely because the political situation on the Continent was then much more fluid. Until late in the sixteenth century Protestantism had continued to make territorial gains, and the defeat of the Armada, the accession of the former Protestant Henry of Navarre to the French throne, and the survival of the Dutch rebels and their eventual success in forcing a truce on Spain were all events offering hope to the Protestant cause. Some of those who sought asylum in England in the earlier period never had any intention of staying and could not have perceived themselves as refugees. The church at Rye, for instance, flourished for short periods when the congregation at Dieppe was disturbed by the tide of events in France in 1562, 1567–9, 1572, 1577, 1585 and finally 1622, then on each occasion disappeared as its members sailed back across the Channel.

For a variety of reasons, then, the sixteenth-century immigrants resisted assimilation rather longer than the more numerous seventeenth-century Huguenot refugees. But while the latter were prepared to face facts, they also wished to keep their options open as long as possible and to preserve memories of their French background. A few of their number, acknowledging that there was no immediate hope of return to their homeland, were concerned to plan for the future: when the minister Charles Piozet urged the establishment of French academies in England, he argued they would maintain the French language and background against the day when God re-established the churches in France and trained pastors again became needed. Most refugees, less farsighted, awaited events more passively, merely preserving such ties as they could. Since it was their religious belief that brought them across the Channel, it is hardly surprising that it was in their congregations that those links were most visibly expressed.

As we saw in chapter 2, geographical factors played a large part in deciding where Huguenots sought safety. Consequently they usually found groups from their provinces already in existence when they arrived in their new home town. Moreover when practicable refugees often travelled in groups. Ninety per cent of the largest single monthly influx of newcomers reaching the French Church of London, in May 1687, came from what is now the Département of Seine-Maritime, almost all from within the triangle formed by Dieppe, Le Havre and Rouen. In such cases provincial ties were not even temporarily disrupted. Ministers also kept a check on the whereabouts of their old flocks, so that when the pastor Estienne Dusoul appealed for assistance he was able to list the present locations of refugee members of the congregation he had once superintended at Rennes,

Britanny.[8] Sometimes they acted as focal points around whom provincial groups gathered. When four ministers founded the church at Hungerford Market in London, they did so, they claimed, at the insistence of former members of their congregations in France. After the closure of the non-conformist church known as 'Le Petit Charenton' in 1705, its members seem to have shown similar loyalty by walking to hear their previous pastors at La Patente, Soho, rather than simply joining the nearest available congregation, which was conformist.

Because refugees wished to maintain contact with others from their home districts in France, individual congregations may have been founded as a result of provincial contacts or have developed a regional bias. This is not easy to prove, since places of origin are given only erratically in the registers according to the whim of their keepers, but an examination of entries in its first five years of existence suggests that La Patente, Spitalfields initially had many members from Poitou (especially Niort) and Normandy. Similarly, the second church of the Artillery drew on Dauphiné and Dieppe; St Jean, Spitalfields, on Normandy (especially the pays de Caux) and Picardy; St Martin Orgars on Paris; and the church of Leicester Fields on Saintonge, Normandy and the Paris basin. The names of some churches ('Le Petit Charenton', 'La Tremblade') also imply continuing regional loyalties, and state relief was at first administered through *bureaux* according to the province of origin of those assisted.

The provincial affiliations of the Huguenots were again shown in the creation of a series of Friendly Societies in the late seventeenth and eighteenth centuries. They proved to be a significant contribution to England's Huguenot heritage, for they were the first in the country (although the old Guilds had had similar functions) and served as models for later English Friendly Benefit Societies. The earliest actually predated the Revocation; the 'Société des Enfants de Nîmes' was founded in 1683 for refugees from 'Nismes, St Cezaire, Cayfargues, Bouillargues, Courbessac et terres adjacentes'. The Society of Parisians claimed to have been formed four years later and that of St Onge – still active today as the Society of St Onge and Angoumois – dates from 1701. For many years 'The Bachelors', instituted in Spitalfields in 1697, admitted only French Protestants and their descendants. The Norman Friendly Society came into existence in 1703 and the more localised Society of Lintot in 1708. Both survived into the 1960s, as did a third body connected with the same province, the Protestant Refugees from High and Low Normandy Friendly Society, which was founded at the remarkably late date of 1764. The Society of Dauphiné was formed in 1702, and that of

Picardy was flourishing by 1708; it is quite likely that others existed by 1710 but have left no traces. A feast of rather uncalvinistic character held at Paddington by the 'Méridionaux' in 1715 is described in a pamphlet in the British Library. 'The Friendly Society' was instituted by Huguenot refugees in 1720, while the 'Société des Provinces du Poictou, Xaintonge, et Pays d'Aunix' was founded two years later and the 'Société du Poitou et du Loudunois' may also have been of early eighteenth century foundation.

These associations had similar aims. As the rules drawn up at the inauguration of the Society of Dauphiné explained, their intention was the creation of 'a kind of family' united in peace and brotherly love. Members met together for occasional communal meals and sermons, but the principal purpose behind the societies was relief of the poor and sick. Funds were accumulated from entry fees and regular subsequent payments, and, once a certain period had elapsed after he had joined, a member of the association became eligible for a weekly pension should the need arise. Assistance was also available to ensure a decent burial for financial members. The societies flourished; 200 years after its foundation the Society of Lintot, paying a sickness benefit of 21 shillings a week and a pension of 6s 6d to members aged 65 and over, had sixty members and a capital of £2,846.[9]

Through such Friendly Societies based on regional ties, the Huguenots tried not only to give one another practical support but to keep alive their past heritage. Present-day experience shows just how hard that is. In modern England, Sikhs may organize themselves in the first generation in terms of narrow homeland loyalties, but in the second they tend to move towards the formation of a broader South Asian ethnic unit; West Indians may be Jamaican or Grenadian in the first generation but share a more general black creole culture in the second. Sociologists commonly view this as a reaction against white discrimination, but it is surely also a sign that provincialism cannot thrive unless the home locality is a known reality. So with the Huguenots; as time passed provincial loyalties slowly came to seem less important, and those families most aware of their continental background identified with one another more and more under a French national umbrella. This process was doubtless encouraged in a negative way by the decline in size of congregations during the eighteenth century, but also influenced positively by the development of institutions coping with the needs of the refugees as a body whatever their place of origin – the *Maisons de Charité* of Soho and Spitalfields, for instance, and especially the French Protestant Hospital (plate 10b). *La Providence*, as this became known, opened its doors in 1718, catering for the elderly and infirm and also, at first, for younger people ill in body or mind. For most of the eighteenth century it housed around 225 residents, offering them security and a caring environment at a time when London was a frightening place for most such afflicted people. A fascinating if critical tribute to the continuing quality of care offered by *La Providence* in the nineteenth century was provided by one of the Charity Commissioners' Inspectors in 1875. Imbued by a deep sense of what he conceived to be proper class distinctions and evidently appalled that the poor should be so well housed, he praised the economy with which the Hospital was run (the Treasurer, Secretary and Architect all providing their services free of charge), but continued:

> The Hospital including the Chapel is a handsome building, too handsome indeed for the purpose for which it was designed viz: the board and lodging of aged weavers and weaveresses, ordinary labourers and domestic servants who are at the most but second poor. . . . This Institution . . . is eminently adapted to aged and decayed French Protestant Governesses who in exercise of their vocation have been accustomed to more care better accommodation and greater consideration than were ever dreamt of in the wretched hovels of Spitalfields.

La Providence endures today, now transformed and located in Rochester, but still requiring those admitted to prove their French Protestant ancestry. From a meeting of a group of its directors in 1885 sprang the latest but far from least of the groups concerned to maintain a consciousness of their French past, the Huguenot Society of London (plate 15). The mention of London is misleading, for the Society is and always has been a national and international body. Its objects were laid down at its inaugural meeting on 15 April 1885 as the interchange and publication of knowledge relating to the Huguenots, and the formation of 'a bond of fellowship among those who inherit and admire the characteristic Huguenot virtues and who desire to perpetuate the memory of their Huguenot ancestors'. Over twenty-three volumes of annual proceedings and fifty-five larger publications – most notably editions of French church registers – bear witness to its continuing zeal and effectiveness in achieving its aims during the first century of its existence.

Today, while many of the descendants of the Huguenots retain great respect for their ancestors, they are fully English, concerned with the preservation of a collective memory rather than with institutions, church organization or language. Their adoption of English customs and ways is complete. At the turn of this century one of their number, B. J. T. Bosanquet, even contributed variety to that most English game of cricket by inventing googly bowling. The process of assimilation was long and gradual, and not without frustrations. It was retarded by the arrival of successive waves of refugees between the sixteenth and eighteenth centuries, each reminding its predecessor of a joint continental inheritance, each injecting new life and vigour into the French communities in England. It was retarded too by English ignorance, insularity and suspicion of foreign ways. The stereotypes discussed in chapter 7 and implied by the opening quotation of this chapter took many years to disperse; witness Hogarth's *Noon*, published in 1738, with its mincing, elegantly but strangely dressed French congregation (plate 16). But eventually the stereotypes died. Bonds with France, bonds of family, of trade, of charity (generous assistance was sent from Huguenot refugees to their less fortunate co-religionists forced to serve on the French king's galleys), all slackened. Charitable donations by people of Huguenot descent, like the Peloquin Charity still being administered in Bristol, gravitated towards the support of English causes. Ghettos in the London suburbs and Canterbury slowly dissolved as intermarriage occurred and the French language was abandoned. Perhaps most important of all, the Calvinistic drive that had impelled the refugees to flight diminished, or was diverted into new channels.

What, then, are we to conclude from our study of the Huguenots? Professor C. D. Darlington, in *The Evolution of Man and Society* (1969), drew attention to their genetic contribution to English development, remarking that they

> tell us more than any other racial group except the Jews of the distinction between the inbred and outbred effects of migration. At home [in France] the Protestants continued inbred as a useful but not very remarkable section of society. Abroad, so far as they remained inbred, they introduced and developed their manufactures of textiles, glass and metalwork, technical achievements contributing to the new growth of industry. Yet outbred, they yielded over a period of six generations outstanding new individuals in every field of activity and culture.

The present book has certainly confirmed that the Huguenots played a highly significant role in English and European development, a role quite out of proportion to their number. But can it really be argued that their genes were more important than the situation in which, as refugees, they found themselves? Their contribution to sixteenth-century printing or the eighteenth-century Enlightenment gives the lie to Darlington's assertion that 'pure Huguenots were never inclined to literature, learning or the arts'. Might not the mixture of two cultures, in any case, produce intellectual distinction just as successfully as the association of different genes?

Genetic factors may have helped determine which French Huguenots possessed the combination of faith, resolution, endurance, and a will to work for a new future which led them to seek refuge in strange lands. Once they had done so, what strikes the historian is not their genetic inheritance but their potentially profitable connections; their need as refugees to apply themselves to whatever they undertook, and consequently their exceptional degree of motivation; the liquid capital and the new craft skills and techniques they brought with them; their preparedness to experiment and (if need be) to migrate anew and start again. Given good fortune such qualities could be turned to profitable account, and we have seen that this is precisely what happened. In the process, not only the refugees but the society to which they came benefited hugely, to the great detriment of France. The history of the Huguenots in England shows that the right of a minority to exist is more than a moral rule. It is also, as Philippe Joutard remarked, 'the most certain means of enriching a civilization and increasing its dynamism'. At a time when there are more refugees than ever before in human history, yet when governments all around the world are setting up barriers against immigration, the reminder is salutary.

Appendix:
Tracing Huguenot Ancestors

You may believe that you are of Huguenot descent. This appendix is designed to help you trace your ancestors and interpret the information you find in the printed records of the French churches in England. There may be a more or less vague family tradition that you have a Protestant refugee background, perhaps accompanied by a belief that your ancestors were, say, silkweavers or noblemen. Trust the general family tradition rather than the more specific beliefs, unless these are supported by documentary evidence, but explore all avenues.

In genealogical research you should aim to proceed backwards in time, from the known to the unknown. This is not always possible with the Huguenots, and this appendix reviews what the *French* sources in England may have to offer, in the belief that it can be helpful to explore these forwards while *also* pursuing English sources backwards in time. However, work should at least begin from the secure foundation of persons from whom a continuous descent is an unquestionable certainty: great-grandparents, perhaps. Consequently the first step is to make sure of your forebears back to 1837: start in England with the General Register of Births, Marriages and Deaths at St Catherine's House in Aldwych, London. Thereafter you are on your own. Collections of printed genealogies can be investigated; some hints on where to locate them are given below. Should these fail, where are you to turn?

Granted a family tradition or positive indication of Huguenot descent, it is best to start with the invaluable Quarto Series Publications of the Huguenot Society of London. Here you will find almost all the known registers of the Huguenot churches in England and Ireland, together with other material of great use. It is essential to bear in mind that many of these registers of baptisms or marriages were compiled by scribes who listened to names and then wrote them down as well as they could. Sometimes they had no written or printed names before them to give precision to their work, and in any event spelling was not standardized before the nineteenth century. (A volume was published in 1869 under the title *Autograph of William*

Shakespeare . . . together with 4,000 ways of spelling the name.) Moreover scribes from different extremities of France such as Languedoc and Normandy might well pronounce and write names differently. Variants are therefore common. To give one example, Delliers, Lilars, Lislaire are all French scribal variations of the name de Lillers which is frequently encountered in the seventeenth-century records of the French Church of London in Threadneedle Street. Names beginning with a silent 'H' or a vowel pose special difficulties, so that Hemard may appear as Aimart, Emar or Eimar. Therefore every index of names (and some volumes of the series, dealing with the registers of several churches, have more than one such index) must be searched under every possible phonetic variant. Try pronouncing the name aloud initially, and make a careful note of every spelling variant encountered as your search of the records proceeds.

With most names it is wise to begin by assuming that they may on occasion (but not always) be prefaced by 'de', 'de la', 'du', 'le' or 'la'. Some refugees came with names with such prefixes, others added them to make their names more imposing or were credited with them through scribal ignorance. Some names lent themselves to the addition of a prefix, others did not; thus de la Fontaine tended to become Fountain, but de Quesne, Ducane. It is better to search thoroughly but slowly than to skim and perhaps miss some vital connection, so check the name being researched under possible prefixes as well as the stem. Remember that in some indexes a name like de Lillers will appear under D and in others under L.

So far we have considered entries in the registers of the French Protestant churches in England. Whatever the problems involved in their use, at least these registers were prepared by Frenchmen or their descendants. When one approaches records written by Englishmen who were uncertain in transcribing French names, further difficulties become apparent. The ear attuned to one language may not find it easy to appreciate the other: so one finds French scribes making a strange mess of English placenames ('Pigdely' is Piccadilly, 'Crupelgait' and 'Gripel gatte' are Cripplegate, 'Winsor' may be not Windsor but Wandsworth), and English scribes misrendering French surnames ('Garrett' for Gariot, 'Lacklead' for de la Clide, 'Shoppee' for Chapuis). Even a highly literate Englishman with French connections like Samuel Pepys, whose wife was the daughter of a Huguenot, could turn 'D'Esquier' into 'Shar', 'Eschar' and 'Eshar'. A name normally spelt in the French way in French records may appear in direct translation in English ones: 'White' for 'Blanc', for example, 'Marshall' for 'Prévôt', 'All the World' for 'Toutlemonde', 'Byrde' for 'Loiseau', or 'Colt' for 'Poultrain'. Some names, such as Martin or

Robert, posed no problems to their bearers during the assimilation process, and indeed the difficulty for the modern researcher in such cases lies in discerning that these might ever have been refugee names. Others have never been changed or have been altered in only a minor way, so that Minet or de Gruchy remain readily recognizable. But a minority are confusing indeed; Petitoeil ('little eye') became Liddley, the lawyer Solomon de la Penissière was known to his English clients as Solomon Penny, Jean de Bois turns up as both Boyce and Wood, and Jean Pierre Lamblois features in the Court Book of the Weavers' Company, having dropped his last name, simply as John Peters. There is substance behind the opening paragraph of Daniel Defoe's *Life and Adventures of Robinson Crusoe*:

> I was called Robinson Kreutznaer; but by the usual corruption of words in England, we are now called, nay, we call our selves and write our name, Crusoe, and so my companions always called me.

Fortunately such extreme transformations are uncommon; but some idea of the scale of the problem can be gained from the list drawn up by Francis Cross after working on the Canterbury records – a list which, he adds, records only some of the translations, abbreviations and corruptions:

Andrieu	Andrews
Anglais	English
Arnoult	Arnold
Bachelier	Batchelor
Bacquelé	Backley
Barbier	Barber
Behaghel	Hagell
Belinguier	Bellinger
Blanc	White
Boulanger	Baker
Caloué	Callaway
Charpentier	Carpenter
Clarisse	Claris
Cotignie	Cotone, Cotton
Courte	Court
Crespin	Crippen
De Bourges	Burgess, Burge
De Casselle	Cassell
De la Croix	Cross
De la Mere	Dalimer
De la Motte	Dalimote

De la Pierre	Peters
De la Planche	Plank
De l'Eau	Waters
De le Becque	Beck
De le Port	Port
De l'Espau	Shoulder
De Lespine	Lepine
De Pou	Pugh
Descamps	Scamp
Despaigne	Spain
Despersin	Purslee
De Vine	Divine
Dubois	Wood
Du Boys	Boys, Boyce
Ducrow	Crow
Du Forest	Forest
Faidherbe	Fedarb
Forestier	Forrester
François	Francis, French
Gambié	Gambier
Jordaine	Jordan
L'Amy	Friend
Le Cerf	Hart
Le Chevalier	Shoveler
Le Clercq	Clark
Le Febre	Lefevre, Fever
Le Houcq	Hook
Le Leu	Wolf
Le Moine	Monk
Le Poutre	Pout
Le Rou	Rowe
Mahieu	Mayhew
Mareschal	Marshall
Mercier	Mercer
Michel	Mitchell
Momerie	Mummery
Olivier	Oliver
Paramentier	Parmenter
Petit	Small
Pilon	Pillow
Poitevin	Potvine
Reynard	Fox
Rideau	Ridout

179

Senellart	Sneller
Thierry	Terry
Van Acre	Acres, Hacker
Veré	Verry
Wibau	Wyber

The Huguenot Society Quarto Series Publications, consisting of over 50 volumes, can be found through major libraries. While it is perfectly possible to begin with volume 1 and simply work through the indexes, any family traditions about trade or time of arrival or place of origin on the Continent or place of settlement in England may offer logical starting-points. A belief that the family was involved in watch-making or silver-smithing would make the registers of the west London congregations in Westminster, Leicester Fields and Soho a sensible starting place, while a tradition of silkweaving would point rather to those of the French churches in the City and eastern suburbs of London, or Canterbury. If family roots are thought to be in south-west France, the Bristol and Devonshire congregation registers are worth early inspection; if in the southern Low Countries, try first the registers of the old French/Walloon churches of London, Canterbury, Norwich and Southampton, which must also be the advice if the family is thought to have come to England before 1650. Do not be disheartened if your early efforts fail – these are no hard and fast rules, merely initial guidelines suggested by experience. If good fortune does not smile early, you will need to work steadily through the indexes, backtracking where necessary if new variant spellings are encountered in later volumes.

The French church registers consist mostly of baptisms and marriages from the late sixteenth to the late eighteenth centuries; the Huguenots were not particularly interested in recording burials, and did not normally maintain their own burial grounds. The baptismal and marriage entries are more complete for the Elizabethan wave of refugees, not merely because the foreign churches then in England were fewer and better organized, but because of subsequent English legislation. Marriage law acts in 1694 and 1696 imposed taxes on every marriage graded according to the groom's social position, insisted that marriages in 'exempt-places' should be performed only after banns had been called or licence obtained according to law, and imposed savage penalties on clergymen trying to bypass this legislation. As a result, those choosing to be married in the French churches could expect to pay double fees, and the number of celebrations in French declined. This partly explains why the records of the Huguenot congregations deteriorated more rapidly during the eighteenth century than did those of the Walloons during the seventeenth.

Three other sources of information are *abjurations*, *reconnaissances* and *témoignages*. *Abjurations*, conversions from Roman Catholicism, were infrequent, but the *reconnaissances* and *témoignages* can be of the greatest value in providing information as to the date of arrival of a new refugee and the place from which he had come. Calvinist Consistories expected a traveller to bring his *témoignage*, or certificate of sound doctrine and good behaviour, when he applied for admission to a new church. After the Revocation of the Edict of Nantes in 1685 there were no Protestant churches in France to provide such certificates, and consequently refugees could only make their *reconnaissances* or professions of faith in the church to which they went. Where these *témoignages* or *reconnaissances* were recorded in special registers or with baptismal and marriage entries they have been published, and volume 21 of the Quarto Series (the *témoignages* presented at the Threadneedle Street church, the first port of call of many new arrivals in London) is of special value. Others remain hidden in Consistory minute books that have not yet appeared in print; it is particularly to be hoped that the Threadneedle Street minutes for the later Stuart period, which contain some 3,000 *reconnaissances* for the three years 1686–8 alone, will soon be published. Along with *témoignages* may be found records of first communion, commonly received around the age of 16 in Calvinist churches.

Working through the Huguenot Society Quarto Series, you will encounter various volumes that have no connection with church registers. Some of these – the minutes of Colloquies and Synods, for example, or despatches from Venetian ambassadors at the French Court – can be ignored. But others are of great genealogical value. Volumes 8, 18, 27 and 35 record grants of letters of denization and acts of naturalization throughout and beyond the period of Huguenot immigration, and volume 10 lists returns of aliens in London between 1522 and 1625. Both of these collections record all aliens, not just Protestant refugees, but Huguenots predominate. However, the scribes were normally English and consequently spelling is often strange. This can also be the case with the extracts from the Court Books of the Weavers Company (1610–1730) reproduced in volume 33, although by the end of the seventeenth century there were so many Frenchmen employed in the weaving trade in the east London suburbs that the Company found it convenient to appoint a French-speaking clerk.

In recent years the series has begun to make available new sources of information, with the production of volumes 49 (relief distributed through the Threadneedle Street church, 1681–87) and 52 and 53 (inmates of and applicants to the French Protestant Hospital, 1718–1957). These new sources relate to the help given refugees and their descendants on the borderline of destitution, and are particularly important because historians have too often ignored such people. The volumes can be supplemented by the printed lists of assisted refugees which appeared from 1705 onwards, the *Estats de la Distribution* . . . , but it is not easy to gain access to such lists.

Inevitably, it is always easier to obtain information about men of greater wealth or importance. If they became elders or deacons, Consistory minutes recording their election to office may give their places of birth. When refugees or their descendants possessed enough of this world's goods to make wills, they opened up in so doing a profitable avenue for the genealogist. For wills, you must use English records; refer to a work such as J. S. W. Gibson, *Wills and where to find them* (Phillimore, 1974). A useful starting-point is the Huguenot Library at University College, London, with its formidable collection of abstracts compiled by Henry Wagner. Although by no means exhaustive, this collection is indexed and the abstracts are normally reliable, providing a valuable short cut and a base from which to launch further investigations in English repositories of wills. (Do not be content with the abstract, if you find one; go back to the original.) Also in the Library are housed genealogical notes regarding some 900 Huguenot families, put together by Wagner around the end of the last century; and a growing collection of files compiled by research assistants of the Huguenot Society of London, who are prepared to make initial genealogical searches on payment of a fee. (The Huguenot Library is not open to the public, and has no full-time staff. To use it, you must first become a Fellow of the Huguenot Society of London and then write to its Administrative Assistant to obtain permission to visit the Library.)

Wagner's notes tend to be concerned with the more important members and descendants of the refugee community. So too are the many printed and manuscript biographies, monographs and family histories of Huguenot interest also to be found in the Huguenot Library. Similarly, it is the more important Protestant families who tend to be the subject of the biographical entries in E. and E. Haag, *La France Protestante* (10 vols, Paris, 1847–59; second edition, 6 vols up to letter G only, 1877–87).

For wealthy families, there is a comparatively good chance that a more or less complete family tree, linking original refugees to their modern descendants, may be constructed'– although it is never easy. Lacking access to wills and family possessions, it will be harder for descendants of the poorer refugees – the vast majority – to overcome the most formidable obstacle facing the Huguenot genealogist: linking traces of those who first came to England and their immediate successors with the family information likely to be available from 1837 (when compulsory civil registration began). Again and again it proves possible to document the arrival and establishment in England of a refugee from Louis XIV's France, only to find traces of his family disappearing during the middle or later eighteenth century. This is the result of the process of assimilation, and the keys to the solution of the problem lie in ordinary English records which, though crucial, are outside the scope of this appendix. (If you know nothing about them, start by consulting the publications of the Society of Genealogists, particularly the latest edition of *Genealogists' Handbook* and the Society's leaflet *A Bibliography for Beginners in Genealogy*. A booklet on Protestant refugees in the Society's 'My Ancestor' series is due to appear shortly, and should be very helpful. You are also strongly recommended to join a family history society.)

We have seen that Huguenots tended to travel and settle in the company of their friends and relations. Individual descendants of refugees may be traceable (provided the relevant church records survive) as long as they remained members of communities with a common language and worship, but once they left those communities their movements become far harder to unravel. Thus, as the quality and number of entries in the registers of the French churches diminishes during the eighteenth century, so do the hopes and spirits of the genealogist. English church records for the region where the Huguenot was last known to be may fill the void, sometimes showing traces of the process of anglicization. The registers for St Matthew's, Bethnal Green, for instance, include entries of the burials of Elizabeth Lhereux of Princes Street, aged 70, in 1813, and Thomas Happy of Princes Street, aged 35, in 1819. Many interesting references are also submerged among other, non-ecclesiastical papers which may seem to have nothing to do with the Huguenots; to uncover these requires skilled detection, luck and persistence in equal measure, together with the assistance of local experts aware of the possibilities of local archives.

Let us take one illustration to see how the approach suggested in this appendix may work out. Suppose all that is known of a family believed to have a Huguenot connection is descent from John Shoulder, silkweaver, born in the early nineteenth century. The clue here lies in the profession, so the best place to start seems likely to be the Court Books of the Weavers Company. Since the extracts in the Huguenot Society Quarto Series volume cease in 1730 there is no hope of a direct connection with John Shoulder, but nevertheless the volume proves very useful. It provides a reference to John Dela pau [de l'Epaule] *alias* Shoulder, produces a variety of spelling variants (De la Spau, Delaspoo, Delespan, de l'Epaule, Dela pau, de Laspoo, Delespau, Delesparo, Sholder and Shoulder), and connects the family with Canterbury as well as east London. Armed with this information, further search of the Quarto Series volumes – remembering to check indexes under D and L as well as E and S – reveals that the family was established in Canterbury by the late sixteenth century, so was probably of Walloon rather than strictly Huguenot origin, and that many of its members migrated to the east London area in the late seventeenth or early eighteenth century. In the process of searching, it becomes obvious that the de l'Epaules must be distinguished from the Pauls or Pols and from the de l'Espines or de l'Epinnes. It transpires that they were a family of some local significance in seventeenth-century Canterbury, and that they were non-conformist in their religious attendance. These clues in turn suggest directions for further research, pointing the need not only to look for wills but to investigate English Nonconformist as well as Anglican records. The heavy concentration of the family in seventeenth-century Canterbury indicates the desirability of further examining local records there. As it happens, these include a pleasing illustration of the process of assimilation in the form of a petition of 1657 drawn up in the name of various woolcombers including 'John Shoulder' but signed by 'Jean de Lespau'.[1]

The example of the Shoulder family is fairly straightforward, since in both its French and English forms the name is comparatively uncommon. The French equivalents of John Brown and Henry Smith would be far harder to trace. Nevertheless it serves to draw attention to some of the difficulties the researcher may confront: for example, the errors liable to occur in oral family tradition, which has here confused Walloon and Huguenot, and can often be much more misleading; the need to view the period of Protestant immigration into England as lasting from the sixteenth century to the end of the eighteenth, not as something that happened in the 1680s; the persistence in a family of a favourite Christian name, which may provide significant supporting evidence for the genealogist but may also cause confusion between father and son, uncle and nephew, or even grandfather and grandson; the need to search indexes under all possible spellings. There are other traps not highlighted by this particular example, such as possible confusion with the names of old Norman settlers or later French émigrés.

It will be clear to any reader of this book that there was a particularly heavy concentration of refugees in certain London suburbs. This meant that a family might be within easy walking distance of a number of congregations, and consequently appear in several different registers during one decade. Although most of the records of the large Threadneedle Street church have been preserved, this is less often the case with the many small and comparatively poorly-organized congregations that sprang up after the Revocation. There are also gaps in the records of the churches in the country. Here, too, the older refugee churches proved to be better organized, so that source material for the second wave of Huguenots tends to be less satisfactory than for their sixteenth-century predecessors. The Devonshire congregations founded in the late seventeenth century are especially hard to research; they do not feature prominently in local English records, nor have they left many surviving registers. Of the early seventeenth-century Fenland churches, formed as a result of Vermuyden's drainage schemes, the baptismal registers of Thorney have been published in the Huguenot Society Quarto Series, but those of Sandtoft have been lost (147 names are however listed in the Stovin manuscript printed in the *Yorkshire Archaeological and Topographical Journal*, VII (1882), 194–238). The registers for the French church of Dover do not appear in the Quarto Series, having been edited by F. A. Crisp and privately printed in 1888.

Your problems may be compounded by the mobility of many Huguenots. Once having made the break from their country of origin, refugees frequently moved several times before settling permanently. This was partly because of the circumstances of their departure from France; seeking to escape by night and fearful of dragoons and royal agents, beggars could not afford to be choosers, but had to take whatever opportunities presented themselves. If they first crossed the Swiss border, it was likely that they would move on at least to Germany; if they went to the Netherlands they might choose to follow the fortunes of William of Orange across the Channel; from the British Isles they might seek new opportunities in the New World. Where refugees managed to escape with assets, these were in liquid form, and generally did not tie them to any one place. Where they had none, they were likely to head for relief distribution centres and then follow any avenue that might lead to employment. Since the refugees and their descendants tended to be artisans rather than rural peasants, there was nothing to encourage them to settle in one particular area, nothing to prevent them from trying their luck elsewhere.

It may even be that one migration encouraged a subsequent family tradition; is it mere coincidence that the historian of the early settlement of New Zealand encounters such men of Huguenot descent as C. D. Barraud the artist, George Chamier the author and the missionary Thomas Samuel Grace? Certainly earlier Huguenot migration was often a complex process involving several stages and sometimes several generations. Cameron Allen, an American genealogist skilled in researching Huguenot ancestry, warns that

> if a student desires to track his Huguenot ancestor down step by step, chances are that he is going to have to familiarize himself not only with the records of the American colony where the ancestor ultimately settled, but perhaps with those of another American colony, then with those of one or two non-French countries of Europe, and ultimately, he may hope, with the records of France itself . . . almost every successful Huguenot family reconstruction shows that at least three or four migratory steps were involved.[2]

Naturally refugees who reached America had travelled further than most of their fellows, but the warning should also be heeded by researchers of those who stayed in Europe. The *Calendars of State Papers Domestic*, for instance, offer evidence of much transit of Huguenots between the Netherlands, England and Ireland during the reign of William and Mary, and many individual examples of multi-migration could be cited. Abraham Soblet took the land route and reached London via Manheim and Wesel before proceeding to Virginia. David Garrick, grandfather of the actor, travelled to England by way of Saintonge, Poitou, Brittany and Guernsey. Robert le Platrier came from Rouen to London, and (apart from a brief interlude in Amsterdam, where he married) remained there for a quarter of a century, only to return to his birthplace. Robert Miré served in an infantry regiment in the West Indies, became a freeman of the city of London, and removed to Dublin shortly before his death. You must be alert to the possibilities of multiple migration; do not try to reconstruct a family tree simply through the register of just one church or place. Once again, you will be drawn irresistibly beyond the confines of the French refugee churches in England – and beyond the scope of this appendix.

As information is gleaned, it can be examined for clues suggesting further research. We have already seen that membership of a Consistory or even the making of a will argues a certain (not necessarily very exalted) social status or degree of wealth. The same good fortune is indicated by an entry in a list of naturalizations or denizations if before 1681. (From this year, special arrangements were made for the Huguenots.) Knowledge of the date of an individual's first communion or apprenticeship can point to a probable date of birth within a couple of years' accuracy. Membership of an east London congregation increases the likelihood that the subject was a weaver; membership of a west London congregation makes this an improbable trade. Membership of a conformist church suggests that the subject's descendants would eventually be found as Anglicans, while descendants from a non-conformist background might equally well join Anglican or English Nonconformist churches.

You must make a thorough investigation of all possible sources, but you may save a good deal of time by using clues like those suggested here to try the more profitable approaches first. As a cumulative picture of a family develops, something like a jigsaw with an annoyingly large number of missing pieces will gradually take shape. How many of those blanks can be filled will depend upon perseverance, ingenuity of approach, and good luck in the survival of relevant records. The hunt will be time-consuming. It should also prove worthwhile, and not just from a sense of personal satisfaction or family pride. The more data on families of Huguenot descent that can be collected and collated, the more clearly we shall understand the process by which the refugees became integrated into English society. Herbert Lüthy's study of Protestant banking in France[3] illustrates the importance of genealogical studies in understanding those business circles. Similarly, family histories may eventually shed considerable light on the development of English cultural and trade patterns during the late seventeenth and eighteenth centuries.

Notes

Works cited in these references without author's initials or date of publication will be found listed in the Bibliographical Note that follows. For books published in the last twenty years, the publisher's name is given in preference to place of publication. If no place is given in a full entry to an earlier work, London should be assumed. The number of footnotes is small but, between text, footnotes and the Bibliographical Note, it is hoped that interested readers can track down detailed references without undue difficulty. The author intends to deposit a more minutely referenced copy of the book in the Huguenot Library, University College, London. The following abbreviations have been used:

APC	*Acts of the Privy Council*
Bodl.	Bodleian Library, Oxford
CSPD	*Calendars of State Papers, Domestic*
FCL	Library of the French Church of London, Soho Square
HSP	*Proceedings of the Huguenot Society of London*
HSQS	Huguenot Society of London Quarto Series Publications
PRO	Public Record Office

Introduction

1 See *HSP*, VI (1898–1901), 327–355, and H. Naef, '"Huguenot" ou le Procès d'un Mot', *Bibliothèque d'Humanisme et Renaissance*, XII (1950), 208–27.
2 T. J. Archdeacon, *New York City, 1664–1710: Conquest and Change* (Cornell University Press, 1976), p. 49.
3 R. L. Poole, *A History of the Huguenots of the Dispersion at the Recall of the Edict of Nantes* (1880), pp. vii–viii.

Notes

Chapter 1   An Exposed Minority

1 The estimate of Protestant aristocratic strength and analysis of Genevan missionary activity are taken from Kingdon, *Geneva and the Coming of the Wars of Religion in France*, p. 6 and *passim*; the quotation from the Seigneur of la Ferté-Fresnel from Parker, *La Rochelle and the French Monarchy*, p. 96.
2 Letter to Duke of Somerset, 22 October 1548.
3 Léonard, *History of Protestantism*, II, pp. 148–9.
4 Sutherland, *Huguenot Struggle for Recognition*, p. 56.
5 Quoted in P. Erlanger, *St Bartholomew's Night* (1962), p. 238. Better than Erlanger in suggesting why the massacre occurred are Sutherland, *The Massacre. . .* ; and A. Soman (ed.), *The Massacre of St Bartholomew: Reappraisals and Documents* (Martinus Nijhoff, The Hague, 1974). Figures given for casualties in the massacre have been taken from Salmon, *Society in Crisis*.
6 The full texts will be found translated in appendix 4 of Mousnier, *The Assassination of Henry IV*.
7 See Parker, *La Rochelle and the French Monarchy*; and Grant, *The Huguenots*, pp. 120–1.
8 *An Edict of the French King, prohibiting all Publick Exercise of the Pretended Reformed Religion in his Kingdom. . .* (2nd edn, 1686), p. 9. For the process by which the Edict of Nantes was undermined, see Benoît, *Histoire de l'Edit de Nantes*; Orcibal, *Louis XIV et les Protestants*; and Scoville, *Persecution of Huguenots*.
9 H. G. Judge, *Louis XIV* (Longman, 1965), p. 65.
10 S. Mours, *Les Eglises Réformées en France: tableaux et cartes* (Paris, 1958), pp. 176–8.
11 G. Picarda, 'The Evolution of the French Law of Nationality Relating to Returning Huguenots', *HSP*, XXII (1970–76), 449–52.

Chapter 2   The Huguenot Settlements in England

1 A. G. Dickens, *The English Reformation* (Batsford, 1964), pp. 68, 76; *Letters and Papers, Foreign and Domestic, of the Reign of Henry VIII*, Dec. 1531 (vol 5, no. 564, p. 261) and Feb. 1535 (vol. 8, no. 189, p. 73).
2 For the figures given in this paragraph, see *HSP*, XVI (1937–41), 31; HSQS, vol. 4, pp. 3–4, 7–9; HSQS, vol. 1, pp. 34, 36; HSQS, vol. 15, p. 22; HSQS, vol. 12, p. 105.
3 *HSP*, XVI (1937–41), 33; HSQS, vol. 1, pp. 44–5; HSQS, vol. 4, pp. 19, 102–4; HSQS, vol. 12, p. viii; HSQS, vol. 15, p. 36.

4 J. B[ulteel], *A Relation of the Troubles of the Three Forraign Churches in Kent. . .* (1645), p. 22.
5 J. Strype, *Annals of the Reformation* (4 vols, Oxford, 1824), IV, pp. 114–15; HSQS, vol. 15, pp. 24–5.
6 HSQS, vol. 54, pp. 5–7.
7 Gwynn, 'Number of Huguenot Immigrants', *passim.*
8 *HSP*, XXI (1965–70), 372.
9 The figures for immigrants given here can be set against the total London population as presented in R. Finlay, *Population and Metropolis . . . 1580–1650* (Cambridge University Press, 1981), p. 68, and E. A. Wrigley, 'A Simple Model of London's Importance . . . 1650–1750', *Past and Present*, 37 (1967), 44–70.
10 Mayo, 'Les Huguenots à Bristol', p. 18.

Chapter 3   The Refugees and the English Government

1 *HSP*, XIV (1929–33), 427.
2 *APC*, 1558–70, p. 380; 1571–95, pp. 306, 345–6; 1581–2, p. 213; 1586–7, p. 25.
3 R. B. Dobson, *The Peasants' Revolt of 1381* (Macmillan, 1970), p. 201.
4 For the foreign churches under Edward, see Schickler, *Eglises du refuge en Angleterre*, I; Hall, *John à Lasco*; Denis, 'Les Eglises d'étrangers à Londres'.
5 Collinson, *Archbishop Grindal*, pp. 107–8.
6 Schickler, *Eglises du refuge en Angleterre*, I, p. 85, n. 2.
7 The minutes of all Colloquies (until 1654) and Synods are printed in HSQS, vol. 2.
8 J. M. Krumm, in Littell (ed.), *Reformation Studies*, p. 141; B. R. White, *The English Separatist Tradition: From the Marian Martyrs to the Pilgrim Fathers* (Oxford University Press, 1971), pp. 95, 112.
9 HSQS, vol. 38, p. xiii; J. A. Van Dorsten, *The Radical Arts: First Decade of an Elizabethan Renaissance* (Leiden University Press, 1970), p. 120; G. D. Ramsay, *The City of London in International Politics at the Accession of Elizabeth Tudor* (Manchester University Press, 1975), chap. VII.
10 HSQS, vol. 38, pp. 51, 126.
11 Sir Simonds D'Ewes, *The Journals of all the Parliaments during the Reign of Queen Elizabeth. . .* (1682), p. 506; HSQS, vol. 38, p. 97.
12 For Laud, see J. P. Kenyon (ed.), *The Stuart Constitution 1603–1688* (Cambridge University Press, 1966), pp. 153–4; J. B[ulteel], *A Relation of the Troubles of the Three Forraign Churches in Kent. . .* (1645); HSQS, vol. 1, pp. 271–2; Schickler, *Eglises du refuge en Angleterre*, chap. X; Campbell, 'Walloon Community in Canter-

buty', chap. V. For what follows, see the Introduction to HSQS, vol. 54, which is fully documented.

13 Plummer, *London Weavers' Company*, p. 17.

14 Sundstrom, *Huguenots in England*, pp. 22–42; Gwynn, 'Ecclesiastical Organization', pp. 291–2.

15 *CSPD*, 1680–1, p. 437.

Chapter 4   Crafts and Trades

1 R. H. Tawney and E. Power (eds), *Tudor Economic Documents* (3 vols, 1924), III, p. 212.

2 For this paragraph, see H. J. Yallop, 'The Making of a Myth – the Origin of Honiton Lace', *Devon Historian*, 28 (April 1984), 20–4; E. Hockliffe (ed.),. *The Diary of the Rev. Ralph Josselin 1616–1683*, (Royal Historical Society, Camden 3rd series, XV (1908)), p. 16; Pilgrim, 'Cloth Industry', p. 253; *CSPD*, 1703–4, p. 354; *APC*, 1618–19, p. 264; HSQS, vol. 15, p. 29; C. W. Chalklin, *Seventeenth-Century Kent* (Longman, 1965), pp. 31, 115–16, 123–8; Plummer, *London Weavers' Company*, chap. 1; Southampton Record Office, Exhibition of Documents for the 5th Anglo-Dutch Conference of Historians (1973), no. 20; Norwich Book of Orders, Johnson transcript, p. 5.

3 *HSP*, XIII (1923–9), 126, 130; Thirsk, *Economic Policy and Projects*, p. 44; Pilgrim, 'Cloth Industry', pp. 258–9; Norwich Book of Orders, Johnson transcript, pp. 252–3, 262–3, 266–7. These works continue to be important sources for what follows.

4 P. Corfield, in P. Clark and P. Slack (eds), *Crisis and Order in English Towns* (Routledge & Kegan Paul, 1972), pp. 275, 297–9.

5 D. C. Coleman, *The Economy of England 1450–1750* (Oxford University Press, 1977), pp. 65, 81.

6 *CSPD*, 1666–7, p. 191; W. Cobbett, *Parliamentary History of England* (26 vols, 1806–20), V, col. 855; Thornton, *Baroque and Rococo Silks*, pp. 18–30; *A Satyr against the French* (1691), p. 7.

7 Jones, 'London Overseas-Merchant Groups', pp. 40–1; HSQS, vol. XX, pp. xxv–xxvi; R. L. Poole, *A History of the Huguenots of the Dispersion. . .* (1880), p. 89; Davies, *History of Southampton*, pp. 410–11; Corfield, *op. cit.*, p. 282; Lee, *Huguenot Settlements in Ireland*, especially chap. 7; Mason, 'Weavers of Picardy', *passim*.

8 Thornton, *Baroque and Rococo Silks*, pp. 55–63; HSQS, vol. 15, pp. 202–5; Thornton and Rothstein, 'Importance of the Huguenots'; Plummer, *London Weavers' Company*, chap. VI; W. H. Manchée, 'Some Huguenot Smugglers. . .', *HSP*, XV (1933–7), 406–27; Mason, 'Weavers of Picardy', 5; C. S. Davies (ed.), *A History of Macclesfield* (Manchester, 1961), p. 128; W. White, *History,*

Gazetteer and Directory of Suffolk (3rd edn, 1874), pp. 197–8.

9 J. S. Burn, *History of the French . . . Refugees* (1846), since cited by other writers with no further details; Plummer, *London Weavers' Company*, p. 295; Corporation of London Record Office, MS Companies 2.23 (undated but late 1682); Brett-James, *Growth of Stuart London*, pp. 491–2; (for Putney) N. Luttrell, *The Parliamentary Diary . . . 1691–3*, ed. H. Horwitz (Oxford, 1972), p. 286; G. Unwin, *Industrial Organization in the Sixteenth and Seventeenth Centuries* (Oxford, 1904), pp. 217ff, 248–51; *CSPD*, 1685, pp. 58, 379, and 1695, p. 104; Scoville, *Persecution of Huguenots*, pp. 185, 228–30, 329–30.

10 Scoville, *Persecution of Huguenots*, p. 325; PRO 31/3/164, 11 Feb 1686 NS (Bonrepaus); HSQS, vol. XXXIII, pp. 50, 52 (emphasis added); Thornton and Rothstein, 'Importance of the Huguenots', 68; E. Lipson, *The Economic History of England: III, the Age of Mercantilism* (2nd edn, 1934), p. 61.

11 HSQS, vol. 11, p. xx; Minet, 'Notes on the Threadneedle Street Registers', p. 99; HL, Bounty MS 2, pt 3, p. 20; Poole, *op. cit.*, pp. 94–5; Bodl., Rawlinson MS C 984, f. 228; Bevis, Strangers in the Fens, pp. 7–9.

12 R. E. Duthie, 'English Florists' Societies and Feasts in the Seventeenth and First Half of the Eighteenth Centuries', *Garden History*, 10 (1982), 18, 33; Thirsk, *Economic Policy and Projects*, p. 46; *HSP*, II (1887–8), 216; Kensington and Chelsea Public Libraries, Chelsea Branch, Dr John King's manuscript account of Chelsea, p. 24.

13 Hayward, 'Huguenot Gunmakers', *HSP*, XIX (1952–8), 354 and XX (1958–64), 139; R. N. Hill, 'Huguenot Clock and Watch Makers. . .', *Connoisseur*, CXXI, no. 507 (March 1948), 26–30, 62; M. Wood (ed.), *Extracts from the Records of the Burgh of Edinburgh 1665 to 1680* (Edinburgh, 1950), pp. xlvii, 276; *CSPD*, 1619–23, p. 334.

14 P. Thornton, *Seventeenth-Century Interior Decoration in England. . .* (1978); E. T. Joy, 'Huguenot Cabinet-Makers and Designers in England in the Late Stuart Period', *HSP*, XXI (1965–70), 545–9; E. A. Wrigley, 'A Simple Model of London's Importance . . . 1650–1750', *Past and Present*, 37 (1967), 44–70.

15 Through people associated with the Court, French ideas in architecture and interior decoration spread into the provinces. At Dyrham Park, near Bath, William's Secretary at War William Blathwayt exploited an otherwise unknown Huguenot architect named S. Hauduroy by paying him only ten pounds (of which four went on travel expenses) for providing a new façade for his

Tudor manor house and redesigning the rooms behind. Fine examples of Huguenot work at the end of the seventeenth century are to be found at Boughton House in Northamptonshire, with its Chéron ceilings, flower paintings by Jean Baptiste Monnoyer and Marot furnishings.

16 *HSP*, XII (1917–23), 322; R. A. J. Walling, *The Story of Plymouth* (1950), p. 144; *HSP*, XXI (1965–70), 536–8; *HSP*, XXIII (1977–82), 118, 320, 323–6; *HSP*, XXII (1970–6), 120–2.

17 HSQS, vol. 4, pp. 70, 95, 121; HSQS, vol. 18, pp. 64 ('Cardinall'), 70; Southampton Record Office, D/FC 1, f.10r; Gwynn, 'Ecclesiastical Organization', appendix 1B.

Chapter 5   Professions

1 G. P. Judd IV, *Members of Parliament 1734–1832* (New Haven, 1955), pp. 17–18, 81 (Judd states a firm 65, but the true figure is higher, since even a cursory glance shows that he has not counted the families of Bouverie, Brooke-Pechell or Papillon). Most individuals named in this chapter will be found in the *Dictionary of National Biography*.

2 *HSP*, IV (1891–3), 322 and IX (1909–11), 480–1, 498; J. Childs, *The Army, James II, and the Glorious Revolution* (Manchester University Press, 1980), p. 175.

3 For this paragraph, see HSQS, vol. 15, p. 15, and vol. 38, p. 20; Watson, 'Notes and Materials'; *HSP*, XVIII (1947–52), 74; *History*, no. 216 (1981), 127.

4 FCL, MS 7, pp. 77, 85–7 and MS 8, ff. 107v, 157r, 161r; Bodl., Rawlinson MSS C 982, f. 155r, and C 984, f. 228; R. A. Barrell (ed.), *French Correspondence of Philip Dormer Stanhope. . .*, vol. 1 (Borealis Press, Ottawa, 1980), p. 10.

5 At an earlier date, in the Cambridgeshire Fenland, David Culy had formed an independent sect – the Culimites – which began in the area of Guyhirn and Parson Drove, where there were many Walloons (including David's father, John Cuuelie) and their descendants; by the end of the seventeenth century it reached as far afield as Ely, Newmarket, Thetford, Soham and into Lincolnshire, and it survived into the Victorian era.

6 For this paragraph and the last, see Carter, *Getting, Spending and Investing*, pp. 100, 106; *HSP*, XX (1958–64), 76, citing *The London Gazette*, 5–8 Oct. 1745; G. L. Lee, *The Story of the Bosanquets* (Phillimore, 1966), pp. 37, 42, 55, 64, 80, 106; *HSP*, XVIII (1947–52), 90–91. For the information regarding modern insurance connections, I am indebted to Dr Tessa Murdoch.

7 M. Edmond, *Hilliard and Oliver* (Robert Hale, 1983); C. Avery,

'Hubert Le Sueur, the "Unworthy Praxiteles" of King Charles I', *Walpole Society*, vol. 48 (1982), pp. 135–209 and plates 31–62.

8 T. Murdoch, 'Louis François Roubiliac and his Huguenot Connections', *HSP*, XXIV (1983), 26–45 and plates I-VI.

9 In addition to the *Dictionary of National Biography* and Le Fanu, 'Huguenot Refugee Doctors', see A. Eccles, *Obstetrics and Gynaecology in Tudor and Stuart England* (Croom Helm, 1982), p. 14; F. N. L. Poynter, 'Gideon Delaune and his Family Circle', Gideon Delaune Lecture 1964, published as the Wellcome Historical Medical Library Lecture Series, no. 2, 1965, p. 17; Benoît, *Histoire de l'Edit de Nantes*, IV, pp. 622–3, V, pp. 818–19; *HSP*, XXII (1970–6), 348.

10 C. MacKechnie-Jarvis, *Grand Stewards 1728–1978* (Prestonian Lecture, privately printed, 1978); *HSP*, XXIII (1977–82), 423 and XXIV (1983), 32–33; J. F. Austin and A. McConnell, 'James Six F.R.S. – Two Hundred Years of the Six's Self-Registering Thermometer', *Notes and Records of The Royal Society of London*, 35 (1980), 49–65.

Chapter 6   The Huguenots and their Churches

1 Léonard, *History of Protestantism*, II, p. 443; Marteilhe's *Memoirs*, narrative of Sorbier and Rivasson; *Bulletin de la Société de l'Histoire du Protestantisme Français*, XLIX (1900), 281ff.

2 Gwynn, 'Ecclesiastical Organization', p. 161; the arguments advanced in the present chapter are developed in this thesis with detailed references, see especially chapters 5 and 8.

3 The 'prophets' are not considered in this book; they are discussed in H. Schwartz, *The French Prophets: . . . a millenarian group in eighteenth-century England* (University of California Press, 1980).

4 Sundstrom, 'Huguenots in England', p. 31.

Chapter 7   Opposition

1 PRO, SP/29/274, no. 205, f.397r. Detailed references for much of this chapter will be found in Gwynn, 'Ecclesiastical Organization', pp. 233–68.

2 *APC*, 1589–90, p. 413, and 1586–7, pp. 322–3.

3 B. Coward, *The Stuart Age* (Longman, 1980), p. 60.

4 *Analytical Index to the . . . Remembrancia . . . of the City of London 1579–1664* (1878), pp. 520–1; Plummer, *London Weavers' Company*, p. 163.

Chapter 8   The Huguenots and the Later Stuarts

1 K. H. D. Haley, *Charles II* (Historical Association, 1966), p. 10. I owe the point about Charles's relationship with Louis to Dr John Miller. For the gratitude felt by the foreign Protestant community in England in 1666 and 1681, see L. Hérault, *Remerciment faict au Roy. . .* (1666); PRO, SP/29/143, no. 149; Hessels, *Ecclesiae Londino-Batavae Archivum*, vol. 3, part 2, pp. 2640–3; PRO, SP/30/ case G, Factum of the French, p. 2.

2 R. D. Gwynn, 'James II in the Light of his Treatment of Huguenot Refugees. . .', *English Historical Review*, XCII (1977), 820–33, provides detailed references for the first half of this chapter.

3 For what follows, see Miller, *Popery and Politics, passim*; J. P. Kenyon, *The Popish Plot* (Heinemann, 1972), chap. I; and J. R. Jones, *The Revolution of 1688 in England* (Weidenfeld & Nicolson, 1972), chap. IV.

4 L. Maimbourg, *Histoire du Calvinisme* (Paris, 1682), pp. 505–6; Orcibal, *Louis XIV et les Protestants*, p. 105, n. 64; *The Diary of John Evelyn*, ed. E. S. de Beer (6 vols, Oxford, 1955), IV, pp. 486, 511; N. Luttrell, *A Brief Historical Relation . . . [1678–1714]* (6 vols, Oxford, 1857), I, p. 376; Surtees Society, *Miscellanea* (Publications, vol. 37, 1861 for 1860), p. 215; Dr Williams's Library, Morrice MSS, P, p. 490.

5 *HSP*, VII (1901–4), 332–42; Jones, *op. cit.*, pp. 177–9, 206; *The Diary of Thomas Cartwright* (Camden Society, 1843), p. 48; N. A. Robb, *William of Orange: A Personal Portrait. Volume Two: 1674–1702* (Heinemann, 1966), p. 239; Dr Williams's Library, Morrice MSS, P, p. 499.

6 PRO, Baschet transcripts, 31/3/162, 19 Nov. 1685 NS; [G. Burnet], *An Apology for the Church of England* [Amsterdam, 1688], p. 8; British Library, Add. MS 41,805, f.50.

Chapter 9   The Huguenots and the Defeat of Louis XIV's France

1 For most of this section, see Lart, 'Huguenot Regiments'. The incident at Alicante is recounted in *HSP*, IX (1909–11), 46–54, and that at Almanza in the *Dictionary of National Biography, sub* Cavalier. Nottingham's argument is from *CSPD*, 1702–3, p. 670.

2 *CSPD*, 1689–90, pp. 269–70.

3 J. Childs, *The Army, James II and the Glorious Revolution* (Manchester University Press, 1980), p. 206.

4 For this paragraph, see D. B. Horn, *The British Diplomatic Service 1689–1789* (Oxford, 1961), p. 112; *CSPD*, for instance 1691–2, pp.

205, 408; 1694–5, p. 122; and 1699–1700, p. 320. It is astonishing that J. Ehrman, *The Navy in the War of William III, 1689–1697* (Cambridge, 1953), should not mention the Huguenot refugees even once in 700 pages!

5 Jones, 'London Overseas-Merchant Groups', table 1:1.
6 Gwynn, 'Ecclesiastical Organization', appendix 1B.
7 PRO, SP 8/1, pt 2, pp. 149–50.
8 Agnew, *Protestant Exiles* (3rd edn), II, p. 372.

Chapter 10   The Process of Assimilation

1 H. F. Whitfeld, *Plymouth and Devonport* (Plymouth, 1900), appendix, pp. 8–9.
2 FCL, MS 7, p. 87; A. R. Wagner, *English Genealogy* (2nd edn, Clarendon Press, 1972), p. 266.
3 Hessels, *Ecclesiae Londino-Batavae Archivum*, vol. 3, pt 1, p. 266; HSQS, vol. 1, pp. 255–6, and vol. 15, pp. 140–2.
4 Norfolk Record Office, Norwich City Records, 'Liber Albus', ff. 142–5; FCL, MS 5, p. 486, and MS 7, p. 130; Bodl., Tanner MS xcii, ff. 152, 162–3.
5 Minet, 'Notes on the Threadneedle Street Registers', p. 95.
6 FCL, MS 135A, *Subjection Generale*; Hessels, *op. cit.*, vol. 3, pt 2, p. 2400 and see also p. 2228.
7 G. Ascoli, *La Grande-Bretagne devant l'opinion française au XVIIe siècle* (2 vols, Paris, 1930), II, p. 2; Bodl., Rawlinson MS C 982, f.21v; A. T. Hart, *William Lloyd 1627–1717* (1952), p. 69; *Bulletin de la Société de l'Histoire du Protestantisme Français*, 39 (1890), 459; *Forms of Prayer*, preface.
8 Bodl., Rawlinson MS C 984, ff. 278–9.
9 In addition to Waller, 'Early . . . Friendly Societies', see *Establissement de la Société des Enfans de Nismes* (1683), pp. 4–5; Guildhall Library, MS 9899; HSP, XXI (1965–70), 308; *La Dicipline de la Société de Dauphiné*, (1710), conclusion; FCL, MS 8, f.278r; P. H. J. H. Gosden, *Self-Help* (Batsford, 1973), p. 7.

Appendix: Tracing Huguenot Ancestors

1 Canterbury Cathedral Library, U47-H2-84.
2 C. Allen, 'Records of Huguenots in the United States, Canada and the West Indies. . .', World Conference on Records and Genealogical Seminar, Salt Lake City, 1969. The Conference also produced papers on the records of Huguenots in France (by J. T. Du Pasquier) and French Switzerland (by O. Clottu).
3 H. Lüthy, *La Banque Protestante en France de la Révocation . . . à la Révolution* (2 vols, Paris, 1959–61).

Bibliographical Note

For works published in the last twenty years, the publisher's name is given in preference to place of publication. In the case of books published over twenty years ago for which no place of publication is given, London should be assumed. The following abbreviations have been used:

HL   Huguenot Library, University College, London
HSP   *Proceedings of the Huguenot Society of London*
HSQS   Huguenot Society of London Quarto Series Publications
[Tr.]   Translation from a French original

Works on the Huguenot refugees in England are few, and copies are often hard to locate. The pioneering study by J. S. Burn, *The History of The French, Walloon, Dutch and other Foreign Protestant Refugees settled in England. . .* (1846), is now of little use. S. Smiles, *The Huguenots: Their Settlements, Churches and Industries in England and Ireland* (1867), went through numerous editions, and can still be readily found; it is readable, but contains too many half-truths alongside some good stories. R. L. Poole, *A History of the Huguenots of the Dispersion at the Recall of the Edict of Nantes* (1880), remains valuable; it covers the whole diaspora, not just Britain. The biased D. C. A. Agnew painstakingly but indiscriminately assembled a remarkable collection of facts and quotations in his *Protestant Exiles from France, chiefly in the Reign of Louis XIV*; the best edition is the third (2 vols, Edinburgh, 1886), but it is easier to find the second (1871). Far superior to any of these, although more limited in scope, is Baron F. de Schickler, *Les Eglises du refuge en Angleterre* (3 vols, Paris, 1892). Schickler's book ends with the Revocation, but is thorough and accurate, and of enduring value. It includes a volume of supporting documents. Published at the same time as Schickler's *magnum opus*, J. H. Hessels (ed.), *Ecclesiae Londino-Batavae Archivum* (3 vols, the third in 2 parts,

Cambridge, 1887–97) is a magnificent collection of source material. This edition of the archives of the Dutch Church of London is also an important source for the history of the Walloon/French communities of the sixteenth and seventeenth centuries; entries are summarized in English.

No books in English dealing directly with the subject as a whole have appeared since the days of Smiles and Agnew. However, the Huguenot Society of London has published over 23 volumes of *Proceedings* and 56 Quarto Series publications during the century of its existence, enormously extending the material available to scholars; and some excellent work is hidden away in theses. The Huguenot Society Quarto Series has been devoted to editing primary sources – William and Susan Minet between them hold the remarkable record of having edited over twenty French church registers, appearing between HSQS, vol. 3 (1891) and vol. 45 (1956) – but a few volumes interpret those sources through important historical accounts, including:

Vol.	Date	Author	Subject (not title)
1	1887–8	W. J. C. Moens	Walloons at Norwich
12	1905	W. J. C. Moens	Dutch church, Colchester
15	1898	F. W. Cross	Walloon/Huguenot church, Canterbury
31	1928	W. & S. Minet	Churches of Castle St/Le Carré, London
37	1935	W. & S. Minet	Church of St Martin Orgars, London
38	1937	E. Johnston	French Church of London, 1560–5
54	1979	R. D. Gwynn	French communities in England, 1640s/1650s

The Society's *Proceedings* consist primarily of articles, of variable quality. Some of the many useful contributions are mentioned below. In addition to detailed indices to each individual volume, there is a short index to the first twenty volumes; this should soon be superseded by a combined index to the *Proceedings* and the Quarto Series publications, currently being prepared by C. F. A. Marmoy.

A Refugee Communities outside London

Schickler and Hessels are valuable for the history of the settlements in England until the Revocation, and HSQS, vol. 54 for the mid-seventeenth-century decades. R. D. Gwynn, 'The Distribution of

Huguenot Refugees in England', *HSP*, XXI (1965–70), 404–36, has useful footnote references on many of the smaller settlements.

The BRISTOL community has been exhaustively examined by R. Mayo, 'Les Huguenots à Bristol (1681–1791)' (unpublished University of Lille doctoral thesis, 1966), partly summarized in *HSP*, XXI (1965–70), 437–54. A booklet by the same author is being published by the Bristol branch of the Historical Association in 1985.

The volume by Cross on CANTERBURY in the Quarto Series publications listed above is particularly good. It can be supplemented by J. Campbell, 'The Walloon Community in Canterbury, 1625–49' (unpublished University of Wisconsin Ph.D. thesis, 1970); also B. Magen, *Die Wallonengemeinde in Canterbury von ihrer Gründung bis zum Jahre 1635* (Herbert Lang, Bern, 1973) (see also her article in *HSP*, XXII (1970–6), 307–17).

For the CHANNEL ISLANDS, see M. Syvret and J. Stevens, *Balleine's History of Jersey* (Phillimore, for La Société Jersiaise, 1981); Schickler's *Eglises du refuge en Angleterre*, vol 2; and the rather disorganized article by J. W. de Grave, 'Notes on . . . the Churches of the Channel Islands', *HSP*, V (1894–6), 125–78.

COLCHESTER: see HSQS vol. 12, and L. F. Roker, 'The Flemish and Dutch Community in Colchester. . .', *HSP*, XXI (1965–70), 15–30.

Work on DEVON and CORNWALL is gravely hampered by lack of surviving documentation. The loss of Bishop Lamplugh's papers leaves a gaping void. Although the French communities in Exeter and Plymouth, in particular, were substantial, there are only three articles that can be suggested: C. W. Bracken, 'The Huguenot Churches of Plymouth and Stonehouse', *Report and Transactions of the Devonshire Association*, 66 (1934), 163–79; C. E. Lart, 'The Huguenot Churches and Settlements in the West of England', *HSP*, VII (1901–4), 286–98; and R. Pickard, 'The Huguenots in Exeter', *Transactions of the Devonshire Association for the Advancement of Science, Literature and Art*, 68 (1936), 261–97. Lart in particular needs to be used with caution.

DOVER: G. H. Overend, 'Strangers at Dover', *HSP*, III (1888–91), 91–171, 286–330; W. Minet, 'The Fourth Foreign Church at Dover, 1685–1731', *HSP*, IV (1891–3), 93–217.

For the settlements involved in draining the FENS, see H. G. B. Le Moine, W. J. C. Moens and G. H. Overend, 'Huguenots in the Isle of Axholme', *HSP*, II (1887–8), 265–331; T. Bevis, *Strangers in the Fens* (Westrydale Press, 1983).

GLASTONBURY: H. J. Cowell, 'The French-Walloon Church at Glastonbury, 1550–1553', *HSP*, XIII (1923–9), 483–515.

IPSWICH: V. B. Redstone, 'The Dutch and Huguenot Settlements of Ipswich', *HSP*, XII (1917–23), 183–204.

IRELAND is beyond the scope of this book, and the subject of considerable current research. The obvious starting point at present is G. L. Lee, *The Huguenot Settlements in Ireland* (1936).

The standard work on NORWICH remains HSQS, vol. 1, by Moens. The Norwich 'Book of Orders' has not been printed, but an excellent modern transcript by Frederic Johnson is held amongst the Norwich City Records.

RYE: W. J. Hardy, 'Foreign Refugees at Rye', *HSP*, II (1887–8), 406–27, 567–87.

SCOTLAND: A. Fleming, *Huguenot Influence in Scotland* (Glasgow, 1953), is inaccurate and very general. Of greater use are two specific articles. D. E. Easson, 'French Protestants in Edinburgh (I)', *HSP*, XVIII (1947–52), 325–44 (no second part appeared), and Mason, 'Weavers of Picardy', (secion E below).

The SOUTHAMPTON church register (HSQS, vol. 4) is the earliest surviving, commencing in 1567, and is of more than normal historical value. See also J. S. Davies, *A History of Southampton* (1883), pp. 403–22; W. J. C. Moens, 'The Walloon Settlement and the French Church at Southampton', *HSP*, III (1888–91), 53–76; and the *Minute Book* (section D below).

SUNBURY-ON-THAMES: C. E. Lart, 'The French Colony and Church at Sunbury-on-Thames', *HSP*, XIII (1923–9), 474–82.

THORPE-LE-SOKEN: W. C. Waller, 'The French Church of Thorpe-le-Soken', *HSP*, X (1912–14), 265–97; E. A. Wood, 'Some Descendants of Thorpe-le-Soken Huguenots in the Eighteenth and Nineteenth Centuries' (unpublished typescript [c.1974], in HL).

B   Refugees in the London Area

While works on Canterbury and Norwich were published many years ago, there is nothing on the much larger and more important London-French community. This gap is only partly filled by several unpublished theses: P. Denis, 'Les Eglises d'etrangers à Londres jusqu'à la mort de Calvin' (Liège University, Licencié en Histoire, 1973–4); R. D. Gwynn, 'The Ecclesiastical Organization of French Protestants in England. . .' (London University, Ph.D, 1976); and I. Scouloudi, 'Alien Immigration and Alien Communities in London 1558–1640' (London University, M.Sc (Econ.), 1937). To these should be added two 1983 doctoral theses which I have not seen at the time of going to press, by A. Pettegree, 'The Strangers and their Churches in London, 1550–1580' (Oxford University), and O. P.

Grell, 'Austin Friars and the Puritan Revolution: the Dutch Church in London 1603–1642' (European University Institute).

The conclusions reached by I. Scouloudi in her thesis are summarized in her article of similar title in *HSP*, XVI (1937–41), 27–49. Other available articles include R. D. Gwynn's examination of the London churches after the Revocation in *HSP*, XXII (1970–6), 509–67; C. F. A. Marmoy, 'The Huguenots and their Descendants in East London', *East London Papers*, XIII, no. 2 (1970–1), 72–88; F. H. W. Sheppard, 'The Huguenots in Spitalfields and Soho', *HSP*, XXI (1965–70), 355–365; and J. T. Squire, 'The Huguenots at Wandsworth. . .', *HSP*, I (1885–6), 229–42, 261–312.

N. G. Brett-James, *The Growth of Stuart London* (1935), includes some excellent maps, showing the expansion of the built-up area, and an interesting case study of opposition. Various volumes of the London County Council *Survey of London* make reference to the Huguenot presence; see especially vols 27 (Spitalfields and Mile End New Town) and 33–34 (St Anne, Soho).

Because of the close relationship between the French and Dutch churches of the capital, J. Lindeboom, *Austin Friars: History of the Dutch Reformed Church in London 1550–1950* (The Hague, 1950), has relevance to the Huguenot story. Also of interest are W. Minet's 'Notes on the Threadneedle Street Registers' (undated typescript in HL).

C The Huguenots in France (chapters 1, 6)

The literature on this subject is vast. A. J. Grant, *The Huguenots* (first published 1934; Archon books, 1969), remains a good, short, simple introduction in English.

Several editions exist in both French and English of Jean Migault's *Journal* and the *Memoirs* of Jacques Fontaine, Jean Marteilhe and Samuel de Péchels. More formidable as a contemporary indictment of what happened in seventeenth-century France is [E. Benoît], *Histoire de l'Edit de Nantes* (3 vols in 5, Delft, 1693–95). For information on guides and routes out of France, see the *Bulletin de la Société de l'Histoire du Protestantisme Français*, XLVII (1898), 507–19, 561–93, 634–51, and XLIX (1900), 281–91.

The many books produced during the last generation include J. Garrisson-Estèbe, *Protestants du Midi 1559–1598* (Privat, Toulouse, 1980); *Histoire des Protestants en France* (Privat, Toulouse, 1977); R. M. Kingdon, *Geneva and the Coming of the Wars of Religion in France, 1555–1563* (Geneva, 1956); E. Le Roy Ladurie, *The Peasants of Languedoc* (University of Illinois Press, 1974) [Tr.]; E. G. Léonard, *A*

History of Protestantism, ed. H. H. Rowley, vols 1–2 (Nelson, 1965–7) [Tr.]; S. Mours and D. Robert, *Le Protestantisme en France . . . (1685–1970)*, (Librairie Protestante, Paris, 1972); R. Mousnier, *The Assassination of Henry IV* (Faber & Faber, 1973) [Tr.]; J. Orcibal, *Louis XIV et les Protestants* (Paris, 1951); D. Parker, *La Rochelle and the French Monarchy* (Royal Historical Society, 1980); J. H. M. Salmon, *Society in Crisis: France in the Sixteenth Century* (Ernest Benn, 1975; Methuen, University Paperback edition, 1979); W. C. Scoville, *The Persecution of Huguenots and French Economic Development 1680–1720* (Berkeley and Los Angeles, 1960); N. M. Sutherland, *The Huguenot Struggle for Recognition* (Yale University Press, 1980); N. M. Sutherland, *The Massacre of St Bartholomew and the European Conflict, 1559–1572* (Macmillan, 1973).

D   The Huguenot Churches, and their relationship with the Church of England (chapters 3, 6)

The basic works are those by Schickler and Hessels, and the theses by Denis and Gwynn mentioned in section B. All available French church registers have been published in HSQS except that for Dover, which was edited by F. A. Crisp and privately published in 1888. Unfortunately no registers survive for Canterbury before 1581, Norwich before 1595, or London before 1600. Consistory minutes are largely unavailable; exceptions are those of the French Church of London, 1560–5 and 1571–7 (HSQS, vols 38 and 48) and E. Welch (ed.), *The Minute Book of the French Church at Southampton 1702–1939* (Southampton Records Series, vol. 23, 1979).

Useful biographical studies are E. Carpenter, *The Protestant Bishop: . . . Henry Compton, 1632–1713* (1956); P. Collinson, *Archbishop Grindal 1519–1583* (Jonathan Cape, 1979); and B. Hall, *John à Lasco 1499–1560* (Dr Williams's Trust, 1971).

F. H. Littell (ed.), *Reformation Studies: Essays in Honor of Roland H. Bainton* (Richmond, Virginia, 1962), includes F. A. Norwood, 'The Strangers' "Model Churches" in Sixteenth-Century England' (pp. 181–96, 273–6). HSQS, vol. 54 considers the situation prevailing between the fall of Laud and the Restoration. No adequate study exists covering the eighteenth century.

E   Crafts, trades and professions (chapters 4, 5, 9)

For the craft scene as a whole, see Scoville, *Persecution of Huguenots* (section C above); W. C. Scoville, 'The Huguenots and the Diffusion of Technology. I', *Journal of Political Economy*, 60 (1952), 294–311; J.

Thirsk, *Economic Policy and Projects: The Development of a Consumer Society in Early Modern England* (Clarendon Press, 1978); J. Thirsk and J. P. Cooper (eds), *Seventeenth-Century Economic Documents* (Clarendon Press, 1972); L. Williams, 'Alien Immigrants in Relation to Industry and Society in Tudor England', *HSP*, XIX (1952–8), 146–69.

As far as individual crafts, trades and professions are concerned: there is remarkably little on the ARMY, and nothing whatsoever on the NAVY. When it appears, it will be interesting to see if the last volume of John Childs's trilogy on the English army 1660–1700 concerns itself with the Huguenot contribution. At present there is only C. E. Lart, 'The Huguenot Regiments', *HSP* (1909–11), 476–529.

BANKERS, STOCKBROKERS and MERCHANTS: W. M. Acres, 'Huguenot Directors of the Bank of England', *HSP*, XV (1933–7), 238–48; A. C. Carter, *Getting, Spending and Investing in Early Modern Times* (Van Gorcum, Assen, 1975); P. G. M. Dickson, *The Financial Revolution in England: . . . 1688–1756* (Macmillan, 1967); D. W. Jones, 'London Overseas-Merchant Groups at the End of the Seventeenth Century. . .' (unpublished Oxford University D.Phil thesis, 1971).

CLOTHING, NEW DRAPERIES, SILKWEAVING: D. C. Coleman, 'An Innovation and its Diffusion: the "New Draperies" ', *Economic History Review*, 2nd series, 22 (1969), 417–29; J. Mason, 'The Weavers of Picardy', *Book of the Old Edinburgh Club*, XXV (1945), 1–33; J. E. Pilgrim, 'The Cloth Industry in East Anglia', in J. G. Jenkins (ed.), *The Wool Textile Industry in Great Britain* (1972); A. Plummer, *The London Weavers' Company 1600–1970* (Routledge & Kegan Paul, 1972); P. Thornton, *Baroque and Rococo Silks* (Faber & Faber, 1965); P. Thornton and N. Rothstein, 'The Importance of the Huguenots in the London Silk Industry', *HSP*, XX (1958–64), 60–88; W. C. Waller (ed.), *Extracts from the Court Books of the Weavers Company of London 1610–1730* (HSQS vol. 33, 1931).

DOCTORS: W. R. Le Fanu, 'Huguenot Refugee Doctors in England', *HSP*, XIX (1952–8), 113–27.

EDUCATION, and the ENLIGHTENMENT: E. S. de Beer, 'The Huguenots and the Enlightenment', *HSP*, XXI (1965–70), 179–95; P. J. F. Luget, 'A Study of the Educational Aspect of the Huguenot Settlements in England' (unpublished London University M.A. thesis, 1952); S. Minet, 'Ecole de Charité Française de Westminster', *HSP*, XII (1917–23), 91–117, and XIII (1923–9), 374–92; J. W. A. Smith, 'French Influence on English Higher Education . . . 1660–1730' (unpublished Leeds University Ph.D thesis, 1956); and F. Watson, 'Notes and Materials on Religious

Refugees in their Relation to Education in England before . . . 1685',
HSP, IX (1909–11), 299–475.

GLASSMAKING: E. S. Godfrey, *The Development of English Glass Making 1560–1640* (Clarendon Press, 1975).

GOLD and SILVERSMITHS: J. Evans, 'Huguenot Goldsmiths in England and Ireland', *HSP*, XIV (1929–33), 496–554, and XV (1933–7), 516–20; J. F. Hayward, *Huguenot Silver in England 1688–1727* (1959); H. Tait, 'Huguenot Silver made in London (c. 1690–1723): the Peter Wilding bequest to the British Museum', *Connoisseur* (August and September 1972).

GUNMAKERS: J. F. Hayward, 'The Huguenot Gunmakers of London', *Journal of the Arms and Armour Society*, VI (1968), 117–43.

PAPERMAKING: D. C. Coleman, *The British Paper Industry 1495–1860* (Oxford, 1958), and 'The Early British Paper Industry and the Huguenots', *HSP*, XIX (1952–8), 210–25; G. H. Overend, 'Notes upon the Earlier History of the Manufacture of Paper in England', *HSP*, VIII (1905–8), 177–220.

F Huguenots in the England of the later Stuarts and thereafter (chapters 7–10)

Numbers of the Huguenot refugees of the later seventeenth century and their time of arrival have been analysed in articles by R. D. Gwynn: 'The Arrival of Huguenot Refugees in England 1680–1705', *HSP*, XXI (1965–70), 366–73, and 'The Number of Huguenot Immigrants in England in the Late Seventeenth Century', *Journal of Historical Geography*, IX (1983), 384–95.

Relevant to English attitudes are: E. S. de Beer, 'The Revocation of the Edict of Nantes and English Public Opinion', *HSP*, XVIII (1947–52), 292–310; H. T. Dickinson, 'The Tory Party's Attitude to Foreigners', *Bulletin of the Institute of Historical Research*, XL (1967), 153–65; M. Priestley, 'Anglo-French Trade and the "Unfavourable Balance" Controversy, 1660–1685', *Economic History Review*, 2nd series, IV (1951–2), 37–52; and M. R. Thorp, 'The Anti-Huguenot Undercurrent in Late-Seventeenth-Century England', *HSP*, XXII (1970–6), 569–80.

A. P. Hands and I. Scouloudi (eds) consider the financial support for the refugees inaugurated by Charles II in *French Protestant Refugees relieved through the Threadneedle Street Church, London, 1681–1687* (HSQS, vol. 49). Later aid is examined by R. A. Sundstrom in two unpublished works, 'Aid and Assimilation: . . . 1680–1727' (Kent State University Ph.D thesis, 1972) and his subsequent 'The Huguenots in England 1680–1876: A Study in Alien Assimilation' (undated typescript in HL); note Raymond Smith's comments in *HSP*, XXII (1970–6), 248–56.

W. C. Waller investigated 'Early Huguenot Friendly Societies' in *HSP*, VI (1898–1901), 201–35. For the French Charity School, see section E above. Arthur Giraud Browning reviewed the early history of the French Protestant Hospital, *La Providence*, in *HSP*, VI (1898–1901), 39–80 and VII (1901–4), 193–216, and the story was continued by Arthur Hervé Browning in *HSP*, XV (1933–7), 14–32. In recent years C. F. A. Marmoy has worked extensively on the Hospital records (see *HSP*, vols XXI (1965–70), 335–54 and XXII (1970–6), 235–47, and HSQS, vols 52 and 53), as well as on those of the Spitalfields *Maison de Charité* (*HSP*, XXIII (1977–82), 134–47; HSQS, vol. 55).

Index

Index